THE RADIANT PAST

MICHAEL BURAWOY AND JÁNOS LUKÁCS

THE RADIANT PAST

**IDEOLOGY AND REALITY IN
HUNGARY'S ROAD TO CAPITALISM**

THE UNIVERSITY OF CHICAGO PRESS · CHICAGO AND LONDON

The University of Chicago Press, Chicago 60637
The University of Chicago Press, Ltd., London
©1992 by The University of Chicago
All rights reserved. Published 1992
Paperback edition 1994
Printed in the United States of America

00 99 98 97 96 95 94   5 4 3 2

Library of Congress Cataloging-in-Publication Data

Burawoy, Michael.
    The radiant past : ideology and reality in Hungary's road to capitalism /
Michael Burawoy and János Lukács.
          p.   cm.
    Includes bibliographical references and index.
    ISBN 0-226-08041-2. — ISBN 0-226-08042-0 (pbk.)
    1. Labor—Hungary.   2. Class consciousness—Hungary.
3. Efficiency, Industrial—Hungary.   4. Communism—Hungary.
5. Capitalism—Hungary.   6. Hungary—Economic
conditions—1968–1989.   7. Hungary—Economic conditions—1989–
I. Lukács, János.   II. Title
HD8420.5.B87   1992
338.9439—dc20   91-13817
                                                                      CIP

For Jutka and Kriszti
from Michael

For Ilona, András, and Péter
from János

Contents

Preface

The essays which appear in this volume have been written over the last six years, during which time Hungary has undergone major transformation.[1] Rather than rewrite our earlier essays in the light of all that has happened in the last two years, we have shown how the logic of our research led us from one case study to the next, as well as how we were affected by the political transformation. The first chapter in this book is therefore a sociological diary of research written in a time of transition. The last chapter brings together what we have learned from our studies in order to cast light on the transition from state socialism toward capitalism.

One theme runs through the entire book, namely, the relationship of ideology to reality. Contemporary commentaries all too often treat Eastern Europe like a blackboard, to use Ken Jowitt's felicitous metaphor, on which, first, Marxist-Leninist ideology is written. This is then rubbed off and the ideology of free enterprise and market capitalism is inscribed. Concentration on ideology hides the diverse realities that constitute the blackboard, making it impossible to study the relationship between ideology and reality. We argue, therefore, that ideology has been taken too seriously, but also not seriously enough.

To take the first proposition, that ideology has been taken too seriously: The old totalitarian models and their successors either saw ideology as an all-powerful tool of domination and Marxism as the root of
all evil, or they were concerned to demonstrate the gap between
Marxist-Leninist ideology and reality. The result was the same in both
cases: an overly homogenized picture of state socialist societies which
overlooked the great variety of societies that lived under the umbrella of
Marxism-Leninism. They could not come to terms with the diverse institutions of, the adaptations to, and the struggles against state socialist
regimes which varied within and between countries as well as over time.

Soviet studies have been victims of ideology in yet another sense,
through the use of what can be called false comparisons. Too often studies compare the reality of one society with an ideal typical notion, often
implicit rather than explicit, of another. Thus, the *ideology* of capitalism—the efficiency of market competition based on private property
and the freedoms of liberal democracy—is contrasted with the *realities*
of state socialism—the waste and inefficiency of planning and the
repression of the one-party state. Such ideologically motivated views of
state socialism deny it any dynamics and have been unable to understand, let alone predict, its demise in 1989.

Part 1 of this book is concerned, therefore, to show just how variable
is the reality under state socialism, by pointing to a Hungarian machine
factory (Bánki) more efficient at the micro level than an equivalent
United States factory. Chapter 2 compares Burawoy's experiences working there in 1984 with his experiences working in a South Chicago plant
in 1974. Chapter 3 examines the pressures which can lead state socialist
firms to be efficient and capitalist firms to be inefficient. The point of
this chapter is not to argue that socialism is more efficient than capitalism, but rather to open eyes to possibilities that have been systematically foreclosed—namely, that under certain conditions socialism can
be efficient and capitalism can be inefficient, at least at the level of the
shop floor.

We can now turn to the second proposition, that ideology has not
been taken sufficiently seriously. Precisely because they have been so
concerned to discredit Marxism-Leninism, most studies have not examined its effects, and specifically the different effects for different
classes and in different spheres of life of the discrepancy between ideology and reality. In part 2, which is based on field research at the Lenin
Steel Works between 1985 and 1987, we show how ideology becomes
embodied in rituals of socialist affirmation. These rituals draw attention
to the discrepancy between ideology and reality, leading workers to crit-

icize state socialism for failing to live up to its promises. State socialism develops a negative class consciousness within its work force, hostile to the dominant class of "Red Barons." Chapter 4 presents the "economic reality" of production in a shortage economy, while chapter 5 describes how the juxtaposition of "economic reality" and "ideological reality" leads workers to interpret their experiences in class terms.

The dominant class is also acutely aware of the gap between ideology and reality. For a dominant class to rule effectively it must believe in its ideology. This became increasingly impossible as neither political coercion nor economic reform could bring reality into conformity with ideology. Recognizing that state socialism engenders class rebellions from below and consonant with its own professionalization, the ruling class abandoned the project of transforming reality and instead rejected socialist ideology in favor of the ideology of free enterprise. But, as we make clear in the last chapter, this dramatic shift in strategy does not in fact close the gap between ideology and reality. Celebrating capitalist free enterprise no more transforms a centralized state-owned economy into a privatized market economy than celebrating Marxism-Leninism brings about democratic socialism.

While it is now fashionable to compare the transitions in Eastern Europe to processes of democratization in Latin America, perhaps more appropriate would be comparisons to decolonization in Africa. In Africa, just as in Eastern Europe, independence was to bring about a double transition—an economic transition of modernization and a political transition of democratization. Each side of the double transition was supposed to fuel the other. Just as they are now doing in Eastern Europe, so then, too, armies of social scientists from the West combed the continent promoting the magical virtues of free enterprise and democracy. But it wasn't long before optimism turned to pessimism as countries plunged further into underdevelopment. Democracies proved fragile, giving way to military regimes or one-party states. Enclave economies could not escape the vice of international capitalism. Modernization theorists threw up their hands and blamed the Africans, who were deemed unprepared for democracy and free enterprise. It was said that they were too bound into the primordial loyalties of tribalism and tradition. They were not in possession of the "correct" values or orientations. The famous winds of change did indeed bring change, but not the change that had been hoped for. Now the intellectuals have largely departed, the experiment is buried in history, and Africa, with the exception of its southern tip, is a forgotten continent, riddled with AIDS, poverty, and famine.

To be sure, Eastern Europe has not been underdeveloped to the same extent as countries of Africa. Indeed, by many measures state socialism was a success. Certainly, the extremes of poverty and wealth to be found in a country such as the United States were absent in Hungary. But there is little room for optimism about the future—that these countries will be able to grow economically or sustain democracy. As in Africa, we are already witnessing the unleashing of national and ethnic conflict that had been kept in check by state socialism. As in Africa, all the signs point toward economic decline and the rise of authoritarianism. The radiant future that is to be capitalism is no less utopian than the radiant future that was to be communism.

Acknowledgments

The acknowledgments for this book could make a book themselves. I first visited Hungary in the summer of 1982 at the invitation of Iván Szelényi, who had himself just returned after eight years in exile. Although the directions of our research have diverged, his work continues to exercise considerable influence over my own. His book, *The Intellectuals on the Road to Class Power,* written with György Konrád, provides the theoretical point of departure for the studies presented here. The other signal intellectual influence has been János Kornai's book, *The Economics of Shortage.* Indeed, the framework we develop combines Kornai's microeconomics and Szelényi's class analysis.

During those two weeks in the summer of 1982 I was introduced to a number of Iván's former students, in particular Bálint Magyar, Gábor Kertesi, and Robi Manchin. Especially in the beginning they gave me the bearings to negotiate my way through Hungarian society. With wry smiles and benign tolerance they watched a Western Marxist grappling with socialism on earth. Péter Galasi and Zsuzsa Hunyadi adopted me as their helpless child—until Zsófi arrived. They always made me feel at home, listened with amusement to my stories from the factory, visited me in towns across the country, and tried to steer me away from huge intellectual errors.

Between 1983 and 1990 I visited Hungary twice or even three times a year, spending three entire semesters as well as every summer there. Laci Bruszt, through his father, found me my first job in the village of Izsák. There I worked in a champagne factory of a state farm and was looked after by the family Tege. Bálint Magyar and Pali Juhász made the contact in the village of Felsővadász where I worked in a small spinning factory of the cooperative. That was in November and December of 1983. I have returned countless times to Felsővadász to play chess with Lajos Papp, to eat the sumptuous meals of Klára Papp, to attend weddings, to watch the cooperative grow under its ebullient president, Pista Tóth, and to gossip with villagers.

In the summer of 1984 I made my first entry into industry, working as a radial drill operator at the enterprise we have called Bánki. During this time Laci and Julia Kelemen and their little boy eased my passage into the rhythms and discipline of industrial life. In February 1985 I began work in the Lenin Steel Works and continued working there until the end of July, returning the following summer for two months, and then the spring after that for three months. Each time I joined the October Revolution Socialist Brigade. Józsi, Gyuri, Béla, Csaba, Karcsi (all pseudonyms), and many others welcomed me back every time I returned. They showed me what it was like to be a steelworker in the twilight of socialism. As constant companions outside work, Jutka and Kriszti taught me more about Hungarian life than I could ever express in writing.

Wherever I went I found the same extraordinary hospitality, warmth, and charm. It was the most enjoyable fieldwork—if fieldwork can ever be enjoyable—I have ever undertaken, although also the most exhausting. I had the advantage of being a Westerner and so could easily move between different social strata. The major obstacle to my research was language. Without the patient teaching of Kati Pusztai in Budapest and Ágnes Mihalik in Berkeley, I would have given up Hungarian as a lost cause. Whether it was on the shop floor, or in the bar, or at home, if at first I didn't understand, then I learned to ask and ask again. Early on, Robi Manchin, always one to turn a handicap into an advantage, suggested that lapses in understanding forced me to be more alert in my observations. I had to continually formulate theories about what transpired, and therefore I was more sensitive to unexpected happenings that had to be accommodated into an emerging framework. So he claimed!

Throughout the research I had the good fortune to collaborate with János Lukács. Without him the entire research would have been impossible. As I make clear in the first chapter, he orchestrated my entry into Bánki and the Lenin Steel Works; he interviewed managers while I was working on the shop floor. We discussed our experiences and ideas in local bars and restaurants for long hours after shift or before shift. We worked closely together on chapters 3 and 4. Chapter 6 is largely based on his experiences. Ilona, András, and Péter stoically put up with János's disappearance for days at a time. His absence has intensified during the last year as he became absorbed in promoting employee ownership. Lukács undertook the task of convincing managers and workers, trade unions and workers' councils, members of parliament and civil servants, that employee ownership is economically viable. His efforts have paid off, as he was recently asked to prepare the draft legislation for an employee stock ownership program for Hungary.

We would both like to thank the managers and workers at Bánki and the Lenin Steel Works for all their cooperation in the conduct of our research. Lukács, in particular, would like to thank the workers and managers of Weirton for introducing him to the ins and outs of the employee stock ownership plan (ESOP) as well as to United States steel production during the six weeks he spent there in the summer of 1989.

The Institute of Sociology of the Hungarian Academy of Sciences played the crucial role of official sponsor for our research. Here Csaba Makó, László Cseh-Szombathy, and Elemér Hankiss willingly gave their advice and support. In different ways, either through commenting on our work or though discussion, the following have been particularly helpful: in Hungary, István Gábor, Péter Galasi, Gábor Kertesi, Pali Tamás, Ilona Erös, Miklós Haraszti, Gyuri Lengyel, Laci Bruszt, Ernö Kemenes, and Anna Halustyik, and outside Hungary, Martha Lampland, Wlodzimierz Brus, Ed Hewett, Pierrette Hondagneu-Sotelo, Michael Liu, Brian Powers, Gay Seidman, Vicki Smith, Linda Fuller, Stephen Wood, Rob Wrenn, Linda Blum, Ellen Comisso, Vedat Milor, Mary Waters, Gail Kligman, David Stark, and Ron Weitzer. Numerous discussions with Joanna Goven about her study of Hungarian factory women reminded me of my own blinkers. In Arthur Stinchcombe and Andrew Arato, we couldn't have asked for two more challenging and encouraging referees. We have tried to respond to their criticisms in our revisions. It was a pleasure to work with Doug Mitchell who guided the manuscript smoothly through the editorial process. From the beginning to the end, Erik Wright commented on and enthusiastically supported my work, magically producing a stream of fourfold tables that he hoped would give analytical precision to my inchoate ideas.

A number of institutes and foundations supported our research. My own research was supported by a grant from the National Science Foundation (1984–87), by the Hungarian Academy of Sciences, and by several institutes at Berkeley—the Institute of Industrial Relations, the Institute of International Studies, and the Institute for Slavic and East European Studies. Lukács's research was supported by the Institute of Economic Planning, Budapest, the Hungarian Academy of Sciences, the American Council of Learned Societies, and the International Research and Exchanges Board (IREX), which twice brought him to the United States, once for six weeks and once for a year. For the periods he spent in the United States he was hosted by the Institute of Industrial Relations at Berkeley.

My closest friend and conspirator, Carol Hatch, tragically died in June 1989. Throughout my fieldwork she sustained me with letters, rich in gossip, news, photographs, advice, humor, interrogation, and analysis. From the time I set foot in the Berkeley department, she was my most relentless critic and dogged supporter. Life is much the hollower without her.

Michael Burawoy

1   A Sociological Diary

"Where the Avenue of Marxism-Leninism meets Cosmonaut Square, a great permanent slogan was erected: LONG LIVE COMMUNISM—THE RADIANT FUTURE OF ALL MANKIND!" The fate of this slogan is the subject of *The Radiant Future*, a novel written by Soviet dissident Alexander Zinoviev.[1] Erected with great pomp and ceremony to celebrate the triumphs of communism, the sign soon becomes the meeting place of the rejects of Soviet society—drunks, drug addicts, youth gangs, and homosexuals. An embarrassment to the future it portrays, the slogan is fenced off so that its desecration now takes place in secret. Its titanium letters are filched by apparatchiks for their villas, while pigeons decorate what remains with their droppings. The slogan is reconstructed with the same triumphal, hollow speeches extolling the virtues of the radiant future.

The fate of the slogan symbolizes not only the fate of Soviet society but also the career of the narrator, head of the Department of Theoretical Problems in the Methodology of Scientific Communism. *The Radiant Future* portrays his daily life as a saga of instrumentalized relations, petty careerism, betrayal of lovers, denunciation of friends, jealousy of colleagues, exploitation of subordinates, corruption of

1

power brokers, worthless academic writing, prostitution of ability, and ruthless pursuit of ambition. Obsessing about his prospects for becoming a corresponding member of the academy, our narrator denounces the writings of his close friend and colleague, Anton, to the police. But Anton's ideas take their revenge as our head-of-department is persuaded that the negative features of communism derive from its purported positive features. Anton becomes his alter ego, struggling for freedom inside him. He is plagued by self-doubt and his bosses lose confidence in his judgment. Just as the slogan celebrating the Radiant Future is desecrated, so our narrator's reputation is steadily besmirched, until finally he is beaten out of the academy by his hated rival from the party school.

According to Zinoviev it is not the discrepancy between ideology and reality but the ideals themselves and the attempt to realize them that lead to the degradation of social, economic, and political life. For our head-of-department, his family, his friends, and his colleagues, Marxism is not an irrelevant covering of society but the very stuff of life. Ideology has a reality of its own which imposes itself on people in the form of congresses, meetings, plans, obligations, overfulfillments, conquests of new fields, new departures, demonstrations, decorations, applause, folk-dances, farewell ceremonies, arrival ceremonies, and so on. Life under communism is the daily living-out of Marxism as ideology.

Zinoviev writes only about intellectuals. But how do workers experience communism—this radiant future of all humanity? How do they experience the great slogans erected in their name? We know much more about the reaction of intellectuals to what we shall call state socialism than we do about the reaction of workers. Intellectuals usually speak for themselves, if not always about themselves, and they are very removed from the working class. For all the repression, they are still in a position to make themselves heard more effectively than workers. In a "worker's state" workers don't speak, they are spoken for—by journalists, poets, academics, politicians, bureaucrats; by apologists for state socialism as well as by its dissidents. Each embraces the interests of workers as their own, as that is the reigning discourse, while workers themselves are without an independent public voice. Workers give expression to their interests through their deeds: in hidden day-to-day skirmishes and in occasional revolts which are as unexpected as they are threatening to the ruling ideology. To penetrate the refractory and highly politicized debate and to hear workers themselves it is necessary, therefore, to partake directly in their lives.

I had originally intended to go to Poland in 1982. Martial law put an end to that possibility, but it was with Solidarity in mind that I began my research in Hungary. The Polish workers' movement was after all the first workers' revolution in history. It was both nationwide and led by workers who presented their interests as the interests of all. Yet it was not without its paradoxes. It took place in a socialist society, or at least a society that proclaimed itself socialist, rather than an advanced capitalist society. Its rhetoric was anti-Marxist, anti-Soviet, and sometimes even antisocialist, even if its project was socialist. That is, as a workers' movement it sought to regain control over society. Was this somehow a freak episode, a cultural plot? Or did it say something about state socialism on the one hand and advanced capitalism on the other? And, if so, why did Solidarity take place in Poland rather than Hungary? Turning history back to 1956, who would have guessed that Poland rather than Hungary would have spawned a workers' revolution some two and a half decades later?

If the decade began with Solidarity, it ended with the equally unexpected collapse of state socialism in Eastern Europe. The year 1990 saw communism swept away in the ballot box. Solidarity turned from a workers' movement into a workers' government, proclaiming its devotion to capitalism. So we can now ask: What was this "radiant past" that had seemed so indomitable during the previous four decades? How could it be swept away so easily? In particular, how was it that the same workers who sought to transform state socialism into some form of democratic socialism in 1980 voted so resoundingly to destroy all traces of socialism in 1990? What has happened in the last decade?

Our research is bound between these two puzzles. It began by asking, Why Solidarity in the East rather than the West, and in Poland rather than Hungary? and ends by asking why the transition to capitalism has so far met with so little resistance. We ask why Solidarity's project of turning state socialism toward democratic socialism was replaced ten years later by the project of turning state socialism into capitalism, and we address the difficulties facing this new project.

Our case studies of work organization and working-class consciousness took place in real historical time—the decade leading up to world historical transformations. With the exception of the first and the last, which are original to this book, the essays were originally published between 1985 and 1989. We have decided to keep them intact in order to reflect the changes in the Hungarian political and economic scene as well as the evolution of our own thinking. Each chapter absorbs the truth of previous ones and at the same time marks out new terrain. To have rewritten the essays in accordance with our thoughts at an arbitrary point in time would have given finality to a process without finality. History would have quickly overtaken any such freezing of the past, particularly if undertaken from within the quicksand of contemporary political and economic transitions.

The purpose of this introduction, therefore, is to present both the logic and the social processes behind our successive studies. It is only appropriate that the authors of a book devoted to production and its producers should also examine their own work process. As so often happens in fieldwork, the genealogy of research—entry, normalization, and exit—reveals as much about the society as the research itself. Resistance to novel and potentially threatening research, such as that we undertook, exposes deeply held values and interests of the actors—both the ties that bind and the conflicts that divide.

Theoretical Prolegomenon

This book is in part a sequel to *Manufacturing Consent*, which defended two theses about the consolidation of advanced capitalism.[2] First, the character of the capitalist enterprise itself created a distinctive class consciousness, irrespective of the consciousness carried in from outside. It was not simply that individuals are not centers of consciousness and only respond to the logic of their immediate situations. Rather, it was a historically specific argument that enterprises of advanced capitalism had established their own institutions—the internal state, the internal labor market, and the constitution of work as a game—which sealed workers off from their lives outside work. Family and community compelled workers to deposit their labor at the factory gates, but from there management took over.

The second thesis concerned the logic of the workplace, how it turned that potential for work into real work. Contrary to the Marxist orthodoxy that the interests of workers and capitalists are irrevocably opposed, I argued that not just commodities and social relations but also consent were manufactured at the point of production. There was no need to turn to the realm of the superstructures to explain the quiescence, the compliance of workers—it was organized there in the workplace by the political regime that regulated it. This hegemonic regime of advanced capitalism had three defining attributes. The application of force took place only under certain specified conditions and was itself the object of consent. The interests of workers and capital were concretely coordinated through a common material interest in the expansion of profit. Workers were constituted as individuals—industrial citizens with rights and obligations.

Theories of the political, ideological, and legal institutions would have to be significantly refashioned if the workplace has its own political apparatuses which perform the crucial function of organizing consent to and legitimacy of capitalism. But how true is this? Of course, critics could point to conflict between labor and capital, but this hardly challenged the thesis of consent. The two are far from being mutually exclusive: Consent presupposes conflict. It is the product of conflict. What seemed more tendentious was my claim that the organization of consent was a function of capitalism rather than industrialism per se. I argued that capitalist regimes of production were engendered by the problem of securing surplus that was simultaneously obscured. This could not be effectively evaluated by comparisons within or between capitalist societies but only by comparison with noncapitalist societies. Specifically, I expected state socialist societies, characterized by different mechanisms of surplus extraction, to generate regimes of production very different from the hegemonic ones of capitalism and with correspondingly different effects on the consciousness of workers.

It was a stroke of good fortune when in 1974 I landed a job in the same South Chicago machine shop that Donald Roy had studied thirty years before. The change over the postwar period had laid the basis for the argument about the rise of hegemonic regimes. I now had a second stroke of good fortune when I came across Miklós Haraszti's wonderful ethnography of a Hungarian machine shop, *A Worker in a Worker's State*.[3] Once more the technology, the organization of work, and the piece-rate system were broadly the same at Allied and at Red Star Tractor Factory. What was clearly different was the tempo of our work. Although originally puzzled by the intensity of my fellow operators at Allied, I now found Haraszti's account simply beyond belief. He had to gyrate between two milling machines which operated simultaneously. There was no guaranteed wage as there was at Allied and so he couldn't relax when the rates were impossible to make. Quite the contrary, he had to work all the harder. Instead of Allied's wage security and job insecurity, he confronted job security and wage insecurity. The despotism of the piece-rate system was buttressed by the arbitrary rule of the almighty foreman. Party and trade union were in no sense defenders of worker interests but instruments of managerial domination. How different from the relative autonomy of the hegemonic regime, which guaranteed the space for engineering consent.

My book *The Politics of Production* was largely devoted to distinguishing this "bureaucratic despotic" regime from other varieties of despotism: market despotism, found in nineteenth-century textile industries of Britain, the United States, and Russia; colonial despotism, and the "hegemonic despotism" which emerges under advanced capitalism in the era of global competition.[4] How generalizable were the case studies upon which my typologies rested? In particular, was it reasonable to characterize Haraszti's depiction of Red Star as typical of state socialism? Certainly, his experiences seemed to belie conventional wisdom that workers had won one right under state socialism—the right not to work hard. Other accounts of life on the shop floor in Hungary pointed to a more complex picture. The work of Héthy and Makó underscored the considerable countervailing power of core workers. Inspired by their work, a number of labor economists and industrial sociologists undertook case studies to describe the balkanization of internal labor markets, with some claiming that management depended on the self-organization of core workers.[5]

If Haraszti's experience was not typical of the contemporary Hungarian worker's, what did it signify? First, as an intellectual he was shunned by his fellow workers, leading to a portrait of atomized workers battling alone with their machines. Second, as an inexperienced newcomer he was in a peripheral position and was given the most difficult jobs. He couldn't be expected to make the rates. Third, and most significant, Red Star was a test case for the New Economic Mechanism of 1968. As such it was under a stringent budgetary constraint, leading to tight piece rates and regular "norm revisions." Who he was, where he was in the production process, and the relationship of the enterprise to the state were the hidden sources of his portrait of bureaucratic despotism.[6] These conclusions were reinforced by our research in Hungarian factories.

Discovering the Impossible?

I met Lukács in 1982 on my first trip to Hungary. Already then we found a common interest in case studies of the socialist enterprise. I was sufficiently encouraged that some research was indeed possible that I returned to Budapest in June of 1983 for six months to learn Hungarian. I also wanted to find some work. Knowing how politically sensitive were questions about the working class, I thought it would be impossible to get an industrial job. So I looked for one in agriculture. With the help of friends and acquaintances I managed to find unpaid jobs in a champagne factory of a state farm for two months and in a textile factory of a collective farm for another month. But having never worked in either industry, I found it difficult to determine what was distinctive about these places. In December 1983 Lukács managed to organize a week-long visit to a division of one of Hungary's major heavy-vehicle enterprises. A few months earlier, I had thought even such an expedition unthinkable for a Westerner.

Just walking through the plant made it obvious that it was much more efficiently run than Allied, the South Chicago plant where I had worked. We had stumbled on the impossible—an efficient socialist enterprise! During that week we managed to talk to all sorts of managers and to take workers off the line and interrogate them. We turned our attention to the details of the piece-rate system, whose operation seemed similar to Red Star's. But it was much too short a time to examine carefully the differences between Red Star and Bánki on the one side and Allied and Bánki on the other.

It was then that we proposed to the director that we return the next summer to conduct an intensive case study. He was not opposed to the idea, but would leave it to us to figure out a way of getting me permission to work there! It was the organizational genius of Lukács that made it possible. Already, in arranging our single week's visit, Lukács had faced bureaucratic resistance from the headquarters of Bánki's parent enterprise. The general director insisted we clear the visit with the local branch of the Ministry of Interior—the ministry concerned with internal security. But how to approach such an august body? Time and again the key which unlocked bureaucratic doors was a relative of Lukács's—R—who worked in the Central Committee. In this first case he had referred Lukács to someone in the Ministry of Interior in Budapest—M—who then requested the county authorities to allow me to enter the factory for a week.

Now Lukács had to figure out a way of getting me a work permit. He again got in touch with his contact in the Ministry of Interior, who said he would look into it. At their next meeting, M did not explicitly oppose the granting of a work permit but asked why they should do a favor for someone who hobnobs with dissidents. They knew that I had been to an open party attended by members of the opposition. They were naturally suspicious of my strange intentions to work in a factory. In questioning Lukács about our research he made it amply clear that the Ministry of Interior already knew a great deal about me. If M was to do Lukács a favor, then he wanted us to know that there were risks in it for both himself and for Lukács. Even though he could be accused of co-operating with the hated Ministry of Interior, with unknown effects on his own career, Lukács nevertheless decided to persuade M to organize the work permit.

This was not the end of the story. Having cleared the Ministry of Interior made it possible to send a formal request from the director of the Institute of Sociology (Hungarian Academy of Sciences) to the general director of Bánki's parent company. The general director replied that according to his discussions with the head of the Cultural and Scientific Department in the Central Committee of the party, our research was *nem actuális,* which meant that it didn't exist. This was an effective way of blocking our request without saying no. He was opposed to the research but didn't risk an open denial for fear that the request came from someone who possessed considerable political influence and was prepared to exercise it. What to do? The general director refused to see Lukács, and so once more he reluctantly turned to his relative in the Central Committee. R obligingly talked to the head of the Cultural and Scientific Department, who then called the general director to say she had no objections to the research. He in turn left a message for Lukács, saying that we could now go ahead, but he never wrote this down or withdrew his original letter. To the end he was covering himself against any eventuality. Finally, Lukács asked R to notify the party headquarters at the county level and had no difficulty getting their OK. That was how I got my first real job in a socialist factory.

While I slaved away on my radial drill, Lukács visited the plant regularly, talking to managers on the shop floor and above. My experiences there are described in chapter 2. They point to a very different atmosphere than the one described by Haraszti. Although I was an intellectual, as far as my fellow workers were concerned I was first and foremost an American and the object of great curiosity. I was quickly absorbed into the social groups of the workplace. I was struck by the autonomy of shop-floor organization. The rates were manageable—if not for me, then certainly for most operators. The foreman was a benign figure rather than a despot. The structures of work organization, of payment system, of internal labor market, and of trade union and party had the potentiality but not the reality of bureaucratic despotism. The point was, of course, Bánki was not under the enormous fiscal pressure that Red Star was experiencing in 1971 and therefore did not experience those crippling norm revisions that Haraszti wrote about.

I was, however, more struck by the comparison with Allied than with Red Star. They were strictly comparable in the sense that they were of similar size, were similarly situated as a supplier to other divisions within a single enterprise, and produced a similar product with similar technology, work organization, and payment system. At the same time they seemed to belie the stereotypes of capitalist and state socialist firms. Thus, at Bánki operators worked harder and there was less restriction of output (either quota restriction or goldbricking), not only because there was no minimum wage but also because the norms were better adjusted to the jobs. At Allied, mountains of scrap used to accumulate on the shop floor, while scrap was hard to find at Bánki. There were none of the half-finished products waiting for parts that used to line the aisles at Allied. There were far fewer shortages of materials and parts and fewer urgent "hot jobs" than at Allied. Auxiliary workers such as truck drivers, inspectors, setup men, and crib attendants were not in scarce supply as they were at Allied, where they held up work and generated disruptive lateral conflicts. Although bureaucracy was supposed to characterize state socialism, shop-floor life at Allied was much more bound by rules than at Bánki—rules which protected workers against managerial arbitrariness, but also arbitrary managerial rules that were used to strangle spontaneous initiatives.

What were we to make of this? Here was a capitalist plant that conformed to the socialist stereotype of inefficiency, wastage, and bureaucratic red tape, and a socialist plant that conformed to the capitalist stereotype of efficiency, abstemiousness, and worker initiative. We certainly didn't believe that this was generalizable across economies or that technical efficiency at the level of shop-floor organization implied anything about global efficiency at the level of the economy. Moreover, we were working with a static conception of efficiency. A dynamic view would have to incorporate relative propensity to innovate rather than simply adapt to the economic environment—something which, supposedly, state socialist enterprises have great difficulty accomplishing.

These caveats aside, our case studies nevertheless did pose the question of the conditions under which a state socialist plant might be as efficient as a capitalist enterprise, and equally the conditions under which a capitalist plant might be as inefficient as a state socialist plant. The answer we arrived at, described here in chapter 3, was to draw an analogy between the capitalist corporation and a socialist economy. Both are based primarily on the hierarchical organization of economic units. Allied was a division of the multinational corporation Allis-Chalmers, just as Bánki was part of the Hungarian economy. Allis-Chalmers plans just like the Hungarian state. The divisions of Allis-Chalmers compete for resources from its central executive committee, just as Hungarian enterprises compete for resources from the state. Both centers act in a paternalistic manner toward their divisions, protecting them against bankruptcy, giving rise in both cases to soft budget constraints. Although both operate in an external world market which ultimately becomes crucial, nevertheless it is heavily mediated by hierarchical organization, whether of the corporation or the national economy. Consequently the division of the large corporation has the same urge to expand as the socialist enterprise without being subject to hard budget constraints. We should not be surprised to find the division of a capitalist corporation conforming to the stereotype of a socialist enterprise, even exhibiting the same shortages, wastage, and inefficiencies.

We are, of course, not suggesting that this is the norm, but rather that it is possible for capitalist firms, particularly when embedded in a large corporation, to both survive and be inefficient. Some corporations prove to be much better at planning and compelling efficient organization of their divisions than others. If we can explain why Allied as part of a multinational corporation might conform to the stereotypes of a socialist plant, how are we to explain the capitalist character of Bánki? Here we have to be much more tentative. There were nevertheless certain features that were distinctive. Bánki had a stable and guaranteed market. It had only a limited number of product types, and of these, half were built according to a license from a West German firm. There was little pressure for innovation. Its standardized production process was easier to insulate from the pressures of a shortage economy.

Although we did not appreciate it at the time, the implications of these conclusions suggested drastic rethinking about the nature of state socialism and capitalism. In effect we argued that property relations mattered less than organizational attributes for the microefficiency of the firm. Whether an enterprise was state owned or privately owned was not as important as the combination of organization forms—hierarchies and markets. At this point the distinction between capitalism and state socialism began to blur. But it did seem that Bánki's relative autonomy within the larger enterprise and its insulation from direct state intervention were necessary if not sufficient conditions for its effective performance. Such an argument was consistent with Chandler's claims about successful corporate transitions to the multidivisional form, as well as with explanations for the relative success of the East German economic reforms, which relied on enterprise associations insulating enterprises from direct state intervention.[7] So for our next study we turned to an enterprise that was not so protected from state intervention.

Bungled Entry

When I went north to my various workplaces I often passed through Miskolc—the capital of Hungary's industrial heartland. It is strung out along the bottom of a valley at one end of which are the great Lenin Steel Works (LKM) and its sister factory, the Diósgyör Machine Works. From the hills I had seen the steelworks sprawling over its vast area with its complex of railroad tracks, the familiar tangle of defunct chimneys that had been its Siemen's-Martin furnaces, the covered buildings that were its rolling mills, its blast furances, and its glowing dump of molten slag. I often wondered what it must be like to work down there in the heart of socialist industry. What had happened to those steelworkers—once glamorized as the proletarian heroes of socialism?

Surely I was the only person to dream about working in the Lenin Steel Works. Not entirely aware of all the difficulties Lukács had had with the Ministry of Interior in getting me the first job, I blithely asked him if there was any way he could arrange it. He once more approached M to see if he could obtain another work permit for me. M agreed and informed the county-level offices of the Ministry of Interior as well as its man within the Lenin Steel Works. At the same time the relative in the Central Committee informed the city and county organizations of the party. At this point Lukács was getting uncomfortable about what they might ask of him in return for all these favors. When asked why he was doing all this, his relative replied, "Who knows what favor you will be able to do for me one day." This was the primitive gift exchange which bound the party apparatus together in a maze of reciprocal ties.

I arrived in January 1985 to discover that my request was being held up within the LKM. Fearing that the project would fall through, I contacted an acquaintance who was the director of research in the National Planning Office. He made an appointment for me with the deputy to the general director of LKM, since the general director was away. I went to Miskolc to explain my mission to the deputy, who accepted my unusual request with equanimity since it had support from high up in the government. He assumed that I would want to work in the new Combined Steel Works, which, he boasted, could produce any type of quality steel. Its state-of-the-art technology from West Germany, Japan, and Sweden had been the only major investment in the last decade. He took me down to the personnel manager to prepare the paperwork for my employment. I was shown round the Combined Steel Works and told to report for work on Monday.

With great excitement I returned to Budapest. This was too good to be true. Sure enough, a few days later the general director—just returned from West Germany—rang up the head of the Institute of Sociology demanding to know who was this Burawoy, what was his research, how would LKM benefit from it, had the Ministry of Industry given permission, and was the Institute prepared to take responsibility for me and pay for a personal supervisor who would look after me while I worked? At the Institute, the director and his deputy were quite unprepared to answer these questions. In my impatience I had tried to circumvent official channels, with catastrophic results. Only Lukács, who had been away, could charm the project back into existence by pursuing the official channel he had already established through M. But first, the Institute director had his own position to protect and demanded that Lukács respond to each of the six demands of the general director.

At heart the issue was a simple one—who was going to take responsibility for me? The general director had told the Institute director that someone from outside LKM had just been killed on his premises—what would happen if I had a fatal accident? He could imagine the headlines: "American professor killed while working in the Lenin Steel Works." He was not unrealistic. During the three years I worked at the converter one worker was burned alive by molten slag and another had his leg chopped in two. The director was covering himself by insisting that the Academy of Sciences or the Ministry of Industry assume responsibility for me. Like the general director at Bánki's headquarters, he was saying no without saying no, but he did it in a different way. Recently transferred from being secretary of the Miskolc Party Committee, he did not have influence at the national level. He didn't have access to the Central Committee and instead confronted the Institute himself in this very crude manner.

There is a comparative lesson to be learned here. In a market economy, where failure of an organization leads to its demise, mistakes generate their own costs, whereas in a hierarchical economy, individuals, not organizations, are at risk. The distribution of responsibility becomes a terrain of struggle. Rather than trying to save their enterprises, bosses try to save their skins. To gain entry into a capitalist enterprise I would have to demonstrate that my research would produce profit for the company, whereas here I had to demonstrate that it wouldn't redound against the general director. As ever, entry, particularly when it is resisted and even bungled, reveals much about underlying social forces—even if these become understandable only later in the research process.

Men of Steel

In February I finally took up a job as a furnaceman at LKM's basic oxygen converter. It was to be the first of three stints—six months in

1985, two months in 1986, and three months in 1987. Although I'd never worked in a steel mill, I soon preferred it to the machine shop. Instead of struggling alone with a machine, recklessly pursuing norms, I worked with other furnacemen. Together we tended the converter, taking samples and temperatures, tossing carbon bags into the molten steel, shoveling alloys in barrows or slag into dumpers, signaling to crane drivers to deliver this or remove that. Much of the time we were simply waiting for the cycle to complete itself or a new one to begin. We'd then be in our little eating room. On night shift we sometimes cooked our famous steelworkers' soup. There I learned about the life of the steelworker.

It was not always easy to persuade management and workers that I was for real—an American professor wanting to enter the mill as a furnaceman and be treated like any other furnaceman. Right at the beginning, management worried that I wasn't going to get paid enough so, unbeknownst to myself, they started me on a basic wage that was higher than most of my coworkers'. I was pretty annoyed and so were my mates when we discovered this. Management justified it on the grounds that I would not be working on shifts, and therefore I should be compensated for not receiving the shift differential!

Management's insistence that I remain on morning shift was another way of making me exceptional. It meant that I joined whatever brigade was working mornings that day. Some teams included me in their activities, while others would have nothing to do with me. From the point of view of my own sanity as well as of my research this was very unsatisfactory. It took some considerable pestering to persuade management to let me join one particular group—the October Revolution Brigade—and rotate shifts with them. Either management wanted to keep me in their gaze, which is most easily done on morning shift, or they simply didn't believe I'd be able to cope with the four-shift system. Indeed, no one gets used to the shift system—three morning shifts and one day off, then three night shifts and one day off, then three afternoon shifts and one day off. The rotation continues like clockwork. It pays no attention to the normal world around, to weekends, to holidays, to the demands of a decent family life. However, as far as I was concerned, rotating with the same brigade had the advantage of sure companionship in the mill. Membership in the October Revolution Brigade became the basis of immersion in communities both inside and outside the factory. But it was exhausting—physically and emotionally. The more involved I became, the more field notes there were to write each day, and the less time I had in which to do it.

I had deliberately picked the October Revolution Brigade not only because its members had welcomed me into their midst but also because they were a particularly interesting bunch. Each time I returned to LKM I made sure I worked in the same brigade. Its leader was Gyuri, a chief steward in the union, who had won many enterprise and government medals for his services and had been on union delegations to Scandinavia, the Soviet Union, and Czechoslovakia. I caused him considerable grief when I insisted that, as a matter of principle, I enroll in the union. Surely, if the slogan "workers of the world unite" has any meaning I should be allowed to join the union. He approached the secretary of the union on my behalf, but that came to nothing. Then the personnel manager called me in. He wanted to know if my request was genuine and what nationality I was. Relieved to hear I was British, he said that the union's relations with the British steelworkers were much better than with the American union, and so perhaps it would be possible. Finally I did receive my little blue book with its infamous quote from Lenin about trade unions as unconditional collaborators with the workers' state and as the great educators of the working class. Every month when I turned in my dues (1 percent of my income) my mates chastised Gyuri for cheating me. I would never receive any of the benefits, they said, because I wouldn't be working there long enough. I knew that, of course. They viewed the union solely from the standpoint of the material benefits it provided. Nor was this surprising, since the union never seemed to defend workers' interests against management.

Gyuri had been in the mill since he was nineteen, and in 1985, at forty-four, he already looked forward to retirement in eleven years' time. I sometimes accompanied him home to his village—an hour away—to admire his garden full of fruit trees and his very profitable nutria. He was the only commuter. The rest of the brigade lived in Miskolc—the lucky ones like Józsi, Laci, and Karcsi in two-room or even two-and-a-half-room apartments. Csaba, recently divorced, lived with his parents in a tiny house on the outskirts, while Pista, a Gypsy, had given up a council flat to live in his own community not far from the mill. In those first six months I spent a lot of time with Józsi—an autodidact who had been a joiner and then decided to pursue his studies again. But he never finished and so took up a job in the steel mill. I sometimes went with him to visit his father, who had been a big shot in the rolling mills. Now retired, he tended his garden in the hills surrounding Miskolc. He had won prizes for his wine. There wasn't much Józsi couldn't do, but he never stuck with whatever it was for long. Divorced and frustrated, he was a heavy drinker, and now with heavy bags under his eyes he looked like E.T. So that's what we called him. I'd sometimes follow him after shift past the great statue of Lenin, pointing us in the direction of the "Garden in the Shadows"—the local beer garden. We always joked how tired Lenin must be, always standing there on his pedestal. Then, one night before the elections in 1990, he was quietly taken away, punished for misguiding generations of steel-workers. Still, even without his directions, steelworkers found their way to the Garden in the Shadows.

When I returned the next year (1986), E.T. and Pista had left and I spent more time with Karcsi and his family. They took me to the village where he grew up and where his parents still lived in a large house. His father had been a manager in APISZ—a commercial distribution agency. Without his help Karcsi would never have been able to buy his two-and-a-half-room apartment or own a Trabant car. Cars and fishing were his two obsessions. He was young, bright, and agile, and by the end of my third stint had been promoted to steel maker. His wife hated his rotating shifts since they wrecked any family life and often left her alone at night with her young daughter. He was always thinking of alternative jobs, but none promised security or paid as well as a steel maker's.

How my fellow workers regarded me—an outsider—was as revealing as the answers they gave to any questions. Although my lack of skill and knowledge was a liability, nevertheless I had the advantage of being a curiosity in the mill. Unlike Haraszti, who was so obviously a Budapest intellectual, I was regarded first and foremost as an American. I was eternally plied with questions about how I or an average steel-worker lived in the United States, how much we earned, where we lived, what we possessed, how much things cost. But in time my presence, my funny Hungarian, my eating habits became normalized through a series of jokes that cemented my membership in the brigade. Sometimes my mates called me "Jackson," as in Michael Jackson. But usually they called me Misi, the "kefir furnaceman," because I would consume carton after carton of diluted yogurt. I simply couldn't face, and my stomach couldn't digest, those rancid lumps of pork fat that everyone else carved up for breakfast, dinner, or lunch. They would look on in amusement as I lapped up my "cat food." No wonder I was so weak, they would say. I'd never be more than a 50 percent furnace-man if I didn't eat proper food.

Even my ineptitude bound me to the brigade. There was the memorable but at the time humiliating occasion when I failed to send the sample off to the laboratory. Béla the steel maker was waiting and waiting for the results, storming up and down the podium. He rang up the laboratory and discovered it hadn't arrived and so he ran out to the chute to find it still there. He was livid, flung his hard hat to the ground, and swore in paragraphs until he was blue in the face. Everyone knew who was responsible, but they defended me to the end, saying the air pressure in the chute had been weak. To help me overcome my shame they'd joke and laugh about it, and even to this day they imitate Béla hurling his hat to the ground.

At the end of my first stint I surreptitiously took some photographs on night shift of my colleagues at work. Then Gyuri grabbed the camera in front of the converter and handed me the long and heavy spoon for taking the steel sample—a task requiring skill and strength that was beyond me. I thrust the ladle into the sea of bubbling steel and then drew it out. But I didn't have on the right gloves and very quickly my right hand glowed and swelled with burns—a sure sign of a novice. They still laugh about the time I had my photo taken. These and other symbolic events marked my absorption into the group. I became their kefir furnaceman and they for their part protected me from dangers— human and physical. At the end of each of my stints we had a collective drinking party and I would write in their Brigade Diary—an amusing legacy of the past—what a dedicated group they were, how the bosses exploited them, and how they deserved extra bonuses.

When I worked in the champagne and textile factories and at Bánki I lived with families. Perhaps that was the most effective way to survive in the beginning. But it was also embarrassing to live in a room of my own while everyone else shared theirs. With the exception of pensioners and the three years maternity leave, all women work, so my presence created even more toil for an already overworked wife and mother. It was futile to struggle against the very strict gendering of roles in the home. Therefore, in Miskolc, I was determined to find an apartment of my own. Thus, in 1985 and 1986 I lived in a tiny "all comfort" one-room apartment with its own bathroom and kitchen. It was my "King Mátyás" castle. It had been the flat of an old woman who before dying had handed it on to her granddaughter—a young divorcee with a child of three. She needed my rent more desperately than space and so continued to live with her parents in their relatively commodious two-room apartment. My castle was a real luxury compared to the single room I was to rent during my third stint, in 1987. Then I lived in the huge proletarian housing estate known as the Avas. Almost a city unto itself, it is a maze of identical twelve-story concrete apartment blocks housing some eighty thousand people.

I might have escaped complicity in the family division of labor, but my participation at work and in the community continued to be structured by gendered relations. My fieldwork was founded on male camaraderie at work and on women's toil at home, which released my mates from the burdens of housework. However much I might try to transcend it, my view of the community was structured by my gendered participation.

There is an obvious methodological lesson here. All data, whether collected through interviews, surveys, experiments, demographic methods, or from archival sources, is limited by the context of its production. The limitations are just more obvious in the case of participant observation because it involves unmediated interaction between participant and observer. In the mill we tried to overcome this limitation by combining participant and nonparticipant observation.

What Is Socialist about Socialist Production?

The solidarity of the October Revolution Socialist Brigade contrasted vividly with the authoritarianism of management. Scale, drama, costs, and danger were reason enough for short tempers. There could be no joking around when huge ladles of pig iron, slag, and molten steel at fifteen hundred to seventeen hundred degrees were traveling backward and forward overhead. Here there were real disasters. One day I came in to discover that one of the ladles had sprung a leak. A carpet of eighty tons of molten steel now stuck to the floor beneath the podium. We watched from the podium as acetylene torches cut it apart and the cranes tried to haul it up piece by piece. I asked the person next to me whether this had ever happened before. He nudged his mate and repeated the question to him. They both started laughing. Only someone very naive about socialism would ask such a ridiculous question. But I had already learned to be careful in making attributes to socialism—the same disasters occur in the United States and Britain. So what then is distinctive to the socialist process of production?

As I was immersed in the October Revolution Brigade, my perspective was limited to the processes around the converter, and to the perspectives of my coworkers. I had some appreciation of the interdependence of the converter and the availability of scrap and hot metal on the one side and the continuous caster and the production of ingots on the other, but even this was colored by my confinement to the converter. I certainly remained oblivious to the broader constraints posed by units outside the Combined Steel Works—the rolling mill and the blast furnace and the even wider constraints within which they operated.

Had it not been for Lukács's roving observations and interviews, these wider forces impinging on the converter would have remained a mystery. As before he accompanied managers on their daily tasks and thereby began to appreciate the real problems they faced rather than listening to vague generalities made in their offices. By spending time in the rolling mills and the blast furnaces as well as in other parts of the Combined Steel Works he began to understand the troubles they posed for the operation of the converter. His nonparticipant observation was guided by my participant observation, by the questions and puzzles that emerged during my work in the mill. This was how we located my day-to-day experience around the converter in the broader technological, economic, and political contexts of its determination. Only through such collaboration between participant and nonparticipant observation was it possible to study what was socialist about steel production at LKM.

As before, our analysis leaned heavily on Kornai's path-breaking work on the shortage economy. Producing quality steel is difficult at the best of times, but in the context of a shortage economy, where technology and raw materials are unreliable, scarce, or even absent, it is often a hit-and-miss affair. No wonder the Japanese were quite mystified when they came to inspect their computer system. They are accustomed to being constrained from the side of demand, not supply. Their just-in-time systems are all about the most precise calibration of inputs. Indeed, we were told that some of the steel produced in Hungary was exported to Japan to be used as scrap to make the best steels.

So how then could steel be produced in a shortage economy? By spending time with managers, attending their meetings, listening to their gripes, and watching them hand out punishments and deal with everyday problems, Lukács was able to comprehend the distinctive interplay between informal cooperation among operators and management's dictatorial interventions. Take the case again of that much-boasted computer system, which was supposed to organize and coordinate production within the Combined Steel Works. As a guide to action the computer's instructions were gravely misleading since it worked with erroneous assumptions about the composition of inputs. So operators had to use their own judgment on the basis of emergent patterns of informal coordination. Adaptation to shortages called for autonomy on the shop floor, but the realization of such autonomy or flexible specialization threatened the functions of middle management. So managers would use the computer records against operators, accusing them of violating its instructions. Designed as an aid to operators, it became their surveillant, providing grounds for disrupting the elaborate networks of cooperation established between workplaces, for handing out arbitrary punishments, and for holding inquests into production failures. Operators had no recourse but to defend themselves against this system of bureaucratic despotism, often at the expense of effective plant production.

We wrote up this analysis presented here as chapter 4. But before we could publish it we had to seek permission from LKM management. At the time I happened to be in the middle of my third stint as a furnaceman. We gave the deputy director a draft of the article and he in turn passed it on to management at the Combined Steel Works. There the plant superintendent called a meeting, to which we were not invited, for all managers and supervisors, where portions of the paper were publicly read out. Participants told us how different managers had got up to denounce our work as an outrageous distortion based on rumors rather than facts. In blaming managers for the problems of steel production we simply did not know what we were talking about. Then the deputy director called us in to discuss the paper. He said he didn't object to the theoretical framework but to some of the facts—but it was not clear which. We had better go back and do the research again. Secretly, many would tell us that the paper was right on target but that they couldn't say so publicly. We happily talked to those managers who found it unacceptable, but we came away from those conversations only more convinced that we were correct. When they defended their actions they simply shifted the blame onto the backs of workers, or in some cases upward to top management. What was unacceptable was not what we wrote but that we dared to write it—an obvious challenge to the omniscient dictatorship of management.

Our experiences at Bánki and LKM led us to reflect once more on the pioneering work of Harry Braverman, *Labor and Monopoly Capital*—the original inspiration to the burgeoning literature on the labor process.[8] Braverman's argument that the tendency of the capitalist labor process was toward the separation of mental and manual labor, that is, toward the separation of conception from execution, has been subjected to intensive criticism. But from the standpoint of state socialism, his account of the trajectory of capitalist production assumes a new poignancy. Deskilling leads simultaneously to the lowering of wages and the intensification of control under capitalism because wages are determined through a labor market and the raw materials and machinery are readily available for planned production. The socialist enterprise faces shortages of equipment and materials, so that deskilling often disrupts production by denying workers the capacity to adapt to a changing environment. Flexible specialization is a technical and economic imperative of state socialism.[9] There conception and execution have to be re-unified at the level of the shop-floor production. In other words, we are arguing against the conventional wisdom that capitalism's entry into post-Fordism calls for flexible specialization to meet diversified and specialized markets. To the contrary, we argue that flexible specialization under capitalism is less an economic imperative and more a political stratagem to elicit consent in a period when middle management is under assault. It becomes a means of further expropriating control from the direct producer.[10] Naturally enough, therefore, our studies of the hidden abode of socialist production shed light on the character of capitalism.

Class Consciousness

While the separation of conception and execution may govern capitalist *production*, it does not govern capitalist *appropriation*, which takes place according to the rules of private property. It is the owner of the means of production, not the conceiver of work organization, who appropriates. By contrast, it is under state socialism that Braverman's categories come into their own, not at the level of *production* but at the level of *appropriation*. For here it is indeed the conceivers, the planners, or, as Konrád and Szelényi call them, the teleological redistributors who appropriate surplus from the executors, the direct producers. As they argue in *The Intellectuals on the Road to Class Power*, such centralized and visible appropriation requires a legitimation based on the common interests of all.[11]

When the problem is to mystify the appropriation of surplus, as under capitalism, ideologies play a secondary role in reproducing society. They are diverse and not essential. However, where surplus appropriation is transparent and has therefore to be justified as being in the collective interest, then ideology comes to play a prominent role in everyday life. Thus, state socialism calls on both its dominant and its subordinate classes to proclaim the virtues of socialism—its efficiency, its justice, its equality—in ritual activities from communist shifts, production conferences, brigade competitions, and campaigns to forced marches and public speeches. Everyone is called on to "paint socialism" as the radiant future at the same time that everyone knows that the everyday "reality" is anything but radiant. Through these rituals, ideology assumes a reality of its own which everyone is compelled to recognize—a game that everyone is compelled to play out, but which everyone sees through. The painting of socialism only impresses on people the failure of socialism to realize its promises. It engenders an imminent critique of state socialism, a negative class consciousness, dissent if you please, right at the heart of society in the process of production. In chapter 5, therefore, I juxtapose "painting socialism" to "manufacturing consent." In state socialism it is not simply that exploitation is revealed as domination of the state, but the coincidence of the two calls for legitimating rituals which demonstrate all that socialism is not. Inevitably, state socialism sows the seeds of its own destruction—but how?

Working-class consciousness within all state socialist societies may tend toward critique, but what turns critique into mobilization? Here the relevant comparison is not between the West and the East but within the East, between Poland and other countries. Why did Poland generate a Solidarity and not Hungary? What happened since 1956 to lead Polish workers toward collective mobilization and Hungarian workers toward strategies of individual survival and mobility? First of all, the opportunities for material advancement through the second economy were available to Hungarian workers and much less so to Polish workers. While Polish workers were lining up in queues for basic consumer items, Hungarian workers were cultivating their gardens, plying their trades, and selling their wares. Basic and indeed not-so-basic consumer items were in plentiful supply, so Hungarians didn't have to spend hours in lines or in greasing contacts. Furthermore, those extra hours of work were worth the effort, since the forints earned purchased desired goods. Second, the resources for collective mobilization were available to the Polish workers but not to their Hungarian counterparts. The Roman Catholic church as a symbol of opposition to the party and the crucial role of intellectuals in fostering working-class solidarity after 1976 distinguished the Polish political scene from the Hungarian.

These at any rate were the arguments that evolved during the time I spent working at LKM between 1985 and 1987 and which were developed in the article that appears here as chapter 5. Looking back on the article demonstrates just how quickly history overtook my analysis. My attention was focused on the working class, whereas the most dramatic changes were already occurring in the party. State socialism appeared to be crumbling from above, not from below. It would be easy to attribute the collapse to changes in the Soviet Union, but that would be to take the erroneous view that Hungary and the whole of Eastern Europe were outside the Soviet Union. The dam may have burst, but it was because the water was rising on every side. Leaders of state socialism also had to paint socialism; in fact, they were leading the show, and they saw through it as well as any. With less and less to show for it, the pretense became less and less bearable to party elites. Socialism developed a hollowness they themselves could not live with. Once it was clear that the Soviet Union would not interfere, the painting of socialism turned into the rapid dismantling of socialism. Too many attempts at bringing reality into conformity with ideology had failed, so now it was the turn of ideology to be recast. In 1989 communist ideology was replaced by anti-communism and capitalism became the radiant future of all humanity.

Action Sociology in a Period of Transition

But we are getting ahead of our story. Lukács came to Berkeley for the academic year 1988–89 to study work organization and industrial relations in the United States. He became very interested in worker cooperatives and employee-owned companies. Our research at Bánki and other studies suggested that, given the opportunity, workers could show great initiative in making enterprises efficient. All too often, however, the situation was what we found at LKM, where workers were hamstrung by managerial despotism. Lukács had always been interested in the means to releasing the potentiality of worker participation and saw this as one way of improving the efficiency of socialist industry. Since the U.S. steel industry had become the same sort of inefficient monopoly it had become in Hungary, he became intrigued by the successful transformation of Weirton Steel Company into an employee-owned enterprise. Through an ESOP (employee stock ownership plan), Weirton had been turned from a marginal business into one of the most profitable steel companies in the United States. Lukács spent two months there, studying how it was done, and used his considerable knowledge of steel production to explore the details of its operation.

He returned to Hungary in September 1989, enthusiastic about the possibilities of employee ownership schemes. His newly acquired expertise was particularly pertinent since during his absence the Hungarian government had introduced plans for accelerated privatization of state-owned enterprises. The last socialist government was overseeing the most liberal transformation of the state-owned economy. This was the way it sought to maintain itself. It was privatization at any cost, whether this meant selling companies on the cheap to foreign enter-

prises or allowing state managers to buy up their own or other enterprises. The working class was left out in the cold. Lukács saw employee
ownership as one means of including their participation in the transition.

Armed with his experience in the United States—the land of the free
market—he promoted the concept of employee ownership in conferences on privatization and in lectures to government officials, chambers
of commerce, and enterprises. He wrote articles on United States
ESOPs in major newspapers, although their publication encountered
considerable resistance. Together with a small group of lawyers and
economists, concerned about the rapidity of privatization and the absence of any public participation, he formed a foundation that would
provide expertise on ways of introducing employee ownership.

Lukács became the leading expert on employee ownership schemes
in Hungary. In November 1989 he was appointed to a committee assigned to prepare legislation that would enable employees to buy up
shares in their companies. He was one of six members of a select group
of experts, the majority of whom wanted as little as possible to do with
genuine employee ownership. The committee was set up as a concession
to worker participation in the transformation of state enterprises, but it
was intended to be no more than a gesture. The majority view was that
workers should be owners only as individuals and only if they pay a
proportion of their shares. They had to learn the meaning of capital
investment by risking their own earnings. Lukács fought for ESOP legislation in which workers would pay for their shares not out of their
earnings but out of future profits. He also promoted the idea of an employee trust or foundation as a means to facilitate employee ownership
and as a potential instrument of employee representation. His opponents effectively discredited the idea of *any* collective representation or
ownership by associating it with communism. For the same reasons,
trade union participation was just as flatly rejected. The prevailing ideology of anticommunism pronounced all collectivities evil. After much
wrangling, the final proposed legislation was ready in February, containing two alternative plans. But it was too late to submit to the outgo-
ing government, which was then entering its last month.

However disillusioning, Lukács's participation in the advisory committee nevertheless gave him more credibility in defending employee
ownership. In March and April he spent time in London and Washington, making links with organizations such as Job Ownership Limited
(London) and the Center for Economic and Social Justice (Washington)
who advocated employee ownership. With their help he also made con-

tact with international bodies and governments who were preparing aid packages for Hungary, to persuade them to support such schemes.

In Hungary, enterprises couldn't dismiss his ideas as idle dreams. More and more bodies approached him for advice, particularly workers' councils which had sprung up in opposition to the official trade unions. At the famous porcelain factory of Herend, a workers' council had already replaced the trade union when it called on Lukács for advice. The workers' council quickly realized the advantages of an employee buy-out, particularly when privatization seemed inevitable and foreigners were already on the doorstep. But the general director was less than enthusiastic and called in an opponent of employee ownership in order to discredit Lukács by publicly denouncing his plans as unrealistic. The battle for Herend began.

The Herend workers' council had originally sought the support of the Social Democratic Party, but it showed much less interest than the Hungarian Democratic Forum (MDF), who saw workers' councils as part of their Third Road platform. The president of the Herend workers' council stood for parliament on an MDF ticket and won. So Lukács became the economic adviser to the president of the workers' council and moved closer to the Democratic Forum government, which took office in May. As the workers' council assumed more and more power within the enterprise, it became increasingly committed to making Herend the test case for employee ownership. In June it won control of the enterprise council and deposed the general director.

I had talked with Lukács in Budapest in January (1990), and we had decided to follow up our earlier studies into the period of transition. I arrived in April and stayed until the end of June, not to work in a factory but to accompany Lukács wherever he went, studying the transition through his participation in the unfolding events. Our roles were reversed. I was now the nonparticipant observer and he the participant observer. Our research took on an entirely new complexion as Lukács became an activist and consultant. Instead of Lukács requesting facilities for research from enterprises, enterprises were now soliciting Lukács's advice on how to make their way through the maze of privatization and come out ahead at the other end. The tables were turned. We could legitimately gather all sorts of information that would otherwise be unavailable to us, but we now had to be careful how we used it.

In a period of transition, many changes occur dramatically and unexpectedly. It is no time for armchair sociology. Intense involvement is the only way to appreciate the uncertainty of the unfolding processes. Certainly Lukács's lobbying efforts with government, his consultation with enterprises preparing privatization plans, his public lectures to conferences and chambers of commerce, and his search for resources for his foundation and for personnel to prepare new legislation represented intense involvement, but they left him no time to think about what was happening, let alone write about it. He was pushed this way and that, responding to the political pressures of the moment, not knowing what new turn of events each day would bring. There was no time or space for him to sit down and make sense of his involvement. That was my role. Through daily dialogue we interpreted his experiences in terms of our previous research and in terms of the transition taking place around us.

Lukács's lobbying on behalf of employee ownership and broader worker participation in the economy involved all levels of society, from the ministerial level down to the workshop. It revealed the increasing fragmentation and disarticulation of society, and—most specifically from the point of view of our previous research—the separation of production politics from state politics. The autonomy of the legal system and of parliamentary democracy gave at the same time greater autonomy to the politics of production. No longer an arm of the state, new apparatuses of production had to be constructed to dovetail with privatization. Enterprise councils, which had once been a tool of management, now mirrored the tensions of a new political order. In some cases they became arenas of intense struggle, where management prerogatives could be questioned. Privatization plans had to be formulated in the enterprise council, and it was from there that old directors like the ones at Herend and at Raba could be ousted. The old trade union, which justified its collusion with management on the grounds that the real line of division was between the enterprise and the state, lost its raison d'être as enterprises became autonomous from the state. New lines of division between workers and potential capitalists called for new forms of interest representation, such as workers' councils.

As we discovered when we returned to LKM in June, the Herend worker-council model was spreading. When I met with Gyuri in June, he immediately reminded me of my incessant joking about Hungarian trade unions. How often had I asked: What sort of union was it that could count every manager among its membership, that spent its time collecting dues, distributing places in holiday homes, and organizing family outings, that happily signed any managerial decree? He had taken my ribbing to heart. After a major conflict with management and the union (described in chapter 5), he resigned his chief stewardship and in April 1990 began to organize a workers' council in the Combined

Steel Works. This was going to be a real trade union, he told me jubi-
lantly. It would deny membership to managers with disciplinary powers, pursue legitimate grievances of its membership, and build up a
strike fund out of membership dues. But its goals were still more ambitious: to reduce inefficiency and waste by supervising managers, to
champion economic justice by overseeing the distribution of bonuses,
and even to reappropriate control through employee ownership. This
was radical stuff, harking back to the worker councils of 1956. It was a
reaction to years of trade union impotence and collusion, to bureaucratic centralism and political toadying.

The more we learned about the emerging forms of production politics, the better we understood the past. The emergence of worker councils taught us how the old order had limited the role of trade unions and
how apparatuses of production had been bound to the state. We also
once more discovered that property relations were not the all-important
force that orthodox Marxism and liberal economics made them out to
be. Privatization was one thing, reorganizing production was quite another. The real task was to create markets out of hierarchies, to break
up monopolies and allow new firms to enter production, particularly
industrial production. Spontaneous privatization was not the magic
wand that would create a competitive capitalist economy out of the
preexisting centralized system. Our study of LKM, related here in
chapter 6, shows just how privatization can reproduce the worst aspects
of the old order if there is no guidance from the state. Perhaps, as the
Latin American experience suggests and as Karl Polanyi argued for
nineteenth-century England, the creation of markets requires intensive
state intervention.[12] For all the anticommunist ideology, for all the free
marketeering, the state is destined to continue to play a crucial role in
any transformation. And if that is true, then perhaps we should take the
past more seriously rather than dismiss it as a nightmarish detour from
capitalism to capitalism.

During the last ten years, what was to be the radiant future became
the radiant past. It began in Poland with the first workers' revolution and ended with popularly elected governments rushing back to
nineteenth-century capitalism. Without delivering on its promises, socialism can be painted and repainted only so many times before it becomes a hollow activity—even for the leadership that organizes and
benefits from such activity. When the intellectual defenders of "communism," like Zinoviev's professor, lose any confidence in the worth of
what they have done—when those who have dedicated themselves to
justifying "communism" feel cheated—then the system crumbles from

within. What emerges out of the dissolution of the radiant past are equally radical visions of the future. Politically conscious sections of the working class evolve a vision of radical democracy founded on shop-floor control and employee ownership. But for now this is much weaker than the call for the restoration of nineteenth-century capitalism by the intellectuals of the new parties and the mass media. Still, the gap between intellectuals and workers continues to grow, preparing the ground for future conflicts.

Just as capitalism generates a utopian vision of socialism, so now communism generates a utopian vision of capitalism as the radiant future of all mankind. Ideologists of the East join ideologists of the West under the banner of laissez-faire capitalism. But will the real future of Eastern Europe be so radiant? Or will privatization bring the destruction of industry, the further deterioration of the environment, the invasion of foreign capital, the ruthless exploitation of people, and the intensification of inequalities? Is Hungary taking the Third Road to the Third World? In ten years' time will communism, at least its Kádárist version, indeed appear as the radiant past?

PART ONE: IDEOLOGY VERSUS REALITY
Bánki

Introduction

Our point of departure is the model of state socialism developed by Konrád and Szelényi.[1] In their theory, state socialism is a class society. A dominant class of planners, or what they call teleological redistributors, appropriates and redistributes surplus produced by a class of direct producers. Because centralized appropriation is visible, it has to be legitimated. This brings into play the second distinctive component of state socialism, the ideology which presents central appropriation as being in the interests of all. The legitimacy of the dominant class depends on its claim to decide what those interests are and how they may best be satisfied, while consent to state socialism depends on how successful the dominant class is in realizing those common interests.

In this model, ideology and reality are each given their due and not reduced to one other. By contrast, the models of totalitarianism which have so dominated the study of the Soviet Union and its Eastern European satellites take that ideology too seriously. This comes about in two ways. Either they concentrate on the gap between the reality of actually existing socialism and its ideology, or they regard ideology as determining that reality.

Theorists of totalitarianism who have written from within state socialism have stressed the discrepancy between ideology and reality—that socialism turns out to be very different from what it promises. Instead of the dictatorship of the proletariat, state socialism proves to be a dictatorship over the proletariat; instead of a classless society, a "new class" or "nomenclatura" emerges; instead of the realization of needs, we find the dictatorship over needs. From the standpoint of production, the paradigmatic critique is Miklós Haraszti's book, *A Worker in a Worker's State*, which paints a picture of an atomized, oppressed, alienated, degraded working class—the very antithesis of the socialist ideal.[2] In refuting ruling ideology with reality, the totalitarian images present a homogenized society with no dynamics or variation. Haraszti, for example, presents himself as a typical worker in a typical factory in a typical socialist society. He makes no attempt to locate himself, his factory, or his country in any historical context. Socialism on earth is the denial of its heavenly promise. His is preeminently a work of critique, not explanation.

A similarly homogenized portrait of state socialism appears in writings which take capitalism as their point of departure. Their point of critique is not the ideology of socialism but their understanding of capitalist freedoms. They are less interested in refuting socialist ideology than in demonstrating its pervasiveness, as it imposes itself through repressive command from above, and extracts conformity from all. Reinhard Bendix's classic portrait of managerial ideology in Eastern Europe represents this view most clearly.[3] In capitalism, ideology emerges through the open articulation of interests, whereas in state socialism it is imposed through party dictatorship. In capitalism, ideology is as much a rationalization of interests as it is a guide to action, whereas in state socialism the vanguard party compels the unity of theory and practice. The party organization executes centrally defined goals by subordinating to itself all levels of society. For this the party depends upon activists in the factory, selected for loyalty and isolated through differential rewards. Because Bendix regards ideology as an instrument of an all-powerful force, an image itself driven by his understanding of capitalist ideology, he paints a picture of communist uniformity and atomization.

Andrew Walder tries to shed the overweening focus on ideology in his fascinating study of the Chinese factory.[4] Criticizing the totalitarian images of social atomism and impersonal ties between party and activist, he stresses the particularist ties that develop around relations of material and political dependence. The enterprise's control over the distribution of scarce consumer resources gives rise to two patterns of association: first, "principled particularism," in which party activists exchange political loyalty for preferential access to resources and careers, and second, "nonprincipled particularism," in which workers obtain needed goods and services through bribery and the manipulation of personal ties. Walder claims that "communist" societies are all evolving toward a "new system of institutionalized clientelism; a neo-traditional pattern of authority based on citizen dependence on social institutions and their leaders."[5]

If Walder moves beyond Bendix in capturing the social networks that govern the Chinese enterprise, his model still suffers from false generalization and homogenization. First, without gathering empirical support, he extends his model to all state socialist regimes. Second, in elucidating what is distinctive to all communist patterns of authority, he makes unexamined assumptions about the typical form of capitalist authority. In this sense he too is trapped by ideology, namely the ideology that workers in a capitalist society are not bound by relations of dependence and particularism. As we shall see, the factory regime in the United States can more closely approximate his model than the Hungarian factory regime.

Concerned to generalize across time and space, Walder fails to thematize the social, political, and economic forces which lead to the *specific* form of factory regime he observes. Like Haraszti and Bendix, he does not examine historical change of factory regime, nor thematize, let alone explain, differences either within or between state socialist societies. All these theorists concentrate on establishing the prototype factory regime of state socialism, isolated from the forces that explain its variation.

A major development in the study of state socialism comes with what David Stark and Victor Nee call "the new institutional analysis."[6] They argue that the old paradigms of totalitarianism (in which state socialism is convergent with fascism) and modernization theory (in which technology and modern values lead to a convergence between state socialism and capitalism) give way to the recognition of state socialism as a society with a logic of its own. Within this framework, the focus shifts from parties, ideologies, and elites to alternative institutional forms such as the second economy and to group formation in civil society. Fine-grained studies reveal a rich diversity of social relations in what was once regarded as a repressive uniformity.

In comparing such countries as Poland, China, and Hungary, the contributors to Stark and Nee's volume show just how different these societies are. As a reaction to the homogenizing effects of earlier frameworks in which ideology figured prominently, ideology now completely drops out of the picture. The new institutional approach leads to the study of mixed economies so that the differences between capitalism and socialism become blurred. Equally unclear in these accounts is the extent to which totalitarian and modernization theories were mistaken approaches driven by ideological concerns of cold war and détente, or alternatively, the extent to which they correctly depicted the earlier periods of state socialism. Is the new institutionalism a call for the reexamination of the early Stalinist period, or is it specifically applicable to the 1980s, when in some countries civil society and economy developed new institutions? Having opened Pandora's box of variation it is also important to close it again by developing theories that can simultaneously understand variation as well as similarity—what explains variations of state socialism but also what differentiates it from capitalism.

We are interested in pursuing this task in connection with the character of socialist production. We stress four features of state socialist regimes of production, all of which stem from the central appropriation of surplus. First, the state as both owner and organizer of production is present at the point of production in the form of a triple alliance between management, party, and trade union. From the point of view of direct producers, party and trade union are instruments of managerial domination. Second, central appropriation of surplus leads to shortages of raw materials and appropriate technology, posing distinctive problems for the organization of work and its regulation. Third, central direction of the economy requires ideological justification which becomes embodied in rituals of socialist affirmation, organized within the enterprise. At the same time, enthusiastic participation in these rituals is an expression of loyalty, required by the game of bureaucratic competition. We deal with this component in part 2 of the book. Fourth, the relationship between community and production changes with the extent of distribution of consumer goods through the market. To the extent that consumer goods are available through the market, management loses power over its work force.

We distinguish two types of factory regime under state socialism: bureaucratic despotic and bureaucratic hegemonic. All production regimes are bureaucratic in that they are extensions of the state into the sphere of production. As we will describe in chapter 6, the transition from state socialism to capitalism brings about the institutional separation of factory from the state, production politics from state politics. Under despotic regimes, management, with the aid of trade union and party, extracts submission from workers due to their dependence on enterprise supply of goods and services. At the same time, management is dependent on the spontaneous cooperation of workers to meet the exigencies of uncertain supplies of materials and machinery. Management uses its monopoly over scarce consumer goods to reward a leading cadre of activists—such as Stakhanovites or heroes of labor—who become involved in directing production, set norms to be emulated, or surveil rank-and-file workers. This type of factory regime is the one described by Walder, but it is also the one described by Vladimir Andrle, Lewis Siegelbaum, and Donald Filtzer for the Soviet Union in the 1930s.[7]

At the other extreme is the Hungarian bureaucratic hegemonic regime we describe in chapter 2. The enterprise no longer controls the distribution of scarce goods and services, such as housing, child care, televisions, cars, food, clothing, etc. These are now available either through the market (purchasable with forints) or through distribution by the state. Management loses its capacity to extract submission through its monopoly of scarce consumer goods but does not develop a new power based on the threat of firing or laying off workers. Management has to elicit the consent of workers, through financial incentives, bonus systems and piece rates, the distribution of overtime, or participation in lucrative "economic work partnerships." But there isn't a cadre of party activists mobilizing rank-and-file workers to participate in production campaigns, to achieve plan targets, or to scale new heights in output records.

The contrast with capitalism is instructive. There also we delineate two distinct regimes: despotic and hegemonic. As in state socialism, the transition from despotic to hegemonic regimes is propelled by the independence of workers from managerial control. However, the basis of that independence is different. Under early capitalism, workers feared losing their jobs since this would cut them off from their wages and deny them their means of existence. In that context, arbitrary firing and layoffs, therefore, constituted the basis of coercion. With the development on the one hand of trade unions and procedural guarantees against firing, and on the other hand of social insurance against loss of job (unemployment compensation, social security, etc.), employers lost some of their despotic power. They sought new techniques of eliciting cooperation through hegemonic regimes which concretely coordinated the interests of management and workers. In short, under state socialism it is *market* provision of consumer goods and services that proves the undoing of despotic regimes, whereas under capitalism it is the *state* as organizer of welfare and regulator of industrial relations that undermines despotic regimes of production.

As in capitalism, so in state socialism, we find hegemonic and despotic regimes coexisting within the same society. In capitalist societies this is due on the one hand to the relationship of enterprises and their workers to the market and on the other hand to the uneven regulation of industrial relations by the state and unequal access to welfare. Under state socialism, by contrast, the character of the factory regime depends on an enterprise's relationship to the state and, in particular, its capacity to extract concessions on behalf of its workers, and also in part on the development of the market.[8]

However, there is no natural evolution from despotic to hegemonic regimes in state socialism. The transition in Hungary is due to historically specific factors: the collectivization of agriculture after 1956, whose success rested in part on bringing richer and more skilled peasantry into the cooperatives; the granting of greater autonomy to enterprises as well as the opening up of a legal second economy after 1968; a policy of using foreign exchange to import consumer durables that were not made in Hungary. The state's policy of making goods and services available through the marketplace or by direct application to the state meant that enterprises lost control of these scarce resources, and hence their punitive power over workers came to rest on control over pecuniary rewards. Among state socialist societies Hungary went further in this direction than any other country, with the possible exception of Yugoslavia.

Within a single regime of production, work organization may vary considerably. The nature of a shortage economy requires flexible adaptation on the shop floor. This is what we found at Bánki, as we describe in chapters 2 and 3. When such self-organization threatens management then it may be repressed, with disastrous consequences for production, as we will see in chapter 4. Equally under capitalism, expropriation of control from the shop floor may or may not be effective. Where supply uncertainties exist, due to the hierarchical character of the capitalist corporation, such rationalization is counterproductive, as we argue in chapter 3. The following two chapters, therefore, demonstrate the considerable variations that can occur within both state socialism and advanced capitalism. They demonstrate that just as capitalist production *can* be inefficient, so also state socialist production *can* be efficient. Moreover, they offer an explanation that is based less on property relations and more on the combination of hierarchies and markets.

2 Piece Rates, Hungarian Style

There are three workers: an American, a West German, and a Hungarian.
The American eats five eggs and steak for breakfast and goes to work in his
Buick. At work he is exploited. The West German has three eggs and ham
for breakfast and goes to work in his Opel. He is also exploited at work.
The Hungarian has one egg for breakfast and no meat. He goes to work on
a bus but he is not exploited. At work he rules.

joke from the Hungarian shop floor

Hungary is the consumer paradise of Eastern Europe. The Hungarian
economic reforms of 1968, which gave more autonomy to state enterprises and more scope for private enterprise, have been consolidated
and extended. The shortages of basic consumer goods that continue to
benight other socialist economies have been more or less eliminated.
Queues are now (1984) a curiosity—outside pawn shops, or for Cuban
bananas. Meat, fruit, vegetables, all the basic and many luxury foods
are always available and in many varieties. Every third family has a car,
and almost all have refrigerators. State housing is still in short supply
and apartments are pitifully small, but all over the country people are

building themselves one- and two-story homes. Except among the Gypsy population, one is hard-pressed to find the poverty and insecurity that afflict a quarter of the population of the United States. And the Hungarian welfare system offers basic guarantees in old age, child-rearing, and illness. Consumer paradises, however, like all earthly paradises, are not built out of fine words, economic formulas, or political slogans, but out of hard work. For two months I entered the hidden abode of socialist production.

When I am on the morning shift, as I am today and all this week, I catch the number five bus at 5:32 A.M. It's summer and already light. The bus is jam-packed. Two and three stops back, toward the outskirts of the town, it picked up workers from the housing estate where fifteen thousand people live in one-room, one-and-a-half-room, two-room, and, for the exceptionally lucky, three-room apartments. Although some have managed to buy their apartments from the state, most pay a monthly rent of four hundred to one thousand forints (two to five days' work; the current exchange rate is forty-six forints to one U.S. dollar). Can a family of four ever get used to such cramped quarters in anonymous concrete blocks? Is work, like the open-air swimming baths, a welcome escape? If it is, you wouldn't know it from the grim faces on the bus. Perhaps it's just too early to be jovial. Probably one never gets used to the coercive routine of coming to work. There's silence on the bus, and I avoid catching my foreman's eye. The bus wends its way through the town, and in twelve minutes we are outside the factory. It could be a factory anywhere in the world, except that hovering over it is a dull red star. Its name is inscribed in broken lettering on the front wall.

We pass through a new three-story building, housing the porter's lodge, the security check, and the employment office. But most of the building is taken up by the worker's dormitory, built for long-distance commuters. These are usually young single men with skills to offer, although a few couples live here too. There's room for about a hundred workers, and at present there are about eighty. The rooms would be tiny enough for one person, but they manage to fit three beds together with a small shower and bathroom. At weekends workers go back to their homes, often in distant villages. This is not the sort of life one puts up with for long. But while it lasts it is at least cheap—160 forints (six hours' work) a month for a bed.

After leaving the building I join a straggling line of workers walking toward Department B, the older of the two main shops—older workers and older machines. The entrance to the shop marks the real barrier between the factory and the world outside. Once I cross the line I have to cease daydreaming, wrench myself into the present, and concentrate on the realities at hand. I greet my fellow workers, shaking hands with some and recognizing others verbally. The nuances of social address, complicated enough for Hungarians, are much more so for a foreigner in an ambiguous status like myself. I stumble through it, clock in, and make my way to the changing room. It's 5:48, and already night-shift workers are showering. I open my locker and take out my work boots, still dripping with oil from yesterday, and brown overalls. At least they were brown when I got them four days ago. Now they are more black than brown, covered with oil stains and impregnated with metallic dust—as sure a sign of a novice as any, but no one draws attention to it. Shoes and clothes are given out free, and every two weeks I change my overalls. Brown identifies me as a member of Department B, while the workers in the newer shop, Department A, are decked in a more attractive bright green.

I return to the shop. It could be any machine shop. The familiar smell of oil, the familiar sounds—the screeching of automatic lathes, the hum of drills drowned out by the roar of automatic mills. It evokes the same mixed feelings of dread and awe as did the small-parts department of Allied, the engine division of a multinational corporation in South Chicago where I worked as a miscellaneous machine operator for ten months in 1974–75. It's about the same size—two hundred feet square. There are over a hundred machines, in nine parallel lines separated by five aisles, with another central aisle cutting across the shop. Six of the lines are dominated by lathes, including automatic lathes, while the others are composed largely of mills and drills. Most of the machines are Czech or Hungarian, although one or two of the modern numerical-control machines are West German. There's even a broach used for cutting irregularly shaped holes, such as keyways in steel pulleys. I shudder every time I look at it, remembering the times I nearly killed myself on a similar machine at Allied.

The center of the Allied shop was dominated by the scheduling office, where we would pick up our work orders; the foremen's office; the inspectors' benches; and the crib, where we got our tools. Here the offices and crib are pushed against the wall; one of the inspectors' benches is too, while two are centrally located. But the shop's most central point is marked by a huddle of people around the coffee maker—always kept going by the woman who runs the speed drills. For four and a half forints (ten minutes' work), Zsuzsa will pour you a small glass of strong Hungarian coffee. However, I wait for mine to be brewed by the Dobó Katica Socialist Work Brigade—the women mill operators who have adopted me as one of their own. The noise is temporarily reduced to a hum, as the night-shift workers have left and the day-shift workers are gathered around to exchange gossip about what they did the night before or will do this weekend. The buzzer goes off and we slowly scatter to our machines. The roar begins again.

I operate a radial drill. Unlike with other drills, with a radial drill the piece rather than the machine is clamped into position and the operator moves the spindle from hole to hole. From the steel base rises a column about two feet thick and ten feet tall, with a boom that extends six feet out from the column and swings around it. The head moves along the length of the boom. From its underside drops the spindle, which holds the chuck, into which various tools—drills, reamers, spot-facers, chamfers—can be inserted. So the spindle can be moved in three directions: horizontally, by pushing or pulling on the boom; vertically, by raising or lowering the chuck in the head; and in a horizontal, radial direction by moving the head backward or forward along the boom. A hollow steel table, with grooves used for clamping fixtures, raises the work to waist height.

How did I get landed with such a monstrosity? When I first appeared before the shop superintendent seven weeks ago as a prospective employee, I told him I had operated simple machines before. With no hesitation he marched me over to the vacant radial drill at the end of the line. There seemed to be no doubt in his mind where I belonged. I looked at the giant albatross and panicked. I wouldn't have dared touch such a machine at Allied. I protested feebly that I was not very skilled. Well, try it, he said. This was going to be a nightmare, I was certain. I soon understood why I had been dumped on the radial drill: No one else wanted it. The job was poorly paid and the norms were difficult to make; the machine demanded concentration and strength, and offered few opportunities for private earnings outside work (*maszek*). The trial would begin after I was marched from office to office, collecting a dozen signatures from seemingly every department and organization in the factory, registering me as a genuine socialist worker.

My foreman, Kálmán, seemed pleasant enough—a young engineer, getting practical experience on the shop floor. He introduced me to János, who would or would not teach me the tricks of the trade. János is a slight, mustached Gypsy, a skilled operator with twelve years in the factory and six on the radial drill. That day he had seven tools carefully lined up on the bench to his left. I watched him pick up each in turn, slap it into the whirling chuck, changing the "speed" (revolutions per minute) and "feed" (downward pressure, measured in centimeters per minute) on the head. He then guided the tool to the specified holes by pushing, pulling, and turning the head on the boom, simultaneously bringing down the spindle until the tool cut into the small steel part, shaped like a beer bottle and clamped into its fixture on the work table. When this operation was finished he raised the spindle and detached the tool from the still-whirling chuck, replacing it with the next in sequence and beginning the process again. Periodically, he unlocked the fixture and revolved it on its axis to begin a new series of holes. After about eight minutes the piece was finished, full of holes in different directions, and unbolted from the fixture. A new piece from the large tub to his right was clamped into the fixture, and János began it all over again. The piece-time norm for this job is seventeen minutes; János does it in half. It's an impressive sight—the easy flowing command with which this little man guides his machine in three directions, flicking tools in and out of the chuck. Would I ever be able to remember the exact sequence of tools and the holes each is supposed to cut? Would I ever dare slap a drill in and out of a chuck spinning at a thousand revolutions per minute? Who said industrial work has lost its skill?

János was friendly enough. Realizing my trepidation, he tried to assure me that it was not as difficult as it looked, and in any case my jobs would be simpler to begin with. Soon he took me for a drink of "cola" at the buffet. Then Gabi introduced himself—the setup man on the mills. Laci soon arrived on the scene. Everyone was curious about their new American worker. And then I was introduced to Lajos, the charge hand, who, it turned out, would really be responsible for my training. He is a charming, rotund, mustached fellow with curly hair and ruddy cheeks. I felt I was in good hands. He soon grasped my level and adjusted accordingly. Certainly it was not like my old machine shop in South Chicago, where Bill, the day-shift operator who was supposed to train me, was curt and hostile, showing me the bare minimum. Bill, of course, had every reason to protect job secrets from competition. His power on the shop floor rested in the monopoly of knowledge he had acquired from ten years as a miscellaneous machine operator. For the first three months, I remember, it was a nightmare. Every day I came in nervous, wondering what I screwed up the night before. Here I never worry much. Not only Lajos but the radial drill operators themselves, János and Péter, are always prepared to help me. They show me the real route to success: abandoning the instructions on the blueprint.

Of course, I am not a typical newcomer. I am no threat to János and Péter. I do not compete for their gravy work or show how loose their norms are. That was clear from the beginning. They could afford to be nice to me. I would be here for only two months. Even when they show me the shortcuts I don't make more than 85 percent, compared to everyone else's 100-plus. And there are positive incentives to be friendly. I am Misi, the sociologist from America who has come to write a book about factory life in Hungary, a guest worker with a difference. I am a curiosity that will enliven their days. They exude a natural and genuine generosity so absent from the brittle, competitive atmosphere at Allied (although even there, when I became more experienced and Bill realized that he was going to have to live with me, he became more friendly. We would joke around when our shifts overlapped and even sometimes share a "kitty"—work completed but not handed in, to be used in emergency situations when we couldn't make the rate).

Today is Friday and everyone is thinking about the weekend. Even if it will mean more work, at least they will be working on their own gardens or weekend houses. They will decide the pace and own the product. But before the weekend I still have to get through the housings I began yesterday. The job has a lousy rate, and so I am not surprised Pista has not stolen them from me. When I'm on easier rates he sometimes does four hours overtime on my work after I have left. The gravy quickly disappears. There's nothing I can do about it, despite all the moral support I get from János and the women of the Dobó Katica Brigade. They tell me Pista is a kulák and *csizmás paraszt* (boot-legged peasant). The problem is that Pista's automatic drill across the aisle from me often runs out of work, and if he doesn't manage to find more work for himself, the shop superintendent will—generally lousy work. My first real encounter with Pista was one day when he stormed over to my machine swearing like a trooper about how he'd worked for the company twenty-one years and he was still being pushed around from one machine to another. He protested, "I'm a mill operator, not a rough grinder or a lathe operator. Who the hell does this reactionary management think they are?" That time he knuckled under, moved onto the lathe, worked like fury, stormed out three hours before the end of the shift, and didn't come in the next day. On another occasion, not finding any work to his satisfaction, he marched off home soon after beginning the shift.

At Allied, workers were never punted from machine to machine. When there was no work—it rarely happened—we were guaranteed pay at 125 percent. Here too, at least in theory, we are guaranteed "standstill time" pay at 100 percent, but workers are not satisfied with it. Nor is management. They prefer to transfer workers to other machines. Without the elaborate, union-protected job rights we had at Allied, workers' resistance depends on the bargaining power each can accumulate by virtue of his or her importance in the work process. Management's flexible deployment of labor is enshrined in the special bonus that foremen can distribute, a maximum of three hundred forints a month (about one-and-a-half-days' pay). One of the criteria foremen use is operators' willingness and ability to work on a variety of machines.

But this doesn't affect me at all. I have difficulty operating one machine. My radial drill is not only the last in the line; it's also the oldest. According to the stamp on its base, it came from Csepel Machine Factory in 1959. Over the years it has developed a slight but noticeable wobble. It can shudder on the boom and the speed is difficult to change. But it does OK for the rough work it gets. And I can blame all my broken tools—I must hold the record—on my machine.

It's 6:30 A.M., and there are 104 housings left in the tub. Each requires five holes, carefully spaced around the circumference. I use an eleven-millimeter twist drill and the same speed and feed for each hole. Each piece, about twenty centimeters in diameter, is locked into the fixture by tightening a bolt with a wrench. After I have drilled the holes and taken the piece out of the fixture, I must break the edges of each hole by hand, turning a chamfering tool in the hole. All this takes between two and three minutes, depending on my work mood. The norm time is four minutes. When I first did this job I thought it was gravy. Then János told me there was another operation with another fixture. I assumed he was joking, and so continued merrily at two minutes apiece—200 percent, or so I thought. At last I was making some money. When I finished the series and was feeling rather pleased with myself, Lajos came round and said I had to spot-face them—enlarge the hole to a shallow depth, making a seat for a bolt head or nut, using a special tool called a spot-facer. I looked at Lajos as though he were crazy. "No!" I exclaimed. So he showed me the blueprint, and sure enough there it was, spot-face all five holes. I was furious but powerless. What a rip-off—one norm for two operations. From one moment to the next, gravy turns to dust. The spot-facing takes another two minutes, so even though it is possible to do one piece in four minutes, it would be impossible to keep that rate up for eight hours. In any case, who works for eight hours?

So I never make 100 percent on this work. At Allied this wouldn't be so bad. When confronted with a lousy piece rate we simply took it easy and collected the guaranteed minimum of 100 percent. Here it is quite another story. If you produce at 50 percent, you are paid at 50 percent. This is a socialist piece-rate system—payment strictly according to production. There may be employment security, but it is truly undermined by wage insecurity. The pressure doesn't let up. At the end of the month the piece times recorded on the "work papers" we hand in for each job are totaled and we are paid accordingly. At the end of my first month I received a grand total of 3,600 forints, about seventy dollars. My average percentage was 82 percent, but that included pieces I had produced in the first week when I was paid an hourly rate based on my worker category. These pieces were added into the subsequent weeks' production, so that my actual production level, averaged over an entire month, was more like 70 percent. János, on the other hand, produced at 107 percent and received 8,480 forints for the month, after doing a lot of overtime. He wouldn't stick around the radial drill if he didn't get overtime. That is the way management keeps its radial drill operators.

So as to avoid norm cuts, János doesn't hand in more than 110 percent. But there is also a management-imposed ceiling of 110 percent, which may be lifted on the twentieth of the month if shop supervisors think it necessary. Management wants to avoid arrhythmic work patterns associated with high percentage outputs in some parts of the month and no work available in other parts. It also tries to keep the overall factory percentage below 110 percent so as not to attract big norm cuts from the enterprise's central office. In this respect, workers and management within the firm are in collusion against the central direction of the enterprise.

But there are ways to get around this upper limit without attracting attention from the outside. Today, for example, János is working on the "beer bottles" again. He can produce two shifts' work in one. The night before last he came in at around 9:00. He showed me his time card. Kálmán had written in that he had arrived at 5:45. On other occasions, operators punch in one another for overtime that they don't actually work. This is not as devious as it sounds, since we are paid for the work we do, not the hours we put in. The effect of this manipulation is simply to reduce the official average percentage so that, say, workers producing at 140 percent will appear to be producing at only 108 percent. The company has also begun to pursue an alternative strategy by creating a "VGMK," an "economic work partnership." Workers organize themselves into a collective in order to undertake some particular task assigned by management and to which management assigns a particular price. From the point of view of both management and the workers there are many advantages to this system, but two are particularly important. Income from VGMK work is not counted against the wage bill, and so is not part of the centrally regulated average enterprise wage. And the time spent on VGMK work is not officially recorded. Thus if workers are officially paid at 110 percent, they can receive the value of the extra 30 percent they produce as VGMK earnings. Shop-floor management collaborates with workers, particularly the most scarce and needed workers, to circumvent official limits on their earnings.

At Allied, things were simpler. We restricted our percentages to 140 percent, or at least didn't hand in more than 140 percent, so as not to attract the attention of the industrial engineers who studied our outputs. For all their scientific paraphernalia they didn't know which were the tight and which were the loose rates. But here the system of norm cutting, apparently more arbitrary, is actually more effective. Norm cuts are dictated by the enterprise's head office, based on the firm's overall performance. This figure, about 2 or 3 percent each year, is translated into specific norm changes through bargaining between workers and shop-floor management. Although industrial engineers don't actually know which are the loose norms, worker participation ensures that the looser ones tend to get cut, although the more vulnerable workers obviously suffer most. Surely this is the managerial dream—workers who cut their own rates!

But all this is quite irrelevant to me. I don't have to worry about rate busting or the 110 percent ceiling. I can't even make 100 percent on these damned housings. I can't help but wonder what this system would be like for a newcomer who depended on this wage. For the first week you are on a personal wage. During this time you are "trained" by a fellow worker, and perhaps the charge hand or foreman will show you a thing or two. Then you are on your own. I had all the assistance possible and still made only 3,600 forints. That's hardly enough to support a single person, let alone a family. No wonder new operators don't last long on my machine.

Norms are the true dictator. They drive one to fury and panic. I soon realized that I would have to risk life and limb to make the rates. I came in once to find that Pista had already begun spot-facing some of the same housings I am doing today. The fixture was simple—two steel bars, two centimeters thick, bolted to the table in a V shape. It was obvious what I was supposed to do: hold the piece against the bars with one hand and bring down the spot-facer into the holes with the other. Knowing precisely what this was all about from my Allied experience, I was nervous at the thought. The piece might start shuddering against the bar, perhaps even leap over it, if my left hand wasn't strong enough to keep it in place. This piece of cast iron, the size of an average plate and the shape of a bowler hat, could then rip off a finger and fly into my chest. Machines don't recognize that they are run by fragile and fallible humans; they continue relentlessly.

I hovered around the machine, went for a walk, not knowing what to do. Lajos would never have allowed me to do it this way; he would have found another method. But he wasn't here. There was only Tóni, who wasn't too concerned about safety. He simply showed me how to get hold of the piece with my hand. When Anna saw what was happening she immediately told me to leave it alone and called János. Annoyed that anyone should expect me to do it that way, he knocked the iron bars out of the table, flung them onto the floor in disgust, and found an alternative fixture—the one stipulated in the blueprint, but one that clearly no one used. It required that you bolt the piece in place and, rather than moving the piece, swing the drill from hole to hole, taking twice as long. There was no way I could make the rate.

I am lucky, I don't have to make the rate. I can afford to preserve my body intact, since I still have a second job in Berkeley. And, as often happens in Hungary, my second job brings in more money than my first. The money I earn here is pocket money, *pálinka* money. So why do I care what my percentage is each day? Why do I calculate how many hours' work, "real work" at 100 percent, I complete by the end of the shift? Is it the challenge to accomplish eight hours' work in a shift? The challenge of making the rates? The machine and its rates are an assault on my self-respect. When my performance is particularly low I am depressed and I don't bother to add up the hours. But is challenge the whole story? How much challenge is there for János? He's done those beer bottles so many times now, it can hardly be a challenge—what keeps him going? Yes, money is an underlying factor, but there is something else involved in getting through the workday. It turns out to be much more exhausting to work slowly or irregularly. When one achieves a rhythm, when one is guiding the machine from hole to hole, turning the drill into the hole, flicking the feed on and off, slapping the tools in and out of the whirling chuck with fluency—in short, when one is controlling the machine rather than being controlled by it—time flies by and one is less exhausted. Unfortunately I am usually four or five hours into the shift before I get into rhythm, often already too tired to get moving. Today I am tired at 11:00 and I've done only thirty pieces. There are over seventy pieces still to do. Can I do it? It is certainly possible. So with renewed strength and concentration I begin the final assault. The last hours pass unnoticed as I see the pile gradually diminish.

Here there is no pressure from the foreman to hurry, as sometimes there was at Allied. There are no hot jobs that have to be done an hour ago, that require that I break the setup and start on some new work. There is just me, my machine, the pieces, and the norms. The norms are the decisive power. They are the veritable relations of production. They shape my private relationship with my machine. But it is private—I can seal myself off from everything around me, even the coercive reality of my day-to-day existence. But I can't transport myself into another world without courting danger: The machine and the tools demand my concentration. The holes have to be the right size, in the right place. And I have to be in the "mood for work." How often I see János wandering around the shop waiting for the mood to strike. Today and yesterday it never really came. He had been out on a drinking spree and this upset his work equilibrium. Instead he made himself a stand for his fishing rod out of materials he picked up from a friend in the storeroom. Tomorrow he will lie in the sun on the banks of the Tisza. Fishing is his favorite pastime, an escape from the housing estate and the factory. A city dweller with contempt for peasants, he doesn't grow paprika, grapes, cherries, or potatoes in some garden. For him that's just another work trap.

For the particularly privileged, management superimposes a personal domination on top of the impersonal domination of the piece rates. Typically, it is women who suffer under this double burden. With increasing numbers of women employed, management has devised clever systems of exploiting gender domination. Take the women of the Dobó Katica Brigade, who work on the mills. They have the assistance of Gabi, who sets up their machines and attends to any mechanical problems. But to encourage Gabi to work hard, management pegs his earnings, like the earnings of the individual mill operators, to the average percentage of the group. He is in fact the boss, who tells the women what work to run on which machines and decides if and when they can take their holidays. He is the intermediary between the women and management, and he has every interest in goading them to increase their output. For the most part they put up with his prodding, but when he comes in somewhat tipsy, as he did last week, they ostentatiously begin to gossip with one another.

Why do they put up with this subordination? They explain to me that if they want to work here, they have no alternative. The division into women's jobs and men's jobs is always accompanied by some form of gender domination. If it isn't integral to the jobs, it is added. Thus Zsuzsa, who operates the gang drills, has her independence undercut by having the role of coffee-maker thrust upon her. How she makes her rates I never understand.

Do the Dobó Katica women see themselves, or are they seen, as secondary earners? Certainly not. Anna is forty-one. She has two children, a boy of twelve and a girl of nine. She lives in a small town about half an hour's bus ride away. Two years ago she had serious heart trouble. Her life is hard. Her husband is a lathe operator in the same department, but in the other production cycle. At home he's drunk a lot of the time. One morning Anna came in complaining that he had gone through a week's wages in one night. Anna has to clean and cook at the house of her mother, who is eighty and ill, as well as for her own family at home. At forty-six, Klára hasn't Anna's vitality or toughness, but she's always ready to suppress the seamy side of her life. Today she said she was tired because of her "night work"—her whole face beamed with laughter. Her husband is a printer and drinks a lot. She worries because he also drives a car. She lives in a neighboring village and commutes to work by bus. She also has two children, but they are much older than Anna's. And then there's Ági, the quietest of the three. She is forty-six too, but though she looks wearier than the others, like them she can always break into laughter when the occasion arises. When her daughter, who works in the crib on the other shift, comes by to visit, Ági lights up with pleasure and delight. At work these women feed the mills; at home they feed the family. The two jobs are equally exhausting, although there's no doubt which they prefer. But as Anna told me, "Life is hard but not hopeless." She lives for her two children, and would do almost anything for them.

Anna, Klára, and Ági arrived together five years ago, and they have worked on the same shift and the same machines ever since. With Gabi, they form one half of the Dobó Katica Brigade. The other half is made up of three women and their setter from the other shift. Like everyone else, they switch shifts every week. The department also has another woman who migrated from the shop floor to the office, where she is a clerical assistant to the scheduling man. She records all the brigade's activities in a neatly kept diary, with photographs of the nine members and Kálmán, the managerial representative. The diary records the two Communist Saturdays worked—one day's labor donated for a children's hospital and one day for the National Theater—and three hundred hours of communal work, part on the factory grounds and part donated for the construction of a new cultural center. Then there are records of excursions they've taken together, parties they've had, and political meetings they've attended, such as the big one on war and peace organized by the regional party offices. The Dobó Katica women seem proud of their brigade. Last year they came in first in the brigade competition and won nine thousand forints. That probably about covered their unpaid work. The runners-up got five thousand forints.

What's behind the brigades? They are not obligatory; why does anyone join them? No one really likes the brigades, but pressures from outside the factory, from the enterprise headquarters and the party, demand their establishment. So orders are passed down from on high to the shop superintendent: "Form socialist work brigades!" The superintendent then expects each foreman to establish at least one brigade in his section. Given the hostility, this can be quite a tall order, but his bonuses depend on it. He approaches a likely candidate for leader, holding out the possibility of winning all this money. Whether there are also promises of favorable treatment is not clear. But it is more than likely that the formation of brigades will appeal more to vulnerable workers, such as women, than to experienced and skilled workers, who will have no part of such "nonsense." Certainly, based on my experience here and in the champagne factory that I worked in a year ago, women workers seem to dominate in the brigade competition. By committing themselves to brigade work the women might hope to establish themselves more firmly within the shop, putting themselves in a better bargaining position.

Thus, Anna was furious when she didn't receive any monthly premium, known as *mozgóbér* ("moving pay"), for several months running. It is as if she felt her membership in the best brigade, her diligence at work, her meticulous cleaning of her work area, entitled her to the bonus. In practice, however, the premium is awarded to the more skilled and experienced workers, whose cooperation is essential to the effective organization of the shop. Such workers have no interest in brigade membership, and unlike Anna, they cannot be easily replaced.

There's another side to the feminization of work—deskilling. At Allied everyone set up their own machines, although there was a setter who might sometimes help out. Setting up was the part of the job that required the greatest skill and expertise. I can't imagine Allied workers tolerating the expropriation of that skill, its concentration in the hands of a single setter, while they just feed the machines. Nor can I imagine János, Péter, and the other radial drill operators succumbing to such a system. Deskilling can proceed smoothly only if the old operators find satisfactory jobs elsewhere while the new operators are part of a more vulnerable labor force, and so it goes hand in hand with feminization. It's probably no accident that it was Gabi, a dedicated party member, who oversaw this transition.

The fact that these women face double labor (at home and in the factory) and double subordination (by gender and by class) doesn't mean that the men don't work hard too. Although Gabi is the boss, his hourly wage is not much higher than Anna, Klára, and Ági's. He earns more than they do because he does so much overtime. He too commutes from a village, about an hour and a half away. When he is on overtime and on morning shift he gets up at 4:00 A.M. to arrive at work at 6:00. He leaves at 6:00 P.M. and arrives home not much before 8:00. He has dinner and goes to bed at 10:00 or 11:00. On weekends he works in his garden or helps his friends with theirs. In the shop he may sit around some of the time, but he is always ready to throw himself into his work should anything go wrong with one of the machines. He can look pretty worn out at the end of the shift.

For the men, at least, drinking becomes the quick escape from work. One can get sozzled by oneself at home or in a *kocsma* (pub), or do it in collective style in a private cellar. My first Friday I did it in style. It was Laci's idea. He runs one of the numerically controlled mills. Once he has set up and the machine is running according to plan, he seems to have quite a bit of time to loaf around. He entertained me during my first week. Like Gabi, Laci is an *ingázó* (commuter), but his village is nearer than Gabi's. Laci is in his early thirties and strikingly handsome. Last year his wife had a serious operation in Debracen to remove an ulcer. She's now recovering at home, but is still very weak. Laci seems to have one major obsession: sex. His cupboards are plastered with pin-ups. He's always making passes at the women on the shop floor, who generally greet his advances with bored contempt. He's also a heavy drinker. Together with Gabi he organized my welcoming party at Béla's cellar. Béla, who towers over most of us, works on the horizontal boring machine. After work that Friday, Laci, Gabi, Béla, his mate on the "horizontal," and I all went off to the cellar.

It was an old place hidden away in a hill, a cave with about fifteen wine barrels lining the walls, and a long table in an adjoining room. Béla's parents had been very successful wine growers until they were dispossessed of their land, first in 1945 and again with the consolidation into cooperatives in 1959. Each time his family had to begin again. Béla and his family now work two thousand *négyszögöl*, about three-quarters of a hectare, growing some fruit and vegetables, but mostly cultivating vineyards. He makes about fifty hectoliters of wine a year—two white wines and one red. Béla doesn't sell any—he consumes it all with friends and family. He must have a lot of friends. As a guest I had to drink all three wines, and so was soon *totál*.

I swayed back to the town with Laci and Gabi. On the way we stopped at an *eszpresszó* for a coffee and rum, whereupon they began to pound me with questions about working-class politics in the United States. What does an average worker think about the nuclear arms race? As I was to find time and time again, Hungarian workers cannot understand the mentality that would lead people to vote for a warmonger like Reagan. They had been well disposed toward Kennedy and Carter, but now they have difficulty distinguishing the American bear from the Soviet bear. They want to think well of America, land of opportunity and wealth. I'm always asked how much I earn—an amount that's mind-bogglingly vast to a Hungarian worker. Even when cost of living is taken into account it's much more lucrative to be a machine operator in the United States than in Hungary. In terms of hours of work, a car costs at least four times as much in Hungary; trousers, shoes, and dresses cost seven or eight times as much, and food is also often more expensive. Only transportation, rent, and some entertainment can be cheaper. On the other hand, equally incomprehensible are the levels of violence, poverty, and unemployment in the United States. And when I try to talk about the deep-seated racism in the United States, they compare Blacks to Gypsies, who, they say, are "lazy" and "criminal." In short, the comparison is complicated. But they do know they are much better off now than they were in 1956. Kádár has brought a continually increasing standard of living, but at a cost—an even greater increase in the expenditure of labor. They are running up the down escalator.

Next week will be my last, and Laci is organizing another gathering at Béla's cellar—this time, he promises, with "goulash and shapely Hungarian girls." But Gabi isn't here today to finalize arrangements, and we aren't sure when he will return. He's taken two of his five weeks' holiday to work on the harvest in his village cooperative. In two weeks he gets five thousand forints, almost as much as he would get here in a month if he had no overtime. Miklós, the setter from the other shift, is working four hours' overtime to cover half of Gabi's shift. He's having a frustrating time with the large numerically controlled machine next to mine. It has been breaking down regularly, and now is making a huge racket. As at Allied, the numerically controlled machines are down a lot. When this happens to Laci's mill he loiters around, gossiping, or goes home. It isn't worth taking "standstill" pay. When the mill next to me breaks down, whichever member of the Dobó Katica Brigade is operating it is simply transferred to another mill. There are always more mills than operators.

The maintenance department has every incentive to get on with the job since their bonuses depend on keeping the down time below 320 hours a month for the whole shop. Józsi, one of the maintenance men, told me that they usually get their bonuses, if only because their boss is adept at juggling the figures. Sometimes Józsi has a lot of work to do; other days he has none. He told me that he averages three or four hours of work a shift. On afternoon shift he works less, and he often comes round to my machine to chat. But this week he has swapped shifts; his wife is expecting a baby any day. He is pretty nervous about it because the local doctors do not have a good reputation. He will have to hand over quite a sizable tip, two thousand forints (some ten days' work), if he wants to be sure of proper attention. Józsi, who met his wife while he was working in East Germany, is always comparing Hungary with East Germany, saying that apartments are easier to get and things are much cheaper there. Here they live in a one-room apartment, although it has a television and a hi-fi. He desperately wants to move into a bigger place but doesn't know how he can manage it. A lucky few are now buying apartments from the state—a two-room apartment for about 600,000 forints. One can get a loan from the state bank of 360,000 forints plus 40,000 for each child; with two children a family still has to find about 160,000 forints. The enterprise might help some, but most must rely on some other source, either private work or help from their parents. Józsi just doesn't know where he can get the money, and he doesn't have the time or energy to start building his own house.

On payday Józsi came over and showed me his pay slip for the month—5,300 forints. "That's nothing, Misi. You can't live on that." He has no overtime, but as a maintenance worker he has a skill which can help him find work on the side. Józsi mends washing machines in his spare time, bringing in another 4,000 forints a month. His wife worked in a radiation laboratory until her pregnancy was well advanced. She gets five month's maternity leave at full pay from the state, and then for two and a half years while she is looking after her child she will get 1,000 forints a month. But her earnings are nowhere near what they need for a new apartment. Life must be easier in the West, he assumes, but he knows from his own experience in West Germany how difficult it is to get a job.

So today it seems I have myself to myself without interruptions. Even the mill next to me has ceased its racket. I am concentrating on my housings when one of the seven inspectors comes over to me. He's a little old guy who hides his fussiness behind a veneer of friendliness. He asks me what happened to the two "connectors" that were missing from the series I had completed yesterday. That series, surely the worst job I've ever had, has dogged my existence for over ten days now. The story began a week ago Wednesday. I had just given up a series of "housings" after smashing all available spot-facers because there was too much steel to remove around the hole; so I was already depressed when these un-familiar "connectors" arrived on the scene—skittle-like objects about six inches long with a round head that had been milled flat to make two parallel sides. The blueprint said you had to drill a hole perpendicular to the milled sides through the head, ream (smooth out) the hole, and chamfer the edges. But who takes any notice of the blueprint? With János's help I eventually found the right fixture, and we decided it was best first to drill all the pieces and then to ream them all. All this took time and experimentation, and by the end of the day I had drilled twenty-six pieces.

The next day was sweltering. When I came in at 2:00 P.M. the factory was like an oven—the temperature must have been over one hundred degrees. There's no effective cooling system; the roof is low and part glass. Lajos was away and not a single radial operator showed up until later. It was too hot to work. And then I saw that someone had done another hundred of the connectors but had ruined them by making the hole too small. I didn't know, and still don't know, who left me with this headache. Obviously, they realized what they had done. I finished drill-ing the remaining 170 pieces and then for half a shift hovered around my machine, frustrated, not knowing what to do with the faulty connec-tors—the holes were too small to be reamed. I was very depressed: La-jos wasn't around to help, and János had no suggestions. I told Kálmán I'd had it. I wasn't coming in tomorrow. I'd wasted almost two shifts, and that was enough. I didn't need to waste another one. He tried to strike a deal with me: I could have tomorrow off if I did two lots of four hours' overtime next week. Some deal. Fuck that. There's no point in coming in if there's no work. I'm paid by the piece, not by the hour. So I didn't go in on Friday, and I had already arranged to take Monday off as one of my two paid holidays. By Tuesday, I expected, someone else would have finished the connectors. But there they were, waiting for me, just where I had left them. At least Lajos was back. He started fooling around with the fixture, but it wasn't long before he realized that it wouldn't be possible to ream the defective pieces on my machine. The shop superintendent thought otherwise, so Lajos told him to have a go. To my delight, on the very first piece, with the reamer wobbling, he unhinged it from its sleeve. So we left the connectors and I started on a new series of housings. What a relief!

That was Tuesday. Yesterday, Thursday, Lajos said I really had to finish up the connectors. But how? Well, he found another little fixture in which I could hold the connector by hand while I reamed. But it could only be done on a speed drill. Zsuzsa, who operates the speed drills, helped us set up. But I could see there was going to be trouble. Some of the holes in the connectors were so undersized that when the necessary pressure was brought to bear on the reamer, my hand could not hold the piece steady. Sure enough, on Lajos's first attempt he couldn't hold the piece. It swung against the fixture and the reamer bent. We knocked it back into shape, and after successfully reaming two pieces he handed it over to me. Zsuzsa told me to go very slow, but I guess I wasn't slow enough. On one particularly tight hole which required more pressure on the reamer, the piece slapped against the fixture. I let go with the drill still whirling and the reamer smashed. I was furious. Why the hell was I having to pay for someone else's screwup! I marched to the office and thrust the smashed reamer under Kálmán's nose. He shook his head, told me that would cost me a lot of money, and signed for a new one. I got it replaced, but now I was nervous and agitated. After two more pieces it smashed again. Shit. I'd had it. I was ready to quit.

At this point János and Lajos turned up. They didn't give up as easily as I, but then, they didn't have to run the job. Well, they figured out a way of holding the connector more steadily in the fixture by resting it against a steel bar. This worked. Slowly I got through the hundred pieces with undersized holes without further mishap. Two of the pieces, however, had not been completed in an earlier operation, so I tossed them into the next series and they were not registered as scrap. It is these two pieces that the old man had just come round to query. He says I can't just put them in the next series. That's officious baloney. So he forces me to sign for one more defective connector. It turns out that he really wants to talk me into exchanging some dollars. He hasn't a chance.

In the middle of the fiasco around the speed drill yesterday, Lajos couldn't understand why the holes were so tight. I explained that someone else had done them with a drill that hadn't been ground properly. Zsuzsa on the speed drills and Anna and Ági on the mills all backed me up, telling Lajos it was his fault because he had been on holiday. They continued to beleaguer him about the management's ineptness and how

I had been led round the bush, wasting so much time. What had been a total disaster and humiliation found its compensation in the solidarity the women exuded.

At Allied, while there may have been feelings of class consciousness, there were no such moments of solidarity. For all the trade union's importance, its effect was to atomize the work force on the shop floor, reserving collective struggles for the triennial contract negotiations. The grievance machinery channeled struggles into the defense of individual rights and obligations, while the internal labor market encouraged workers to move to another job rather than fight out the issues in the present one. Here too struggles are individualized, not because of the presence but because of the absence of an effective union. There's no point in going to the union with a grievance, as I discovered when I wasn't paid for three hours' overtime I had worked. I talked to Anna about it, and she laughed at the idea of going to the union representative. We decided to do it as a joke. The two representatives we consulted, both women, thought it was a joke too. I really had to go to the foreman, they said. So I went to Kálmán, who remembered he had given me the three hours and said he would file a grievance. I don't know if he did, but I never did get paid for that overtime.

So no one thinks of going to the union with any serious problem. Last year, when Anna was put on almost continuous weekend overtime, she went to the shop superintendent to complain that she could not do this because she had a family to look after. He simply told her that if she didn't like it she could leave. She explained to me how the union, the party, and management sit together on the "director's council" and decide everything. When I told János that I hadn't gotten my overtime pay, he told me to go straight to the superintendent, rather than the foreman.

"Kálmán has no power."

"What about the union?" I asked innocently.

"What about it? They are useless. *Nulla-nulla*."

"But they at least provide cheap holidays," I protested.

"Yes, but only for those who don't do any work, the bosses. The real workers don't get a chance to go to the holiday homes. I'm not a union member, a party member, or a brigade member."

"If they are all so useless why should anyone want to be a member?" I asked.

"When you want to get an apartment or a place in a nursery, these factors might be important."

In fact, party, union, and brigade membership is becoming less and less important as the enterprise has less control over life outside work. Now flats are distributed largely on a point system linked to earnings, family size, and other factors independent of political activity inside the enterprise.

What is the party's role inside the factory? This is a difficult question. About 15 percent of the workers are party members; these appear to be the more senior, experienced workers. The party secretary in Department B is one of the two scheduling men, a very popular young man. The party members meet every two weeks or so and are told of any managerial problems. They are expected to help in the achievement of production targets and keep an eye open for trouble. But the significant power of the party is a potential one. In theory it can block any decision, from the employment of a given person to the introduction of norm cuts to the approval of the annual plan, since it is a signatory to every important document. In practice it interferes very little. It is this potential power that probably makes workers cautious in their attitudes toward the party. When expressing his bitterness and resentment, Józsi would lower his voice and tell me there are "red ears" all around. While I can joke about the party, no one else does. When a huddle of spectators gathered around my machine one night while I was trying to make out, I cried: "What the hell is this—a party meeting?" They liked that, laughed, and even told the story to others. But I never heard anyone else joke about the party. In this respect the past casts a shadow over the present.

The party and the union are essentially channels for communicating managerial decisions, and the absence of institutional means for expressing workers' collective interests fosters the individuation of struggles. But there is a basis for solidarity rooted in the organization of work. The one abiding characteristic of socialist economies is the generation of shortages, whether of workers, materials, machines, or investment resources. To be efficient in a socialist factory is to adopt a flexible work organization that can improvise effectively and rapidly. Labor is flexibly deployed by, for example, shunting experienced workers like Pista from machine to machine. At Allied, job rights protected by the union and enshrined in the operation of the internal labor market prevented such arbitrary placement. Here, flexibility is facilitated by the ample but by no means excessive supply of auxiliary workers—inspectors, setup men, crib attendants, truck drivers, and supervisors. At Allied these were cut to the bone in the name of capitalist efficiency, which created lines outside the inspector's window and the crib. The truck driver was turned into a king. This effectively turned piece worker against auxiliary worker, a state of affairs compounded by the ridiculous rules that came down from the bosses, further restricting the possibility of cooperation on the shop floor. Here there are also rules about checking the first piece and who should ride the lift truck, but no one takes much notice. Instead of being locked into opposition camps, nurtured by bureaucratic rules, the shop floor is a self-organizing autonomous unit. Every ten days it receives its production quotas and itself breaks them down into daily targets. Completed work and scrap move through the department with amazing speed. Here I have never seen the piles of defective pieces and unfinished engines that lined the aisles at Allied. As we approached the completion date for the half-year plan, I waited for the mythical rush work to begin. Perhaps there was more overtime, perhaps the pace did become a little more hectic, but there was nothing like the rush work at Allied which recurred daily in the form of hot jobs and broken setups.

In order to respond to the constraints of a shortage economy, the socialist firm engenders a limited form of workers' control. So long as piece rates are not screwed down so tight that we are turned against one another in the struggle to make out, so long as there are no arbitrary managerial interventions from on high, conception and execution can be effectively united on the shop floor. But this has consequences for attitudes toward management. Gabi, for example, refers to those who work and those who do nothing. Although a committed party member, he gets very resentful toward the *bürokrácia* in the "white house" where the bosses twiddle their thumbs.[1] "They don't know anything," he said, shaking a blueprint under my nose. The potential for shop-floor solidarity against the white house is always there. Only on my first day in the factory did I see a hint of its reality.

Management wanted to boost output without showing it on the books as an increase in percentage performance. They proposed a 2 percent cut in norms in exchange for an immediate 2 percent increase in basic wages and a promise of no more norm cuts next year. Obviously in some sort of trouble with the central enterprise, management took the extraordinary measure of calling a hasty meeting with the workers. The leader of the economic planning department, essentially the personnel manager, addressed the workers in Department A, while the chief engineer addressed Department B. I attended the meeting in Department A. It was introduced by the union secretary for the department. The personnel manager then explained the deal, suggesting that this was a way of keeping up with wage increases in other parts of the enterprise. But workers were suspicious at this unprecedented move.

Why was management calling this meeting, consulting us? How would management guarantee that there would be no norm cuts next year? Would they put that in writing? Why were they cutting norms across the board, rather than selecting loose ones as they usually do? One party member said he would have to vote against the proposal because under it he would not be able to make the 106 percent that the party expects of him! Among those attending, thirty-four voted against and seven in favor. Those in favor were all party members, union officials, and supervisors.

In Department B, on the other hand, the proposal was unanimously endorsed. This is the older department, with older workers. Relations between management and workers are more harmonious, and the rates are said to be looser. In Department A they make parts under a Western license. The rates are therefore tighter, the machinery more sophisticated, and the workers younger and more skilled. So operators in Department A have more reason to resist norm cuts and greater power to do so, because they are more central to the firm's production and have skills that are badly needed by other enterprises. Nevertheless, they don't believe that their opinion would have any effect on the outcome. Sure enough, the results were referred to the central trade union committee, which rapidly endorsed management's proposal. So why did management even hold the meetings? Perhaps they still remember the one-day strike that took place ten years ago when the new wage system was introduced. At that time the older workers lost their relative advantage vis-à-vis the younger workers and struck. Subsequently many of them left the plant.

Such collective struggle couldn't be further from my day-to-day life on the shop floor. It is 12:45, and the Dobó Katica women are already cleaning their machines and workplaces. On Friday their machines get an extra good cleaning. They are proud of their meticulous housekeeping. But I still have fifteen housings to drill. Determined to finish them off, I am flowing well with my old machine, and the possibility of coming to an end spurs me on to greater efforts. Pista comes round to inspect, to see if there will be any housings left for him to do in overtime. Even he is impressed by my pace, although not too happy about it. By 1:20 I finish the last one, and now I have to clean my machine and sweep up in the work area. I even take a rag to the old albatross itself, revealing a real green beneath the oily grime. I lock up my tools and scrub my hands and arms as best I can with the special soap, and I'm ready for lunch.

Although doing so is not entirely within the rules, I leave at 1:45 to go to the dining room. Lunch consists of a soup, a vegetable or pasta, and meat, and perhaps some fruit for dessert—all for eleven forints, twenty cents, or half an hour's work. Today it's cauliflower soup, liver fried in bread crumbs with potatoes, and cherries to finish off. Tamás, the inspector whose desk is nearest to my machine, comes in with his factory companion, a woman who runs one of the lathes. They sit down next to me. I complain to him about the fussiness of his colleague who gave me a scrap notice for the connectors. He holds up his hands defensively, protesting that it has nothing to do with him. Indeed, Tamás seeks to maintain very friendly relations with the operators. Once when I had been drilling the thick oil-pumps, some hadn't fit into the fixture properly. After they were clamped in place they would still move around when I was drilling, and the holes were skewed. About six were not good and were sent back from the lathe, and another six defectives arrived from a previous series. Jokingly, Tamás asked me what he should do about them, how he should write them up. I told him, "Put them down to bad castings." He was suspicious but amused at my audacity. "I can't do that," he said, but he did. There was a similar problem of castings with the thin oil-pumps. Sometimes the grooves were not smooth enough to fit snugly onto the fixture, so the pumps couldn't be firmly clamped in place. I remember the problem of poor castings at Allied only too well. Some of the pulleys we had to balance came in with huge blowholes in them. It was virtually impossible to drill out the right amount of steel in the right place so that the pressure on the axle would be evenly distributed. Somehow we had to balance them, blowholes or no blowholes. We didn't get much sympathy from management.

I make my way back to the shop, where a number of people are already gathered around Zsuzsa's coffee percolator. They are discussing what they will be doing this weekend. Kálmán beckons me to come over. He tells me Lajos will be mixing concrete for his new house and suggests I help him. "His new house?" I repeat with some astonishment. Yes, Lajos is building himself a weekend house. Pista, it turns out, will also be mixing concrete for his own new house. Tamás, the inspector, will be hard at work with his mates drilling a well in his 2,000-square-meter garden. Indeed, many will be tending to their gardens, plots of land rented from the city council for a nominal sum of sixty forints a year. It's usually the worst hilly land which, to get into shape, takes several years of sustained effort and much money. But then they can grow their grapes, cherries and peaches, cabbages and potatoes. They don't sell their produce but consume it at home. Others will be hiring out their skills, like Józsi repairing his washing machines.

Laci will be running his mill all weekend. For the women, the tasks of unpaid work are endless—washing, cooking, cleaning, and nurturing. And János, I know, will be reclining on the bank of the Tisza, patiently waiting for the big catch.

The buzzer will be going off in five minutes, and already the women are lining up. There's a note of urgency about their escape from this noisy, oily, heartless, metallic factory. I traipse off to the changing rooms to strip off my oily overalls, shirt, and boots. Today I'm rather pleased with myself—I've scaled new heights in the realm of "housings." Bodies rippling with fat around the midriff file into the shower room. Now in the shower cubicle I can feel isolated once more as the hot water floods down from above—refreshing and peaceful. I have to get dried and dressed to catch the bus at 2:23, but that gives me another five minutes of bliss.

I leave, passing through the shop again to punch out. I wave goodbye to Péter, still working away on his radial drill, as diligent as ever. He'll be there for another three and a half hours—his cigarette to comfort him and perhaps a dash of *pálinka*.

3   Mythologies of Industrial Work

Recent developments in sociology have seriously questioned the assumptions about labor markets and labor processes which underpin economic models of capitalism. It is now time for sociology to examine some of the corresponding assumptions in economic models of socialism. Sociological perspectives toward "communism" have been drawn either from political science, which until recently had dwelt on the repressive or totalitarian character of Soviet societies, or from economics, which has insisted on the irrationality of such societies. From these perspectives of terror and waste it remains a mystery how Soviet societies, or what we shall call state socialism, have been able to survive as long as they have, in the case of the Soviet Union almost seventy years. We badly need new perspectives.

In this chapter we study the distinctive social and economic reproduction of state socialism through a controlled comparison of a Hungarian and an American firm. We show how the operation of the socialist firm can belie many of the stereotypes held not just by political scientists and economists, sociologists and Marxists, but also by politicians, managers, and workers, and not just in the capitalist world but in Soviet societies themselves. That these stereotypes have been so tenacious can be attributed in part to political and ideological factors, in part to presumptions of backwardness and inefficiency, but also in part to the absence of studies that compare the actual operation of state socialist and capitalist firms. Where comparisons have been made they generally have been of a macro character and fail to compare like with like, confusing levels of abstraction. This is particularly clear among orthodox Marxists and neoclassical economists.

According to orthodox Marxist analysis, capitalism's historical function is to build up the productive capacities of the human species through the advance of technology and work organization. But there are limits to this process. Eventually the contradictions inherent in capitalism between the private appropriation of surplus and the social transformation of nature stifle the expansion of the productive forces. There ensues a period of revolution: Socialism is installed and releases the fettered productive capacities. Property relations are transformed and, through central planning, economic efficiency is given renewed impetus. Neoclassical economics argues, contrarily, that socialist societies based on central planning are necessarily less efficient than capitalist societies. Private pursuit of profit in a market is the only effective means of advancing efficiency and developing productive energies.

Both orthodox Marxists and neoclassical economists are guilty of a methodological error: comparing an empirical reality of one society with an ideal type of another. Marxists have tended to undertake a critical analysis of capitalism through a usually implicit comparison with a speculative socialism—a society without classes in which individuals are reconciled with the collectivity through their self-conscious making of history. This ideal type is usually left unexamined and is therefore utopian. At the same time they avoid examining actually existing socialism, what Nuti calls socialism on earth,[1] as a relevant contrast to capitalism. They have generally regarded such societies as in transition between capitalism and some "true" socialism,[2] a form of capitalism (usually state capitalism),[3] or a legacy of precapitalist "Asiatic" modes of production.[4] Only very recently has the Marxist tradition attempted to develop either theoretical models or concrete studies of such actually existing state socialisms which compare their distinctive social structures, their dynamics and mechanisms of reproduction, with those of capitalism.

When they have studied state socialism, neoclassical economists, on the other hand, have been guilty of the obverse error. They have compared an empirical reality of Soviet societies with an ideal-type conception of capitalism. They too easily presume that capitalist societies actually operate according to the logic of capitalist efficiency and only rarely undertake controlled comparisons of capitalist and state socialist societies.[5] Furthermore, although neoclassical economists may have gone further in examining the realities of state socialism than Marxists, those realities are usually filtered through official sources, interviews with interested parties, meaningless surveys, or letters to newspapers from purportedly aggrieved persons. Vast areas of state socialist society remain impervious to their eyes, not least the socialist firm.

In short, whereas Marxists contrast the realities of capitalism with an unexamined ideal type of socialism, those Western economists who have examined actually existing state socialism have done so within an ideal-type model of capitalism. The task of the first part of this chapter, therefore, is to elaborate theoretical models of capitalism and state socialism. Based on the work of Iván Szelényi, Tamás Bauer, and János Kornai, these models not only outline the distinctive features of the economic and political contexts within which the two firms operate, but also generate two different logics of work organization if raw materials are to be transformed into useful goods.[6] It is in terms of the transformation of inputs into outputs, that is, the realization of production possibilities, that we assess the level of technical efficiency.

In the second part we see to what extent the actual levels of technical efficiency of the two firms can be explained in terms of their approximation of or deviation from the theoretically derived logics of work organization. We do this by examining how the firms measure up against a series of stereotypes, all of which suggest that capitalist firms are technically more efficient than socialist firms. These stereotypes have never been well grounded empirically, but emerge precisely from viewing state socialism through the prism of capitalist logic and from projecting downward onto the micro level the widely held assumption that at the macro level state socialist societies are less efficient than capitalist societies.[7]

Through our comparison of machine shops in the United States and Hungary we shall not only cast doubt on the universality of the stereotypes but also question the misplaced logic that underlies them. Inevitably eyebrows will be raised at the limited empirical basis of our corrective to prevailing views, but we believe that one such comparative case study is better than none. At the same time we make no claims to the generality of our two cases. There is no evidence that state socialist firms are generally technically more efficient than capitalist firms. But we are saying that technically efficient socialist firms, just like technically inefficient capitalist firms, are possible. Conventional theories do not seriously consider such possibilities and can explain them only in an ad hoc manner. The place to seek answers to such questions is first and foremost in the firm itself, which in conventional analyses has remained a theoretical black box and an empirical void. Only after examining the functioning of the firm is it possible to broach the conditions and mechanisms which produce and reproduce technically efficient and inefficient firms in the two economic systems. We tentatively explore this issue in the conclusion, underlining a fundamental flaw in the models of capitalism and state socialism presented here and elsewhere.

Even if we were to claim that state socialist firms are as technically efficient as capitalist firms, this would by no means imply that the economic systems are equally efficient. Technical efficiency at the level of the firm, what economists have also called *X-efficiency*, cannot be generalized to the level of society. We shall say nothing about what economists call *social* or *allocational* efficiency, the optimal use of resources with given techniques to satisfy competing ends.[8] Nor do we claim that a technically efficient firm is necessarily economically successful—it may, for example, efficiently produce goods that cannot be sold for a profit due to market factors, or be continually held up by shortage of materials. And it is possible for an economically successful firm to be technically inefficient in both systems.

Finally, it will doubtless be argued that not only have we picked two factories arbitrarily, but also Hungary is not a typical state socialist society.[9] Some may even argue that it is not a state socialist society at all. Yet it undoubtedly approximates the model of state socialism presented in the first part of the chapter. To be sure, there is state socialism and state socialism just as there is capitalism and capitalism, but to argue that Hungary is an exception is too easy a solution, a way of avoiding issues. Sociology has too easily accepted the stereotypes supplied by Sovietologists: not only unsubstantiated stereotypes concerning state socialism, but also erroneous stereotypes about the functioning of capitalist societies against which they implicitly and sometimes explicitly evaluate Soviet societies.

Capitalist and State Socialist Logics

Capitalist and state socialist societies vary a great deal, yet it is still possible to work with the distinction between capitalist economies, which operate through the private appropriation of surplus legitimated by the ideology of private property, and state socialist societies, which operate through the central appropriation of surplus legitimated by the ideology of rational redistribution—that is, the direction of society carried out in the name of a "scientifically" produced common interest.[10] Of course, the concrete realization of both systems varies between societies, and some societies can be seen as articulations of both types, with one prevailing. Recognizing this, we can still develop models. But they are models and crude ones at that, which we will modify and elaborate as we proceed through the empirical analysis, as well as in the conclusion to this chapter.

The viability of a capitalist enterprise depends on its *profitability*—a function of the difference between the value of inputs and that of outputs, values which are given independently of the enterprise by the *market*. The market is responsible for the allocation of those inputs and outputs, and also establishes *competition* among enterprises, determining which enterprises will be profitable. The viability of a state socialist enterprise depends on its *success* as defined through *bargaining* between it and the state. The institutional context is the *plan*, which directly or indirectly regulates the allocation of goods and services and establishes "success indicators" or "targets." While the plan is presented as the incarnation of the collective interest, its purpose is better understood as maximizing the redistributive power of the state.[11]

Whereas capitalist enterprises are subject to *hard budget* constraints, which are more or less rigidly determined, state socialist enterprises are subject to *soft budget* constraints.[12] The softness takes two forms. First, prices are subject to political negotiation rather than being defined by market forces. Second, enterprises have a paternalistic relationship to the state, so that their continued existence is ultimately a political rather than an economic decision. The state can decide to extend or withdraw subsidies, change prices, replace management, offer new investment, merge the enterprise with another, or, finally, although very rarely, liquidate the enterprise.

In the pursuit of profit, capitalist enterprises attempt to cut costs, not least labor costs, but also compete with one another for customers by cutting prices. The search for profit by all leads to the reduction of profit for each and, because wages have to be kept to a minimum, to overproduction. This in turn leads to the unemployment of labor and capital which is endemic to capitalism. Thus, the search for profit realizes itself as a constraint of *demand*. The success of the socialist firm involves increasing its bargaining power with the state, which it accomplishes by seeking investment resources. Here the objective is expansion, and the enterprise therefore faces *supply* constraints, be they of raw materials, labor, or machinery. In other words, the problem of shortages in state socialist societies cannot be reduced to economic underdevelopment but is endemic to the functioning of a centrally directed economy.[13]

Capitalist firms respond to overproduction in the short term by idling capital and laying off workers. In the long term they may recompose production by transforming the labor process or what is being produced. There are various theories of this long-term recomposition, such as the theory of long waves.[14] How do socialist firms respond to the problem of shortages? In the short term they search, queue, and substitute for inputs and outputs; in the long term they bargain for investment resources with the state. Bauer has suggested how this leads to investment cycles at the level of the economy as a whole.[15]

The capitalist state responds to the problem of overproduction through the creation of demand, either through warfare and/or welfare state spending or by boosting working-class purchasing power, for example via statutory minimum wages.[16] In other words, functional gaps in the market are filled by state intervention. In the same way, dysfunctions of the plan in state socialist societies are countered by the opening up of the market, in the form of the second economy which permits limited private enterprise to supply state enterprises and consumer needs.[17] Alternatively, socialist enterprises undergo backward integration to control supplies[18] while capitalist enterprises form oligopolies that attempt to shape demand. But these stratagems contain but never eliminate the distinctive constraints of the two types of economy.

The *short-term* problems facing capitalist and state socialist firms pose different challenges for the organization of work, the subject of this chapter. The socialist firm must continually adapt to the exigencies of supply uncertainty—that is, to the continually changing form and flow of materials, labor, and machinery into the enterprise. This requires continual improvisation and readjustment of the labor process, and therefore a flexible managerial organization. To be effective, shop-floor organization must be allowed a certain autonomy to respond to changing supplies; it cannot be controlled from above. The capitalist firm, on the other hand, facing short-term fluctuations in demand does not have to continually transform work organization but rather must expand and contract the *size* of production. Adaptation to uncertainty in the market involves quantitative rather than qualitative change in production organization. This is compatible with the pressure to increase profit through deskilling and the concentration of directive power in the hands of management. In this sense Harry Braverman is correct to identify the separation of conception and execution as a distinctively capitalist rationality springing from the search for profit, but it is only effective insofar as the firm faces demand rather than supply constraints.[19] In a centrally directed economy where shortages necessitate flexibility in work organization, technical efficiency requires managerial restraint in the expropriation of control from the shop floor.

The Two Firms Compared

The plausibility of these schematic models of capitalist and state socialist political economies rests on their provision of superior explanations for the similarities and differences between work organization in actual capitalist and state socialist societies. The examination we offer here is limited but nonetheless unusual for its empirical character. It involves a comparison of two machine shops—one in the United States, where Burawoy worked for ten months in 1974–75 as a miscellaneous machine operator, and the other in Hungary, where he also worked for two months in 1984 as a radial drill operator. Lukács studied the operation of the Hungarian firm for over a year through interviews and nonparticipant observation at all levels of management. We call the U.S. firm Allied. It is the engine division of a large multinational corporation, manufacturing agricultural and construction equipment. It is located in South Chicago, and at the time of the study employed about one thousand people. The Hungarian firm, which we call Bánki, produces parts of gear boxes for the larger parent enterprise that makes vehicles, exported to various parts of the world as well as sold domestically. It too employs about a thousand people. The basic work organization, technology, and system of payment of the two machine shops are very similar. Individual operators run individual machines—mills, lathes, drills, and borers—and are serviced by auxiliary workers—truckers, inspectors, setup men, scheduling men, and crib attendants. In both shops, operators are rewarded for the most part on the basis of individual piece rates, while auxiliary workers are paid on time rates. In short, we have a controlled comparison in which the basic technology is held constant so that we can begin to highlight the importance of the wider political economy for the organization of work.

We shall proceed by examining eight widely held stereotypes about work organization and its regulation in state socialist societies as compared to capitalist countries. The data we use to discredit the stereotypes are not of a hard statistical character but are based on interviews and participant and nonparticipant observation conducted by the two authors. We have tended to present our findings in brief conclusive form rather than use the rich ethnographic and interview data from which they were culled.[20]

1. "Labour in Soviet type economies does not work hard. Our source for this comment is common observation, unbacked by statistics."[21]

The relevant literature expresses a unanimous verdict that the one right socialist workers have retained is "the right not to work hard."[22] Explanations abound. Peter Wiles's list is the longest: national character, hatred of the system of the command economy, lack of tools and supplies, improbability of being fired, and low purchasing power of marginal earnings.[23] David Lane and Felicity O'Dell attribute the "slower pace and more careless style" to the workers' peasant background.[24] Murray Seeger attributes the fact that Soviet workers "do not work very hard and the labour they exert produces meager results" to the "inefficiencies inherent in central planning and the backward nature of the country's technology."[25] Leaving aside cultural and developmental factors, the arguments are convincing. Because there is little significant unemployment, and because it is hard to dismiss employees, workers do not have any incentive to work hard. Moreover, in the absence of the coercive whip of a labor market, workers have a positive incentive to conserve their energy in state-sector jobs for their second jobs or for domestic work.[26] Yet workers at Bánki labored at least as intensively, with as high-quality results, as at Allied.[27] Why?

The piece-rate systems of the two firms begin to provide an explanation. At Allied, operators were paid according to their level of production, but they were guaranteed a minimum wage equivalent to 100 percent output. A worker with a job whose rate was difficult to make could take it easy, produce at 70 percent, and receive a wage equivalent to 100 percent. At Bánki, operators faced a straight piece-rate system; they were paid exactly according to the number of pieces produced, with no guaranteed minimum. Turning in at the 50 percent rate, we received 50 percent pay. Thus, one was always under pressure to make the rates. Accordingly, Allied workers labored under conditions of *wage security* and a certain *employment insecurity* (due to the contraction of production and consequent layoffs), while at Bánki *employment security* was combined with *wage insecurity*. This corresponds to the dilemmas of the two types of economy. In a demand-constrained economy, labor's purchasing power is increased through minimum wages imposed across directly competing industries; at the same time, labor must be expelled and absorbed in accordance with changing levels of production. In a supply-constrained economy, on the other hand, demand is contained by binding wages to production, while labor is compelled to improvise in the face of supply uncertainties (see point 8 below). A straight piece-rate system of remuneration assists both objectives.[28]

2. As compared to capitalist societies, the level of reward for effort is ineffectively determined in state socialist societies.

In capitalist societies remuneration for work and piece rates are fixed scientifically, through the careful specification of tasks and the precise timing of operations. In state socialist societies norms are "statistical"—that is, based on existing levels of output—or "centrally determined" outside the enterprise and therefore insensitive to local conditions, or manipulated by management to redistribute income among workers in the firm. "Norms thus no longer determined earnings, but rather were set at levels that would provide proper levels of earnings."[29] In reality we found that norms matched the corresponding jobs at least as well at Allied as at Bánki, and often better.

It is true that thirty years earlier, time-study men, stopwatches in hand, occupied Allied's shop floor timing jobs they suspected of having loose rates. But they were too disruptive, incurring the hostility of shop-floor management as well as operators. Workers could easily deceive their adversary, and Taylorist practices had to be given up as counterproductive.[30] The time-study men have long since given way to the industrial engineers, scouring through output records in a distant office. Now, so long as operators don't hand in more than 140 percent, their jobs will not be subject to rate cutting. Naturally, operators often produce at more than 140 percent, but they bank the excess for a rainy day. Norms are changed only very rarely and the industrial engineers have little idea which rates are loose.

At Bánki there is indeed an official norming process. Management showed us the super-scientific methods they use to calculate norms based on estimated time of the body motions involved. But, as we soon discovered, this is mainly for show. The reality of the norming process revolves around the annual norm cuts. Of this, about 2 percent is stipulated as having come from norm cuts—called norm maintenance. Industrial engineers examine the output figures and, largely by guesswork, decide where the loosest rates must be.

Proposals for norm changes are then sent to the department heads, who consult with foremen, union officials, and, finally, the operators themselves. Then there is a discussion as to whose jobs and which norms should be cut.[31] Operators are thus actively involved in cutting their own rates, with two consequences. First, the looser rates tend to get cut. Second, workers who have less power in the enterprise might face tougher norm cuts. Thus, the norms on jobs done by women and Gypsies tend to be tougher than those of the more skilled male workers. In short, shop-floor negotiation of norms at Bánki accounts for their closer reflection of the job, while it is their "scientific" character which explains the misfit at Allied.

3. Capitalist economies promote constant innovation in technique and products, whereas in state socialist societies such pressure toward dynamic change is weak.

We have so far been considering processes of "adaptation" of firms to their economic environments. These processes take place continually at Bánki in accordance with the exigencies of supply. Innovation, on the other hand, refers to permanent changes in technology or organization that enhance technical efficiency. In this field, socialist firms are reputed to be particularly inept.

Eastern European societies seem to become less and less able to generate significant innovations in any of the substantial, value creating fields of social life from technology through science to art. With the growth of a social-political conservatism there proceeds the increasingly imitative character of their development in all sectors of society.[32]

Capitalist firms, on the other hand, confronted with competition to produce new and ever-cheaper commodities to satisfy consumer demand, are continually forced to change both what they produce and how they produce it.

Joseph Berliner begins his account of the innovation decision in Soviet industry with the statement, "It is the innovative vitality of the modern capitalist economies that has placed the subject on the agenda of the analysis of the Soviet brand of socialism."[33] The Soviet enterprise, he argues, faces an unfavorable incentive system and decision rules, organizational obstacles, and an unresponsive price structure. Bonuses and sanctions are distributed according to the fulfillment of plan targets, above all output targets (whether measured in monetary or physical terms)—although, according to Berliner, reforms since 1965 have given profitability a more central role. Substantial overfulfillment courts an increase in the targets—but not in the bonuses—in the next period. Like machine operators paid by piece rates, enterprise directors have an interest in not overfulfilling above a certain percentage when plans are slack, and in underfulfilling when the plans are taut. They bargain with central planners for loose plans, concealing capacity rather than innovating.

An innovating enterprise faces organizational obstacles that make the incentive system even more unfavorable. Berliner enumerates the following: the shortage and uncertainty of materials and equipment, particularly if they are not routinely incorporated in the plan; the remoteness of the institutes of research and development from the day-to-day realities of production; and the inadequacy of the sales organization. Finally, the price structure compounds the problems created by the incentive system and organizational obstacles. Prices are important not as a medium of exchange but as accounting devices to decide which decision rule to follow. They are generally based on the cost of production plus a stipulated percentage for profit, without reference to its social or use value. This by itself is a disincentive to introduce new techniques, although it is somewhat counteracted by cost-reduction expectations built into the plan. Since prices are also relatively permanent, older products tend to be more profitable than newer ones, given the high costs of innovation. Taking all these factors together, one wonders how it is that an established state socialist enterprise ever introduces a new technique or product.

The realities at Allied and Bánki do not quite fit this picture. At Bánki there are continual pressures to innovate, and management seeks to reorganize production more efficiently, introducing more modern machinery, reconstructing relations between departments, and improving planning and work scheduling, whereas Allied management seems content to keep on doing things in the same way as before, and visible pressures for innovation are few. In 1974–75 the engineering manager had plans to improve some of the equipment, but he had so little money for research and new equipment that the plans never left the drawing board.

How can one account for this reversal of stereotypes? Allied is a division of a large multinational corporation. Its relationship to corporate headquarters is akin to the stereotypical picture painted above of the relationship between the state socialist enterprise and the central planners. It has few resources with which to innovate, and the central enterprise allows it to enter the open market and seek alternative customers only when it has first supplied the needs of the corporation. The division negotiates annual plans stipulating the number of each type of engine it is expected to produce and the (internal) prices they will be sold for. These plans may be arbitrarily changed during the year with the changing demand for agricultural and construction equipment, for which the division does receive some compensation. During the period of the study (1974–75), the general manager was replaced because of an operating deficit. The sort of pressures that are presented as obstacles to innovation in state socialist firms can be found, for similar reasons, in multinational capitalist corporations.

At Bánki, on the other hand, pressure to innovate comes directly from the recognition that there are limits to planning; it is difficult to plan innovation so it is "forced." In addition to demanding the production of specific numbers of specific parts, the central enterprise expects efficiency to increase by roughly 5 percent every year, of which norm cuts are, say, 2 percent, as outlined above. If left unchecked, this pressure would make norms tighter and tighter, disruptive struggles would develop on the shop floor, or workers would leave. This was precisely what happened at Red Star Tractor Factory in the aftermath of the economic reforms. [34] New machines or new products allow management to introduce new, and therefore looser, norms. Where the ratchet principle operates there are continual pressures to innovate.

Berliner's account of the innovation decision contains only two kinds of actors, enterprise directors and state planners, whereas the above description underlines the role of workers. One must establish not only the external framework within which the enterprise operates but the exigencies of production as well. Here we see that external constraints, including supply uncertainties and cost reduction, require management to continually innovate in order to elicit the cooperation of workers and fulfill its plans. The response of the enterprise, whether capitalist or state socialist, to external pressures for innovation is by no means given, but is instead critically dependent on relations among different managerial departments and levels, as we shall see in later sections. [35] But first we must examine the process of production more carefully.

4. Planning leads to shortage and therefore hoarding, which further intensifies shortage, creating anarchy on the shop floor, whereas the market guarantees the efficient allocation of resources and thus the smooth coordination of work.

But the Plan mentality has also spawned a chaos all its own. . . . The Plan engendered storming, featherbedding in factory work forces, the end-of-the-month hassle over raw materials, the short-changing, phony figures, and systematic deception at all levels. [36]

In both Marxist and non-Marxist literature the stereotype of capitalist work organization is one of effective coordination through managerial domination. The flow of raw materials between machines and the distribution of labor are all smoothly integrated with one another through scientific management and the expropriation of control from the direct producer. State socialist work, on the other hand, is dogged by malcoordination. Planners change the targets; supplies of materials and machinery never arrive on time, in the right quantity, or even in the right form. Production is continually disrupted, especially by "rush work" or "storming" toward the end of plan periods. The literature paints a picture of perpetual chaos as management strives to direct a recalcitrant labor force toward ever-changing production operations and quotas.[37]

Again, the realities of the two firms belie the stereotype. The rush work at Allied is much more intense and widespread than at Bánki. At Allied one frequently breaks setups and interrupts runs of pieces for hot jobs that have to be done "yesterday." Rush work and compulsory overtime intensify as orders are due. The quality of work suffers too. Piles of defective pieces lie strewn over the shop floor, particularly around the inspector's bench. These, together with the uncompleted engines lining the aisles, dissolve the image of efficient capitalist work organization into a picture of confusion and anarchy. At Bánki, materials and completed parts move through the plant much more rapidly. One never sees the piles of scrap; what scrap does appear is quickly removed. One hardly ever breaks setups to begin a new job. Only once during the two months in 1984 did we see this happen. Just before the completion of the half-year plan, a fellow radial drill operator was asked to start a new job before he had finished the one he was on. His fury indicated just how rare such an event was. At Bánki an effective system of work scheduling stipulates what each department has to produce in ten-day periods. As we moved toward the completion of the half-year plan, overtime increased, but there was not the mad panic that could descend onto the Allied shop floor when orders were due.[38]

How can we explain this apparent reversal of stereotypes? Part of the answer lies in Allied's character as a division of a multinational corporation, suffering from precisely the shortages and plan-target changes from other divisions that stereotypically face the state socialist enterprise. Bánki had managed to control the problem of supplies, in part through the use of regional party ties and in part through effective advance planning and reorganization of management so that the material supplies department is firmly under the surveillance of the production manager. But other reasons why the work process is so much better coordinated and directed at Bánki than at Allied relate to the utilization of labor, to which we turn next.

5. Whereas capitalist firms attempt to reduce labor costs, state socialist firms seek to hoard labor in anticipation of fluctuating labor requirements and because it has zero marginal cost.

[A] Soviet director, still basically induced to place priority on the fulfillment of an output-based target, and faced with the combination of short operational plan periods and uncertain supply links with other organizations, can be expected to be loath to part with any resources, however marginal. "Storming," the mad rush at the end of the plan period to ensure plan fulfillment at any cost, is still a key characteristic of the Soviet economic system, and storming is difficult if you do not have spare workers to throw into the melee when the situation becomes desperate.[39]

So long as "excess" labor is built into the wage fund, there is no incentive to reduce this particular cost. In the capitalist firm, on the other hand, managers seek to economize on labor—particularly indirect labor, the auxiliary employees who serve directly productive operators. At Allied these are the truck drivers, crib attendants, inspectors, and setup men. And there is indeed an attempt to economize on such auxiliary work, but it is counterproductive.

First, particularly at the beginning of the shift, there are lines outside the crib and inspector's office, as workers wait for tools or fixtures or for their first piece to be checked, while others hang around their machines waiting for the trucker to deliver their stock. Paid on a daily rate, the auxiliary workers have no material incentive to work quickly, and any incentive would be dampened by the apparently endless demands on their time. Second, the shortage of auxiliary workers leads to considerable lateral conflict between them and the operators straining to "make out." Minutes lost waiting for the trucker, inspector, or crib attendant reduce output, making it more difficult to achieve the prized 140 percent. In short, the attempt to cut direct costs to the bone leads to major bottlenecks, inefficiencies, wasted time, and work disruption—none of which is found at Bánki. There, an adequate supply of auxiliary workers allows production to be effectively coordinated without undue lateral tensions. One might wonder which of the two alternatives is preferable in terms of societal rationality: underemployment inside the factory to absorb tensions created by shortages in the context of rigid output targets, or unemployment outside the factory, with associated attempts to cut labor costs inside resulting in mounting organizational tensions. This brings us to the next conventional wisdom, concerning the mechanisms of distribution of labor power among enterprises.

6. **Administrative allocation of labor and/or central determination of wages in state socialist societies makes the deployment of labor less than optimal, whereas in capitalist societies the market assures the optimal allocation of labor by rewarding it according to its marginal productivity.**

The owner of labour power is under a statutory obligation to sell his labour power for a price which is administratively set and which has in principle nothing to do with the surplus that labour will produce. The owner of labour is not allowed to bargain collectively or individually over the price of his labour power. He cannot decide to withhold his labour and to try to sell the products of his labour rather than his labour power. Under these circumstances we cannot speak meaningfully of a labour market.[40]

This too is more or less the perspective of the official Soviet labor policy.[41] Nevertheless, few now give much credence to the idea that the state directs the distribution of labor between enterprises even in the Soviet Union.

Even under "high Stalinism". . . the bulk of the working population were constrained by essentially negative controls, rather than active direction as such. Since the death of Stalin, the situation has become simpler and we can say that in general terms, only members of the Communist Party and new graduates, for the first three years after graduation, are subject to active direction. . . . Coercion, then, is not a key element in the process of labour planning in the contemporary Soviet Union. . . . When it comes to the allocation of the given labour force between jobs, between enterprises and between regions, it is hardly surprising that the wage system does, and is meant to, play a fundamental role, as it does in the West.[42]

But that stereotype of the West is far from accurate. A considerable literature shows how labor markets in advanced capitalist societies diverge from the model of perfect competition. The original dual labor market perspectives pointed to the balkanization of markets supplying different sectors of industry, to the importance of gender and racial discrimination in the allocation of people to firms, and to the development of internal labor markets, relatively sealed off from the external labor market and operating through a distinctive set of rules based on seniority. Sociologists have come a long way from the early crude models and have begun to specify what structural variables (industrial sector, internal organization of the firm, market dominance of the firm) best account for differences in income, security of employment, and working conditions.[43] Whatever the differences among these writers, one thing is clear—the idea of a perfect labor market is not tenable: Labor is not rewarded according to its marginal productivity, and it does not move freely between firms.

The organization of the labor market at Allied confirms this revisionist picture. There, workers join the firm at the lowest jobs, those requiring the least skill and commanding the least pay, and proceed up an internal "career" ladder by bidding on vacant jobs; the worker with sufficient expertise and the most seniority gets the job. Layoffs operate in reverse, so that through a system of bumping, workers with least seniority get laid off first. Seniority also determines the size of one's benefits. This makes it expensive to move to another firm, where one would begin again at the bottom of the job ladder. The longer one stays with a firm, the more likely one will remain. Equally, management's right to fire workers is restricted to clear and persistent violation of rules recognized by both union and management, which further inhibits the effectiveness of the external labor market.

At Bánki there is no administratively developed internal labor market with its systematic rewarding of seniority. Workers cannot be easily fired, and management has little interest in firing workers in the face of existing labor shortages. But workers can leave of their own accord if they can find better jobs. Although average wages are centrally stipulated, the enterprise is still left with the possibility of rewarding workers according to their market price. Thus, for example, radial drill operators are in short supply, and so management has to find some means of holding on to them. It is not possible to increase their basic wage directly, so instead they are given a lot of overtime, some of which is not actually worked. In other parts of the factory, management in 1984 was considering setting up a Vállalati Gazdasági Munkaközöség (VGMK), essentially a system of internal subcontracting whereby self-selected and self-regulating worker collectives are assigned to and paid for the completion of a given task. This system allows workers to receive higher rates of pay for work done in normal hours without it being charged to the firm's wage fund.[44] These maneuvers to increase workers' pay, also found in the Soviet Union,[45] demonstrate the strength of the external labor market in affecting the distribution and price of labor.[46] Indeed, it is stronger at Bánki than at Allied, whose internal labor market provides insulation from the external one.

None of this should be surprising. Planning meets definite limits in the subjective character of labor power as potential producer and consumer. Dictatorship over needs is impossible; one can only indirectly control productive activities through training and incentives, and consumption through the provision of a limited range of goods. State intervention in the labor market has only limited impact.[47] To be sure, in the heyday of socialist primitive accumulation there were attempts at a true dictatorship over needs, but, like programmatic attempts to minimize state intervention under early capitalism, they had to be given up as hopeless.[48] Just as capitalism necessarily contains an irreducible arena of central direction, so state socialism must contain an irreducible arena of market forces.

7. In state socialist societies, conflict between management and workers is either repressed or atomized; in advanced capitalist societies, it is institutionalized and collectivized.

The totalizing social system of domination which encompasses nearly all areas of individual life and involves each individual in a complicated set of dependencies upon (and complicity with) the apparatus, has, as it were, two faces. On the one hand it means not only the lack of formal safeguards (for individuals or communities) against the actions of the apparatus, but also the actuality of an enormous pressure generated by the latter to disrupt all informal, spontaneous social connections and ties beyond the confines of the family. On the other hand, the ensuing atomization of individuals is accompanied by a system of measures which provide relative protection against chance mishaps and, more importantly, give a safe and orderly character to everyday existence. (This naturally again characterizes the developed social system and not the epoch of its historical establishment.) And most of the "cushioning-off" measures exist not as clearly stated and enforceable rights, but as favours granted for good behaviour.[49]

Seeger states this in a more extreme idiom:

The end result is a collection of sullen, disillusioned, unproductive workers who have little say in economic decisions and who have no outlet for their grievances. The party which claimed to represent them and guarantee them a privileged position in society has failed them. No other institution has been permitted to challenge the party for authority. It is easy to see why the regime reacted so quickly and so brutally to repress the tentative efforts by a few workers to organize independent trade unions.[50]

How do our two factories measure up to these images? At Bánki there are few signs of the union or party defending the interests of workers against management. Indeed, in most workers' eyes the party and the union are instruments of managerial domination. But that does not mean that struggles are necessarily repressed or atomized. Rather, as Michel Crozier has argued in the French context, uncertainty, so characteristic of the labor process in a state socialist enterprise, provides the foundation of considerable worker power and potential resistance to managerial dictatorship.[51] On the one side, shop management at Bánki is very powerful on the shop floor. In particular, the foreman commands a wide range of resources (including the allocation of special bonuses, vacation time, new tools, and "standstill" pay), and is centrally involved in any transfers or promotions in his section.[52] On the other side, key workers are able to pose considerable countervailing power by virtue of their position in the labor process or their particular skill and experience. Management is forced to rely on such workers, so that they are able to extract concessions in defense of their interests. Such key workers are all the stronger when there are union officials and party members in their midst. Similar bifurcation of the labor force has been found among construction workers,[53] among machine operators,[54] among electronics workers,[55] and among transportation workers.[56] As Makó and Kertesi and Sziráczki have argued, within the firm a core and periphery develop, following the character of the production process and reinforced by the distribution of party and union officials.[57]

At Allied, struggles are indeed institutionalized, but for that very reason they are also atomized. The internal labor market and grievance machinery constitute workers as individuals with rights and obligations. Workers' ability to bid off their jobs gives them a definite if limited power vis-à-vis shop-floor management. If this undermines collective organization, it also constrains managerial autocracy. The foreman in particular has less authority than at Bánki, where he is not bound by a set of intricate rules governing the distribution of workers and work, grievances, and collective bargaining. If workers at Allied are protected from arbitrary managerial depredations, at the same time their interests are tied to the firm by virtue of the rewards for seniority and collective bargaining.

In 1974, these institutions appeared to be as natural and inevitable as capitalism itself. Since then, recession, mounting unemployment, and an aggressive assault on union strength have met with relatively little effective resistance from the rank and file, precisely because the organs of collective grass-roots struggles have been eroded. The very institutions that before protected workers and bound them to the firm have been turned against them to extract concessions and reimpose a new managerial despotism in the factory.[58] Conflict is less institutionalized and managerial domination more and more arbitrary. Again the stereotype is confounded.

8. **Bureaucracy pervades state socialist societies, hampering the efficient organization of work and undermining responsiveness to human needs. Capitalist societies, on the other hand, operating through the market, assure the optimal allocation and coordination of resources while catering to consumer tastes.**

The directive planning of state socialism is frequently linked to a vision of a monstrous and inhuman bureaucracy which is unresponsive to pressure from below. "The Soviet bureaucracy has to be inefficient in order to accomplish its true aim: to stem the tide, to defer the satisfaction of the population's needs."[59] Enterprises are hamstrung by rules that lead to suboptimal allocation of resources, to the production of waste. As ever, under capitalism the market guarantees the smooth integration of production functions, as well as linking supply to demand.

In reality it turns out that Bánki is relatively free of restrictive rules while Allied is enshrouded by bureaucratic regulation. We have already noted the importance of the internal labor market, the grievance machinery, and collective bargaining at Allied. And these institutions operate through a set of well-defined bureaucratic rules that protect workers against managerial arbitrariness. At Bánki we noted the absence of such explicit rules and management's ability to direct work and workers within limits defined by the bargaining power of core workers. There may be rules, but no one takes much notice of them.[60]

Rules at Allied have two sources. First, they emerged with labor struggles in the 1930s when the foundations of the existing labor legislation were laid—the period of the depression, when labor sought security above all else, and capitalism was suffering from a crisis of underconsumption. The rules forged out of the struggles gave labor an array of job rights, more or less unique among capitalist societies. But rules on the Allied shop floor have another source: They have been a means for higher management to exercise control over production.[61] Department heads regularly promulgate rules dictating the way their shopfloor agents should behave. Thus, there are always new rules regulating the removal of tools and fixtures from the crib, the inspection of pieces, the distribution of job and setup cards. Each new set of rules disrupts the lateral coordination of work and exacerbates tensions between operators and auxiliary workers. Operators spend most of their time maneuvering around the rules in an attempt to recoordinate work on the shop floor.

At Bánki the union is too weak and collaborative to enforce rules that would defend workers against management. But more interesting is that we did not notice attempts by higher management to direct production on the shop floor. The planning department stipulates what must be produced every ten days and with what materials, but it is up to shop-floor management to organize the production process itself. The department superintendent is as much an emissary and representative of the interests of the department as he is the agent of higher management. In other words, top management grants the workshop a certain autonomy in order to meet the exigencies of an uncertain environment, in this case particularly technological scarcity. We can now see a further function of the piece-rate system. It is not merely a means of stimulating hard work; it also *compels* a creative autonomy in response to disruptions in the production process. Shop-floor control, whether management or worker directed, far from being inimical to planning is the sine qua non of efficient production in the context of endemic supply constraints generated by centrally directed economies. Bruszt's study of foreign management consultants shows how the attempt to impose capitalist rationality in the form of scientific management and bureaucratic lines of authority can lead to chaos in a Hungarian firm.[62]

Conclusion

Can state socialist firms be as efficient as capitalist firms? We have argued that the technical efficiency at Bánki's machine shop was greater than at Allied's. In comparison to Allied, Bánki operators work as hard if not harder and produce higher-quality work, norms are better adjusted to jobs, pressure for innovation is more continuous, planning on the shop floor is more effective, the external labor market is better able to tie rewards to skills and experience, and bureaucratic rules that interfere with production are more limited. This flies in the face of conventional wisdom; the reader may continue to insist that these are two freak cases and that nothing more can be learned from them. However, we believe our comparative case study has more than curiosity value. It does offer clues as to the conditions under which state socialist firms might be more technically efficient than equivalent firms in advanced capitalist societies.

Throughout the discussion of the eight stereotypes, time and again we noted how Allied approximated to the stereotype of the socialist firm and Bánki to the stereotype of the capitalist firm. It is as if we have stumbled across a capitalist firm in a socialist society and a socialist firm in a capitalist society. And there is a kernel of truth here: The capitalist corporation can in some ways be likened to a socialist society. It operates through the centralized appropriation and redistribution of surplus from the member divisions so that the relationships among the divisions are akin to relations among enterprises in a socialist society with a paternalistic relation to the center. This certainly was true of the relationship of Allied to its headquarters, despite its self-financing appearance. It is not surprising, therefore, that this hierarchical relationship should give rise to problems of shortages, rushing, poor-quality work, and so forth. The corporation insulates the division from market pressures. Correspondingly, the socialist enterprise seals off its constituent firms from the state, permitting, although not necessitating, economic criteria to dominate relations among those internal units. Clearly our own models, formulated in the first part of this chapter, and those from which they were derived, do not adequately distinguish different levels, in particular the enterprise and its component firms.

Thus Kornai's models of capitalism and socialism tend to conflate these two distinct organizational levels. This shortcoming is linked to another one: the failure to distinguish different stages of development of capitalism. There is only one model of capitalism, that of classical capitalism in which firms engage in perfect competition. The advent of advanced or monopoly capitalism can be linked to the growth of the large corporation, and with it the development of hierarchical relations among its constituent firms. As Alfred Chandler has shown, the large corporation proved to be successful only where the centralized, functionally departmentalized structure gave way to an organizational structure based on semiautonomous divisions operating as profit centers.[63] Yet no matter how autonomous the divisions, they are still bound into a paternalistic relationship with the center, with all the potentially disruptive effects we discovered at Allied. In other words, like the decentralization reforms in the Soviet Union and Eastern Europe, the transition to the multidivisional structure ameliorated but did not eliminate the transaction costs of the large corporation.[64] We see this reflected in the difficulties facing some of the biggest U.S. corporations today and in the move toward conglomeration. For example, during its demise, United States Steel displayed many of the problems normally attributed to socialist planning. It is not a coincidence, perhaps, that the move toward "mini-mills," that is, small autonomous mills using electric arc furnaces, is most pronounced in the United States, and that United States Steel, for example, has been a front-runner in the diversification of investment.

On the other hand, where Hungarian firms are not insulated from the state by a corporate structure they are more likely to display the features we found at Allied, that is, to conform to their stereotype. Thus, in the following study of the largest Hungarian steel mill, which has no semiautonomous divisions such as Bánki, we found the distinctive problems of shortages, inefficiency, and bad planning. It would seem then that in the present phase of socialist development the chances for technically efficient firms are enhanced by an enterprise structure which contains autonomous units linked by economic ties. While the enterprise center will bargain with the state, its constituent firms are more insulated from the wider political arena. It is perhaps no coincidence that despite all the talk of decentralization, the average size of the Hungarian enterprise has continued to increase since the economic reforms of 1968. Contrary to conventional wisdom, the multidivisional corporate structure, that is, the very structure which is now facing grave difficulties in advanced capitalism, may be conducive to efficiency in state socialist countries.

At a theoretical level, these speculations suggest that the models based on shortage and overproduction economies that we developed earlier in the chapter are inadequate. Both advanced capitalist and state socialist societies display features of both types of economy, but at different levels. However, this is not another version of convergence theory, for the most important determinant of the character of a society is the outermost ring—the hierarchical relations of state to enterprise in state socialism, and the market relations among enterprises in advanced capitalism. To be sure, the market fills functional gaps in the state socialist economy and the state performs a similar plumbing role in advanced capitalism, but these interventions are supplementary. They do not alter but reflect the underlying differences between the two types of society.

PART TWO: IDEOLOGY AS REALITY
The Lenin Steel Works

Introduction

In the introduction to part 1 we argued that theories of totalitarianism took ruling ideology too seriously. Either ruling ideology determined reality, or it became the basis of a restrictive and homogenizing lens through which to interpret reality. Either Marxism-Leninism was a vehicle for extracting conformity from all layers of society, or it was a benchmark against which to contrast the actual lived reality of state socialism. In reaction to these two modes of exaggerating the importance of ideology, two correctives emerged in which ideology largely disappeared. On the one hand, convergence theory argued that technology and economic development, not ideology, were the driving force behind changes in state socialism. On the other hand, institutional life proved to be much more diverse and complex than simply the inversion of ruling ideology would suggest. In this second part we propose to restore ideology to its proper place as shaping the way people interpret and then respond to their lived experience.

We begin, as before, with the contrast between capitalism and state socialism. Unlike all other modes of production, capitalist appropriation of surplus from direct producers is invisible, so much so that people deny that such appropriation even occurs. Because surplus labor is obscured, it does not have to be legitimated. Moreover, capitalism creates the conditions for its own reproduction—workers have to produce a surplus and capitalists have to appropriate it if they are to survive as workers and capitalists. The state must simply protect the external conditions of capitalist development—the sanctity of private property and market competition.

In the economic reproduction of capitalism, ideology is secondary, and for that reason its role is to mystify the essence of capitalism. Capitalism can exist alongside any number of ideologies. It is as comfortable with fascist, national popular, racist, or even socialist ideologies as it is with liberal individualism. Usually, as Antonio Gramsci acutely observed, the hegemonic ideology is some combination of these, with one or another prevailing. Different groups or classes draw from this constellation to defend their own interests. The ideological system is very flexible and therefore easily grafted onto diverse lived experiences. Ideology does not stand out from lived experience. Rather than comparing lived experience with reality, under capitalism we compare one ideology with another. Ideology, indeed, provides the terrain for class struggle. The power of ideology is its ubiquity. Like a panopticon, it acts behind our backs without our seeing it.

State socialism is quite different in that ideology is essential to the appropriation of surplus precisely because it is transparent and therefore has to be legitimated. State socialism is not a self-reproducing system in which economic actors are only agents of forces beyond their control, but an order which is self-consciously directed by a class. The ruling class is also the economically dominant class. There is no state that oppresses *on behalf* of a dominant class of exploiters, a state with "relative autonomy." Here the state coincides with the dominant class which, therefore, has to establish an ideology to justify its domination and exploitation. It has to present the central appropriation and redistribution of surplus as being in the interests of all.

The central importance of ideology means that it is not just a rationalization, something taught in schools or displayed in the mass media, but has to come alive in everyday rituals which affirm socialism. Within state socialism, therefore, people live in two worlds: an ideological world and a lived world. But they are both real. What is clear is the contrast between these worlds. State socialism engenders a heightened consciousness of the discrepancy between ideology and reality, between proclamation and experience, between the affirmation of justice, democracy, and efficiency and the ubiquity of injustice, dictatorship, and inefficiency.

Rituals of affirmation are not simply imposed from above. They are also staged from below. Since goods and services are centrally redistributed, competing claims are adjudicated in terms of loyalty, itself expressed in the idiom of socialist ideals. Employees struggle to define themselves as workers and hide their petit-bourgeois background. Employees try to provide credentials that establish themselves as dedicated to socialism so that they can climb the list for housing, child care, refrigerators, or other scarce goods or services. Enterprise managers seeking scarce capital resources flaunt their commitment to plan fulfillment, to productivity campaigns, to socialist competition. The more intense the competition for resources, the more intense the affirmation of commitment to the ideals of socialism, and the more flagrant the discrepancy between ideology and reality.

Different groups react to this discrepancy in different ways. Intellectuals polarize between those attached to the ruling class, who endorse socialist ideology as expressing reality or tendencies within reality, and those in opposition, who embrace reality as the refutation of ruling ideology. The latter may claim that they are better equipped to realize socialism, or they may reject socialist ideology altogether and embrace alternative ideologies. However, what is of interest to us here is the response of workers. Chapter 5 argues that the response to ritual affirmation of socialism is not to reject socialism because it is a hopeless, corrupt endeavor, but rather to embrace the values of justice, democracy, and efficiency. They become tools of criticism. Existing socialism is rejected for failing to live up to its promises, but those promises are themselves positively evaluated. This is because socialist ideals resonate with the class experience on the shop floor, where workers organize production, do the most menial tasks, are subject to managerial abuse, and at the same time receive the least rewards. Class consciousness is endemic to socialist production even if its expression is handicapped by the dominant class's appropriation of the vocabulary of class.

The contrast with feminist consciousness is instructive. In her fascinating study of changing gender relations in Hungary, Joanna Goven argues that women also experience a wide gap between the state's ideological promise of "emancipation" and the reality of the double or triple shift, of poor pay and marginal status in wage employment.[1] Far from endorsing a feminist consciousness which would condemn state socialism for failing to deliver what it proclaims—namely, the emancipation of women from male tutelage—women of all classes reject feminism altogether. Why? Goven argues that hostility to the state has led to the positive evaluation of the private sphere, in particular the family, as an arena of autonomy and self-determination.[2] But endorsing the family is simultaneously an endorsement of male domination: antipolitics leads to antifeminism. First and foremost, the enemy is the state, and men therefore become allies in carving out liberated zones, free of state intervention. By contrast, opposition to the state from workers, whether men or women, does not involve positive evaluation of the workplace or the embrace of class domination. The workplace is an extension of the state, and resistance takes the form of class confrontation. In short, whereas opposition to the state is quite compatible with *class* consciousness, it is incompatible with *feminist* consciousness because of the very different context within which opposition is forged.

In other words, in order to understand the way the discrepancy between ideology and reality affects class consciousness it is necessary to devote attention to lived experience as well as to socialist ideology. The following two chapters attempt to do precisely that. Chapter 4 describes how the shortage economy creates a specific set of shop-floor tensions in steel production, while chapter 5 elaborates the contrast between that setting and the rituals of socialist affirmation, a contrast that shapes the class consciousness of workers.

Less clear from these chapters are changes over time. In part 1 we spoke of the shift from despotic to hegemonic regimes as the result of the growing independence of the reproduction of labor power from production. The rise of a consumer market in basic goods and services has meant that enterprise management can no longer exercise the same arbitrary power over its work force. It has to appeal to market incentives rather than orchestrate mobilization campaigns such as were familiar parts of the Hungarian economic landscape in the 1950s and which were, of course, central to production politics in the USSR, particularly in the 1930s. It is a distinctive feature of the bureaucratic hegemonic regime that ideology is much more attenuated. The rituals of socialist affirmation degenerate into mere sideshows, ridiculous cabarets—the subject of jokes, an empty shell. Class consciousness becomes correspondingly weaker.

Of course, the attenuation of rituals is in part due to the new forms of control associated with the rise of hegemonic regimes. Without despotic powers, management-orchestrated socialist emulation, production conferences, productivity campaigns, and so on were largely ineffective, and the rituals of socialist affirmation were therefore bound to

be weaker in their effects. But they remained under a system of bureaucratic hegemony not so much for their effect on workers but as expres-
sions of loyalty to the center. The livelihoods of enterprises and the careers of their managers continued to depend on their bargaining power
with the center, which in turn required continual affirmation of socialist
values. Painting socialism, as we call it, continues to be important in a
hierarchical economy where budget constraints are soft and indicators
of financial success are unreliable.

The final disintegration of the rituals of socialist affirmation comes
only when the ruling class itself abandons socialism. As we suggest in
chapter 6, in order to understand the demise of state socialism it is important to consider the way the ruling class itself handles the discrepancy between ideology and reality. Any ruling class has to believe in its
own ideology. In the heroic days of socialism it sought to bring reality
into conformity with its ideology, whether through reform or through
repression. Not suprisingly, reality refused to conform to ideology—a
class society cannot be forced into the mold of classlessness. The reproduction of classes turns democracy, justice, and rationality into unattainable goals. As long as the teleological redistributors are not subject to control from below through radical democracy, the rationality of
planning becomes the irrationality of bargaining within the dominant
class; the principle of reward according to contribution becomes the
injustice of reward according to position.

In the final analysis, even the most degenerate form of Marxism—
Marxism-Leninism or official Marxism—proved to be the undoing of
state socialism. Reality mocked the ideology, and, more explosively, ideology continued to subvert reality. Unable to close the gap by changing
reality, the ruling class decided to jettison the ideology. The initiative to
throw off the chains of Marxism-Leninism came from above, not from
below. *Perestroika* and *glasnost* leading to the enthusiastic endorsement
of markets and private property were the creatures of reform elements
within the nomenclatura. Indeed, in the Soviet Union the adoption of
capitalist ideology as a program for reform was and is actively resisted
from below. The campaign against cooperatives and unearned incomes
is the unanticipated legacy of seventy years of painting socialism. The
struggle for the future of the Soviet Union is just beginning.

4 Production in a Shortage Economy

This is the communist sector. If there's pig iron, then there's no scrap. If there's scrap, then there's no pig iron. If there happens to be both, then someone must have stolen something.

Furnaceman's joke

Are there features which distinguish production in state socialist societies from production in capitalist societies? Can one talk of a capitalist as opposed to a state socialist production process? At similar levels of the development of the forces of production, is the organization of work of industrial societies essentially similar, irrespective of differences in their political and economic systems? After undertaking case studies which compare advanced capitalism and state socialism, specifically the United States and Hungary, we have come to the provisional conclusion that the two types of economy do incline toward different forms of work organization. Specifically, Harry Braverman's now-classic thesis that the tendencies toward the separation of conception and execution shape the character of *capitalist* production finds indirect support from the reverse tendencies we observed in *state socialist* enterprises.

Criticisms of Braverman have often been misplaced since they focus on his failure to explain variations within capitalism rather than on his attempt to establish the "essence" of the capitalist labor process. His focus on domination at the expense of resistance, his mistaking ideology for reality, his recognition of only one strategy of control where a number are operative, his essentialist view of development without adequate analysis of social mechanisms, etc., are all important shortcomings when explaining *variations among and within capitalist economies*. But Braverman set himself the task of identifying features common to all forms of the *capitalist* labor process. So his claim that the tendency of the capitalist labor process is toward the separation of conception and execution can be properly evaluated only through a comparison between capitalist and noncapitalist labor processes. When such a comparison is made, new light is shed on the expropriation of control from the direct producer.

Braverman was primarily concerned with domination and exploitation, the vertical dimension of production, not with the horizontal conditions that make production possible. That is, Braverman took as unproblematic the supply of inputs to and the demand for products of enterprises. Neither supply nor demand can be taken for granted, and we follow János Kornai's distinction between two types of advanced industrial economies: one in which supply exceeds demand, the modern capitalist economy of overproduction, and one in which demand exceeds supply, the state socialist economy of shortage.[1] Contrary to Michael Piore and Charles Sabel, who argue that demand-side constraints generate tendencies toward the reunification of conception and execution, we argue that this is the result of supply-side constraints.[2] Our task will be to identify, on the one hand, pressures toward and compatibility between expropriation of control from the shop floor and overproduction under advanced capitalism and, on the other hand, pressures toward and compatibility between workshop autonomy and shortages under state socialism.

Theoretical Framework

We define a mode of production as composed of two sets of relations: relations *of* production through which goods and services are appropriated and redistributed, and relations *in* production which define the labor process, the production of those goods and services. Under capitalism, appropriation is private with a view to accumulating profit in a context of market competition. Here the pressure is to gain a competitive edge either by process innovation (including reducing wages, developing mass production, reducing inventories, and introducing new technology) or by product innovation. This has two consequences. First is the tendency toward overproduction, for supply to exceed demand. Capitalism is, therefore, characterized by demand constraints; following Sabel and Piore, one can plot the development of capitalism and its national variations in terms of changes in those constraints as well as the way enterprises and states respond to those constraints (fig. 1).

But there is a second consequence of the search for profit in a competitive market which Piore and Sabel overlook. That is, it leads to the insecurity of both capital and labor. Profit is realized in the market but generated in production. Since the market is beyond the capitalist's control and there is no way of measuring profit at the point of production, the resulting endemic uncertainty drives capital to extract an ever-expanding surplus from the productive process. The reproduction of the relations of production depends first and foremost on the relations in production, so the capitalist can afford the latter little autonomy, and all the less so the more intense the competition. Although management might subscribe to all sorts of ideologies defending greater participation by employees, these tend to obscure the realities of greater control over employees. The contemporary context of global competition has created pressures toward centralization within large enterprises, for example, through the elimination of middle managers.[3]

Since labor depends on capital, over which it has no control, its fate

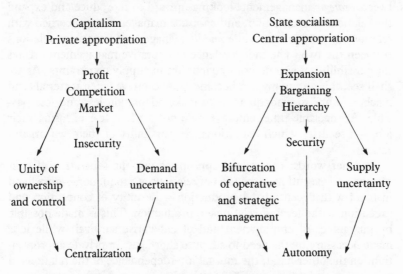

Figure 1. Ideal Type Models of Capitalist and State Socialist Enterprises

is doubly insecure. It has to cope with an arbitrary subordination to capital, itself subject to the caprice of the marketplace. Anxiety at this level concerning material livelihood is inimical to forms of self-organization that do not bring immediate economic gains or that may further endanger jobs.

In state socialism, central appropriation incorporates enterprises into a hierarchical bargaining structure.[4] The accumulation of resources whether of materials or investment depends on the enterprise's bargaining power with the center, which may depend upon its size, its profitability, the political influence of its director, plan fulfillment or other criteria. None of these is a "hard" criterion, but all are themselves subject to bargaining. The results are twofold. First, enterprises develop a seemingly inexhaustible appetite for investment resources, leading to shortages. The source of that appetite can be reduced to a universal urge for expansion, as Kornai argues, but more important in our view is the allocation of new resources which makes it impossible to effectively utilize existing resources. That is, supply constraints stem from the discrepancy between the logic of allocation and the logic of production.

Central appropriation and redistribution gives rise to a second set of consequences. The success of an enterprise is less dependent on the production process than on its bargaining power with the center. Insecurity lies in the competitive relations among enterprises for resources that are centrally allocated. The result is a split within management between *strategic* management, looking upward to reproduce and expand the relations *of* production, and *operative* management, concerned with relations *in* production, while *middle* management negotiates relations between the two. The independence of operative management creates the possibility of autonomous adaptation to supply constraints. As we shall see, this autonomy can become quite coercive when materials and machinery are so inadequate as to make adaptation less and less possible. At the same time, employees do not work in fear of losing their jobs—a security which conditions the possibility of their self-organization.

In other words, centralized appropriation—the separation of conception and execution at the level of relations *of* production—goes hand in hand with decentralized production—the unity of conception and execution at the level of relations *in* production. This is made possible by guarantees of employment and of enterprise survival, while it is made necessary by the need to adapt to shortages. In private appropriation, on the other hand, the mutual interdependence of the relations in production and relations of production leaves no space for autonomous self-regulation of the former without corresponding regulation of the latter. Any attempts at self-organization of work are made more difficult by the insecurities facing both capital and labor, as well as by the centralizing pressures from demand-side constraints.

We will illustrate this theoretical framework by analyzing the Lenin Steel Works, one of Hungary's three integrated steel mills. We will examine, in particular, one section of the plant, where the steel is actually produced. Here the use of the most modern equipment, imported from advanced capitalist countries, allows us to control for the effects of technology in studying how political economy shapes work organization. Following the model outlined above, in the next section we focus on problems in the supply of both investment resources and material supplies, and how shortages are exacerbated by demand constraints. We then turn to the way a shortage economy structures management. At the enterprise level, "strategic" management negotiates external relations, in particular bargaining with the state over, for example, new investments, subsidies, prices, and production profiles. In the plant, "middle" management acts as a coordinating umbrella for "operative" management, the majority of whom are formally skilled workers. Middle management finds it influence restricted on the one side by strategic managers who hand down decisions arrived at through accommodations with the state and on the other side by operative managers who have to enjoy considerable autonomy if they are to adapt to the exigencies of shortages. We describe the forms of this self-organization on the shop floor and managerial attempts to undermine it. In particular, we study two cases of attempted centralization—the use of computers to regulate the system of production and the imposition of a centrally directed system of quality control—and a further case of the scrap yard, where shortages were too intense to permit meaningful self-organization. Finally, we draw some conclusions about the potentialities and tendencies of the socialist labor process.

Shortage Constraints at the Lenin Steel Works

The problem of shortages becomes more or less intense according to pressures from the demand side and from the character of the technology. We examine each factor in turn.

Demand Pressures

The Lenin Steel Works (LKM) produces steel for domestic and foreign industry, including quality carbon steel and alloy steel. Of LKM's total steel production in 1985, 63 percent was used domestically, 14 percent was exported to socialist countries, and 23 percent was exported to the West. The specific site of our study within LKM was the Combined Steel Works, completed in 1980 at the very height of the international steel crisis. Its purpose was to introduce "state of the art" technology into the production of quality and alloy steel at a world level. In the first place it was to supply the growing need of domestic manufacturing industry for specialized quality steels. Proudly boasting that it can produce any type of steel, LKM's management faces intense pressure from the state to accept orders for almost any type of alloy steel required by Hungarian industry. The relatively small scale of manufacturing ventures and a general unwillingness to use higher-quality steel in Hungary have given rise to lots of small-batch production with often narrow quality specifications.

Diverse and small-batch production is also the result of state economic policy. The construction of the Combined Steel Works was part of a larger government plan for the steel industry, namely that in addition to supplying domestic demand it should export finished products to the dollar markets while importing its raw materials from the ruble markets, complementing the opposite strategy of the machine- and vehicle-building industries, which import capital goods from the West and export to the Soviet bloc. The success of this venture has been substantially thwarted by the unanticipated international crisis in steel production, marked by world steel surpluses, competition from both advanced and industrializing countries with their new steel complexes, and falling prices for finished steel. LKM's strategic management has sought to enter into the world market by accepting orders which Western steel makers reject as uneconomic, namely small-batch production of high-quality steels at huge losses. Only by establishing its reputation in such steels can LKM begin to attract orders that might be profitable, but to achieve such a reliability is virtually impossible given the constraints on small-batch production posed by shortages in and/or poor quality of raw materials and investment goods. A further consequence is that the state has to make up the losses of the steel enterprise with subsidies, leaving no resources for the investments necessary to alleviate some of the problems responsible for the losses.

Uneven Development of Technology

Irrespective of demand-side pressures, the Combined Steel Works has to operate in a very unfavorable technological environment. The effectiveness of the new steel-making complex is undermined, on the one side by the backwardness of the technologies that produce the basic ingredients for steel production (the blast furnaces and scrap deliveries), and on the other side by the antiquated rolling mills, which are often poorly equipped to deal with processing high-quality steel. While this problem of uneven technology due to underinvestment can be found in capitalist countries, it is accentuated in the shortage economies of state socialism. Here the distribution of investment resources is based on bargaining with state organs, that is, on political as well as economic criteria. Rather than concentrate all new investment at a single steel enterprise, it becomes politically imperative to distribute resources among all three enterprises, thereby leading to the development of uneven technology.

To understand some of the problems of installing capitalist technology in a socialist economy we have to look more carefully at the character of that technology. The new steel-producing complex gradually replaced the eight old Siemens-Martin open-hearth furnaces with an eighty-ton basic oxygen converter from West Germany, known in the shop as the "LD." Like the Martin furnaces before it, the LD reduces pig iron to steel by combining it with scrap (roughly in a ratio of four to one) under high temperatures. But whereas the Siemens-Martin furnaces used gas to maintain the necessary high temperatures, the LD accomplishes this some eight times as quickly through an infusion of high-pressure oxygen. Here operators face a number of typical supply problems. For example, the amount of oxygen "blown" has to be carefully controlled to produce high-quality steel. The computer assumes that the oxygen is 97 percent pure, whereas in fact its purity fluctuates between 87 percent and 94 percent, so that operators have to blow more oxygen in than prescribed by the computer. Exactly how much depends on the quality of the oxygen, which is often unknown. In addition to the LD, the Combined Steel Works contains an eighty-ton electric arc furnace from Japan, the "UHP," which operates in conjunction with a Swedish vacuum degasser, the "ASEA," to provide the highest quality steel.

Within the same complex are casting facilities. There is a five-strand continuous caster from Japan, the "FAM," which accepts steel mainly from the converter. Money did not permit the two continuous casters, originally planned, to process the bulk of the steel produced. Even at the best continuous casters, casting sensitive alloy steel is a difficult operation usually confined to one or two qualities and not the wide range that would have to be cast at LKM. So there remains a casting bay where ingots are cast and from there taken to the more primitive primary rolling mill via an ill-equipped "soaking pit" where they are re-heated. Stoppages at either of these points affect the casting of ingots at the casting bay as well as the final quality of steel produced in the fine rolling mill. To facilitate continuity in production at the rolling mill, that is to avoid frequent change of the rollers, they try to maintain the same shape of steel for long periods of time, which results in frequent changes in the quality of steel, exacerbating problems in the steel-making process.

Pig iron (hot metal) coming from the blast furnaces is teemed (poured) into a mixer which can hold up to 1,300 tons, enough for almost twenty heats ("vessels" or "ladles" of steel). As well as acting as a buffer, the mixer is designed to homogenize the content of the hot metal so that steel production in the converter can proceed more smoothly. It

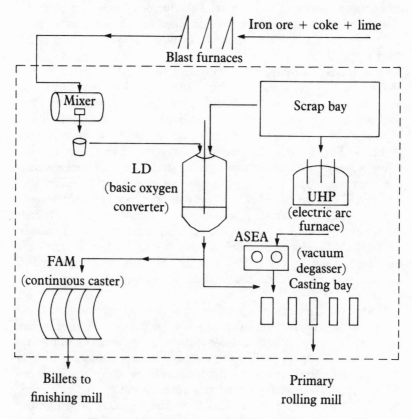

Figure 2. The Combined Steel Works at LKM

is important when the quality of the pig iron from the blast furnace varies considerably over time, as is the case due to the poor and variable quality of the iron ore, the ineffective sinter plant which processes the iron ore, and the now old-fashioned blast furnaces. In practice, due to the shortage of pig iron the mixer is often less than half full so that it does not homogenize the composition of the hot metal charged into the converter.

Finally, there is the scrap, the major ingredient of the electric arc furnace. The quality of scrap poses the critical barrier to the production of high-quality steel. Scrap is also used in the converter together with pig iron, and here too the variable quality means that it is more difficult to control the production process. In an advanced steel mill the scrap is divided up into several grades so that they can be selected according to the steel to be made. Here the scrap is not sorted but heaped onto a single pile. It is often of very poor quality and unprocessed—loose, light, and often mixed with slag. There is neither the space nor the equipment for effective processing. The best scrap comes from within the enterprise, but most of it is used at other electric arc furnaces.

Tightly Coupled Technology

We have seen how surrounding advanced technology with more backward technology intensifies the problems created by shortages. But the character of that advanced technology is itself a source of tension. The different parts of the Combined Steel Works are tightly interconnected and interdependent at the same time that they have their own cycles of production, so that the entire operation is very sensitive to mechanical breakdowns and to the availability and quality of raw materials. Take the relationship between the converter (LD) and the continuous caster (FAM). The cycle of production at the FAM dominates the production process at the LD, but only within limits defined by the LD's own cycle. Once the FAM begins to cast it must be continuously fed with heats from the converter about every forty-five minutes (the exact time depending on the size of the billets being cast and the number of strands working). To be efficient the FAM must be fed at least five consecutive heats. This requires advance planning. There must be enough hot metal and scrap for all five heats and the temperature of delivery (around sixteen hundred degrees) is important; otherwise the FAM will not work properly. It can happen that by the time the heat reaches the FAM it is too cold, or that it reaches the FAM too late, or that something happens at the FAM so that it malfunctions (the strands get clogged up with aluminum coating, steel can leak from the strands due to the presence of bits of slag, or it may have too low a viscosity due to low temperature before entering the strands); then the heat has to be sent to the casting bay where it can be cast at lower temperatures. But that is a complicated rerouting process, and whether there will be space at the casting bay depends on the availability of ingot molds. Such an elaborate coordination in time and space of tightly coupled technology is very susceptible to the types of supply problems that a socialist firm faces. What are the implications for the organization and direction of work?

The Squeeze on Middle Management

Based on the demarcation of three levels of management—strategic management, middle management (directing the plant and working on day shift), and operative or shop-floor management (distinguished by shift work)—our thesis is that the shortage economy tends de facto to polarize managerial direction at the lowest and the highest levels, leaving middle management dependent on both. This is a consequence of a shortage economy which requires strategic management to negotiate with the environment, particularly the state, at the same time that responsibility for dealing with shortages must lie in flexible organization on the shop floor. We shall show in later sections how attempts by middle management to appropriate control over the shop floor undermine effective adaptation to the exigencies of a tightly coupled technology in a context of supply uncertainty. This is not to say that middle management is superfluous. It does carry out important recognizable functions, to which we now turn.

Routine Functions

First, middle management performs certain routine functions. The highest levels create a buffer between the actual shop-floor practices and the attempts by the front offices to dictate alternative practices. Here the authority of the plant manager is critical—with both those above and those below. He has his agents on the shop floor, work site managers and foremen working permanently on day shift. They mediate dictates from above, as when some urgent order requires immediate production, an experiment is run, or preparations have to be made for the visit of a delegation. They are supposed to plan ahead, for example, for the supplies needed at the work points. They redistribute personnel on a temporary basis when there are shortages as well as controlling promotions and demotions. Foremen and work site managers are responsible for coordinating relations among the parts of the plant. In their daily managerial meetings they are held accountable for failures at their work sites. At the same time, we shall argue, steel making in the context of shortages of materials and uneven, tightly coupled technology requires that immediate production decisions be made on the spot by skilled workers who are elevated to what we have called operative managers, specifically the steel makers at the LD, UHP, and ASEA, the casting bay master, and the process controller at the FAM.

Development Functions

Second, middle managers attempt to improve the efficiency and safety of the plant, and thus during the three years of our research we observed considerable increases in the output of the converter. When we began in 1985 the average number of heats was as low as six or seven per shift; when we left two and a half years later it was as high as nine or ten, with a maximum of fourteen. This was made possible by the greater availability of pig iron from the blast furnace and higher quality scrap steel. The crucial factors were the final closure of the remaining four Siemens-Martin furnaces in October 1986, so that all the pig iron could be directed to the converter, and an improvement in the supply of scrap. But who decided to close down the Martin furnaces? Confronted with the necessity of new investment there, strategic management decided to close them down altogether, exploiting the move as a sign of LKM's commitment to modernization. Once they were closed down, many of the advantages to the Combined Steel Works fell into place.

Another achievement of middle management is the increased rollability, that is, improvements in the quality of the steel coming from the Combined Steel Works, permitting more efficient production in the rolling mills. They attribute this to improved organization and a new incentive system. Further investigation shows that the improvement in the rollability can be attributed to the improved quality of the casting powder used in the casting of ingots—although here, middle management was involved in obtaining the new material. Finally, in the second quarter of 1987 middle management proudly announced a considerable increase in the number of heats per converter lining, from a record of 861 to 1,294. The major reason appears to have been the use of magnesium oxide, which reduces the corrosive effects of the slag. This is a textbook solution to the problem, raising the question of why it took so long to be adopted. It seems that the problem became particularly acute when, in a short period of time, the price of the new heat-proof bricks that make up the lining more than doubled from six million forints to fourteen million forints, to be paid in foreign exchange. Strategic management transmitted gradually increasing sensitivity to budget constraints by offering middle managers considerable bonuses for extendng the life of the lining. Such innovation bonuses are a major way for middle managers to increase their income, but not all innovations receive significant rewards. Here middle managers have to take their cue from strategic management, who set the system of rewards. Again, the initiative for development lies with top managers. There is a reluctance to take up small-scale changes on the shop floor which would advance production but offer few material rewards.

Regulatory Functions

The third and perhaps most important function for middle managers is to establish the incentive system for shop-floor operations. While all production workers in the Combined Steel Works receive bonuses according to the performance of their respective sectors, output is beyond the control of all but the key operators, such as the pivotal figure of the steel maker who directs production at the converter. Given a program of production of certain types of steel, the steel maker faces three problems. The first is to obtain hot metal and scrap, that is, backward cooperation. The second problem is to ensure effective production of steel at the converter, and the third is to deliver steel which is of appropriate quality and temperature that can be teemed at the FAM or casting bay.

The official incentive system corresponds to these three problems. Thus the steel maker tries first to minimize the percentage of hot metal per ton of steel. This minimizes the cost of inputs, since at LKM hot metal is more expensive than scrap. Second, he tries to minimize the number of kilograms of charge (hot metal and scrap) per ton of steel produced. This is a measure of the efficiency of the converter. Finally, he tries to maximize the ratio of steel teemed to steel cast. This involves producing steel that is of the right temperature, right quality, and right quantity so that it can be used at maximum efficiency at the FAM or casting bay. At the FAM any amount of steel can be cast, so the steel maker does not worry about the number of tons, but the temperature is critical. At the casting bay, on the other hand, only fourteen ingots of 5.8 tons each can be cast, that is, 81.2 tons. Anything over this will have to be scrapped, bringing down the steel maker's rate of teeming. Here the operative temperatures are lower, because the casting is quicker, giving more flexibility to the caster. As far as the steel maker is concerned, the quantity of steel cast is critical, and therefore the steel maker develops an interest not just in the provision of hot metal and scrap but also in what happens at the FAM and casting bay.

For those whose efforts affect production the official incentive system functions quite well. Sometimes, however, there are breakdowns, most frequently at the FAM, that are beyond the control of the operators but which can adversely affect their pay. On one occasion the personnel officer explained how the FAM had not been working well and workers' wages were being threatened. Extra premiums were introduced to create an effective bottom to their pay—absent in the official pay incentive system. If the official system had operated by itself, then the FAM wouldn't work as efficiently as it does, there would be continual turnover of workers, and their spontaneous cooperation would be lost. A bargain has to be struck on the shop floor between workers and managers outside of and, indeed, in opposition to the official incentive system.

If the incentive system is the carrot, there is also the stick, a punishment system that hung heavily in the minds of operators, arousing fear and fury. In a system so sensitive to shortages, there were ample cases of breakdowns and failures, whether these took the form of production stoppages or production losses or production of scrap. Here the punishment system took its toll. If operators failed to deliver the expected number of heats, then irrespective of the problems they had faced, they were subject to reprimand and verbal harassment. A more serious failure, such as the production of scrap, elicited threats of fines, some of which were actually carried out, for those declared negligent. Any failure to meet expectations, any malfunctioning, has its culprit who must be punished. The punishment system is ritualized in the morning meeting that the plant managers hold with night-shift operators, known to all as "Who knows how to [defend himself]?" after the TV talent show. Each operator has to give a persuasive account of any production failures. Later on there is a meeting of the day-shift managers where fines and reprimands are sometimes distributed. Those who run the meeting are not particularly interested in excuses or explanations but are concerned with allocating the blame to some irresponsible action.

Managers responsible for implementing this punishment system say it is necessary because the steelworks is such a dangerous place. This is less than an adequate response since danger is often the stimulus to self-organization and autonomy. Another explanation lies in the seemingly crucial role the Combined Steel Works plays in the overall profitability of LKM, but in a system of such tight interdependence the roles of the blast furnaces and the rolling mills are no less crucial. More likely is the view that strategic management is no more interested in the complaints and excuses of plant management than the latter is in those of its operative managers. The punitive system is passed down from above. Further, the unwillingness of plant managers to examine the causes of failures lies in their lack of control over the crucial factors of production (supplies and machinery) and their dependence on shop-floor operators to deal with breakdowns, disruptions, and crises as they spontaneously develop on the shop floor. The punitive system represents a frustration with their own powerlessness. What then is the response to this system of positive and negative sanctions on the shop floor?

Self-Organization on the Shop Floor

Given the constraints under which LKM has to operate, it is perhaps remarkable that its productive system is as effective as it is. As we will argue, its success can be largely attributed to the adaptive responses of operators on the shop floor. What are the elements of their autonomy?

Lateral Cooperation

On the basis of criteria established from above, shop-floor management's attention is directed laterally toward cooperation with other units in the Combined Steel Works. Take the steel maker at the LD, like most of the other operators always a male. Since he is dependent on the cooperation of others, he must command the confidence of his fellow operative managers at the other work sites. We observed the strivings of a recently promoted and inexperienced steel maker to establish himself among his peers, his furnacemen, and middle managers. Whenever he made a mistake, for example, they would say how young he was, how much he had to learn, and how in the old days the steel makers were really experienced. The steel maker who does not command respect may find himself waiting for the teeming ladles, for the "pots" into which the slag is poured, for hot metal from the mixer, for scrap from the scrap bay, for space and ingots to be prepared in the casting bay. Cooperation is particularly crucial when steel is being made for the FAM since its operation requires an uninterrupted flow of heats from the converter. The steel maker's adrenalin begins to run and tempers can flare. If operators at the other work sites are not keen to cooperate, he has to somehow persuade them that it is in their interest to do so.

But the steel maker seeks more than simple cooperation from others. In order to protect himself against unforeseen adversity, such as breakdowns at other units, poor service from the overhead cranes, which often need repair, inferior quality or inadequate supply of materials, and arbitrary interference by higher managers, he asks them to undertake two types of manipulations: routine manipulations that make his production record look good and exceptional manipulations to cover up mistakes. First, the amount of scrap and hot metal registered as charged into the converter can be made less than that actually charged, so that at the FAM the amount of steel produced gives a better charging rate—ratio of scrap and hot metal to steel produced. At the casting bay the extra steel gives the leeway necessary to guarantee minimum production of 81.2 tons, and if the casting bay master cooperates there will not be too much officially recorded excess. Such manipulations require the cooperation of crane drivers with the supervisors at the casting bay, scrap yard, mixer, and FAM.[5]

The second set of manipulations takes place when there is a failure at the converter. For example, if the chemical composition of the heat is outside the limits stipulated for the steel being made, it is possible to change the steel being produced to a different type. This requires the cooperation of the "dispatcher"—another operative manager—who plans production of steel from blast furnace to rolling mill during the shift. The steel maker may ask the FAM to accept a heat that is slightly cooler than prescribed. Or he may ask the casting bay master to discount the scrap that was produced from a heat, or ask the FAM to submit a sample from a good piece of steel rather than from the bad one actually produced. In his turn the steel maker can extend favors to those upon whom he depends. He can record lost time due to shortage of scrap, for example (which otherwise would be blamed on the scrap master) as time lost due to shortage of hot metal, for which no one is blamed if there is less than six hundred tons in the mixer because officially this is the minimum. In practice there usually is less than six hundred tons, so that such a doctoring of the record is easy. In short, a system of reciprocal favors develops around the objective of producing steel on the one side and the protection of operative management from the punitive sanctions of middle management on the other.

Any attempt by management to eliminate such manipulations would lead to narrow self-protection on the part of each work site, involving continual and heated arguments as to whose responsibility was a given failure, e.g., in teeming. As it is, the manipulations are the basis of joint cooperation. The steel maker accepts the risk involved, for example, that his teeming ratio (amount teemed to amount of steel produced) may be adversely affected by what happens at the casting bay or the

FAM, but in return he expects his counterparts to undertake compen-
sating manipulations that will make his production record look good
and cover up his mistakes. Instead of interfering directly, the plant
manager allocates fines to those held responsible for lapses. Operators
and steel makers don't forget their punishments in a hurry—not only
because the fines are considerable but also because of the public humiliation. In this way middle management defines what is acceptable and
what is not. Out of this emerges the norms that govern relations and
practices on the shop floor in conditions of uncertain production.

Shop-Floor Culture

This shop-floor culture is further elaborated through a network of social
ties. While drinking groups forge solidarity between operators and their
teams of workers, football competitions and outings, all of which are
organized on a plantwide but shift-specific basis, establish ties between
the different work points. Although workers and operators may move
around from workplace to workplace, they rarely change shifts. That is
to say, their mobility facilitates the development of social ties and a common set of norms. It is interesting to note therefore that the majority of
complaints are made against those who are outside the control of this
system of cooperation, that is, against the laboratory and the maintenance workers. Both groups are outside the moral order of steel production and their cooperation is more difficult to extract.

Shifts compete with each other to teem the greatest number of heats
and to avoid breakdowns. This leads to antagonisms as each shift tries
to push problems onto the next shift. So one shift may postpone repairing the taphole which has become too large or spraying the inner wall of
the converter that has worn thin. Rules about the relative composition
between hot metal and scrap may be flouted to get out a last heat,
thereby emptying the mixer of hot metal and so leaving the next shift
stranded. At the casting bay there might be no ingot molds or the place
left in a mess; at the scrap yard the new crane drivers must begin afresh
with empty boxes, or there may not be any preheated ladles or slag
dishes. Any of these can lead to considerable time loss at the beginning
of a shift. Moreover, the quarterly production conferences are held
separately for the different shifts. All of this cements solidarity within a
shift across work points while building up distance between workers at
the same work points but on different shifts. While middle management
complains about "shift chauvinism," at the same time its own punitive
order encourages lateral cooperation among work sites at the expense of
cooperation between successive shifts.

Obstacles to Centralization

So far we have argued that adaptation to supply constraints is most effectively accomplished through granting autonomy to operative managers on the shop floor. This becomes even clearer when we examine attempts at centralization.

Computer Control

Let us return to the steel maker at the LD and his assistant, who control production at the converter. So far we have talked about how they negotiate relations with other work sites, but what happens at the LD itself? They have to decide first how much hot metal and scrap, and then how much fluorspar and lime have to be charged into the converter, and finally the quantity of different alloys to be charged into the ladle prior to or during the tapping. They are also responsible for the length of the oxygen blow, i.e., the volume and the number of blows of oxygen. The converter, like all the other work points in the Combined Steel Works, is equipped with computer-directed operations, so that for any steel on the program there are instructions as to how the steel should be made.

Given a specific steel to be produced, the computer calculates how much scrap and hot metal have to be put into the converter, and basing its calculations on the average composition (in terms of carbon, silicon, and manganese) of the last ten heats of hot metal, gives up a prescription for the volume of oxygen to be blown in. Where indeed the average composition of the last ten heats of hot metal would predict the composition of the eleventh, and where other factors are held constant, the prescription would be an accurate one. In practice this is almost never the case. Often the mixer is nearly empty and so does not perform its homogenizing role, and the hot metal from the blast furnace can be of very uneven quality. This is the first major variation which the computer cannot take into account. The scrap itself is not sorted, so it can vary in content. Then there are a wide range of miscellaneous problems that affect the length of the oxygen blow, e.g., the purity of the oxygen, the temperature of the ladle into which the steel is tapped, whether the steel is going to the FAM or to the casting bay, the temperature of the hot metal (pig iron), the size of the taphole, whether the argon equipment that circulates the steel once it is made is working. The computer cannot take these and other imponderables into account, so they have to be assessed by the operator.

The computer is not only unreliable but, in roughly 40 percent of the heats, fails to give any prescription at all for the oxygen blow. This is usually because the acceptable limits of silicon or of manganese in the hot metal are exceeded, so that their oxidation generates either too much or too little heat. In practice the steel maker has no such option—not to make a heat when the conditions are not within prescribed limits—so he figures out an appropriate oxygen blow. On one occasion, however, we heard that the production manager had halted the delivery of hot metal from the blast furnace because the silicon was considerably above the prescribed level. Only the top echelons of middle management can intervene in such a manner beyond each plant.

That these problems are largely distinctive to a shortage economy was illustrated when the Japanese who installed the computer were recalled because it was not living up to its promise. The program couldn't take into account the long stoppages due to malfunctioning of equipment or shortages. At first the Japanese were quite baffled by the problems encountered in the plant. They then tried to reprogram the system to meet the specific needs of a shortage economy. But it still does not dictate operations and so its use is confined to information processing.

It is not simply a source of information but actually saves a great deal of time by recording the processes of steel production. But even here it is not always accurate. The shortage economy and the incentive system lead to manipulations that the computer does not register, and so many of the data are misleading. When one of us asked one of the managers if we could examine the computer readings on the amount of hot metal in the mixer, he told us we shouldn't bother since they are hopelessly wrong, registering some minus two thousand tons! The computer system was originally set up so that operators could not change any of the data on the screen. But this proved incompatible with the exigencies of a shortage economy, so that now there is a woman in the production department who is responsible for "correcting" the data in the computer in accordance with shop-floor manipulations. But anyone who wants to make any change has to first register that request in a special logbook.

The following incident highlights the conflicts that can arise over the proper use of the computer. One Saturday morning, the chief metallurgist came in to inspect the production of a very special steel. He was there because of the high cost of the alloys and the importance of the quality of the product. The problem with this steel is that it requires very low phosphorus and sulfur content at the same time as high carbon content. This is difficult to accomplish because the conditions for getting rid of phosphorus and sulfur also bring down the level of carbon.

There is a special desulfurizer, but sometimes this still leaves the sulfur content too high. To further reduce the amount of sulfur requires a very high temperature, but if it is too high the phosphorus that has been eliminated through oxidation and passed into the slag is deoxidized and returns to the steel. The operation is a delicate one in which rather than a single blow of oxygen it is necessary to give two blows, keeping the temperature relatively low and pouring in lime and fluorspar to help oxidize the sulfur and phosphorus, removing them to the slag. Seeing the operator working to keep the temperature relatively low, the chief metallurgist told him he was doing it all wrong and that he should work according to the program, which stipulated a long single oxygen blow. The operator knew that this would not work and took no notice even as the chief metallurgist stood there.

The conclusions are twofold. First, any attempt to use the computer system as a means of control is doomed to failure because of the uncertainties, mainly from the supply side. Second, any attempt at the centralization of control in the hands of those who are not attuned to the day-to-day realities of the Combined Steel Works easily leads to the production of scrap. Although middle management does make such attempts at expropriation of control, for the most part it accepts the necessity of workshop autonomy.

Quality Control

We have shown how shop-floor autonomy helps adjustment to shortages, particularly in the context of tightly coupled work processes. But it cannot be forgotten that shortages exist only relative to demand constraints, so that as the latter become more severe the former also intensify. This can be seen in the case of quality control.

The second half of the 1970s saw government economic policy for the steel industry turn toward the provision of Hungary's developing manufacturing industry and the expansion of the export of steel to the West. In line with this strategy LKM proposed the Combined Steel Works to increase and improve the production of its quality and alloy steels. In 1983, two years after the completion of the new complex, it exported 1,500 tons of alloy steel; in 1984 about 50,000, and in 1985 62,000. Most of these steels were produced in the Combined Steel Works, but at great costs in scrapping. Scrap rates have varied from 5 percent to 40 percent according to the type of steel. In 1986, for every 1,000 tons of finished steel, 1,400 tons of liquid steel had to be produced.

The difficulties of making quality steels underline the dilemmas of production in a shortage economy. Here the diagnosis and solutions of American experts, brought in to advise LKM management but accustomed to problems of a demand-constrained economy, illuminate the distinctive dilemmas of socialist production.[6] The experts attributed increasing rates of scrap to declining effort and diminishing sense of responsibility. As a solution they proposed the creation of an independent and centralized system of quality control which through computerization would trace each heat of steel through its various production processes, pinpointing the source of defective quality, making it possible to correct the problem, and immediately halting the continued processing of substandard steel. In theory their proposal was admirable, but it did not come to grips with the underlying realities of the uncertain conditions of production, whether unreliable machinery or inadequate or even absent materials. It was never implemented.

Frustrated by their apparent powerlessness to affect the quality of production, middle managers in quality control have attempted to follow these plans for centralization.[7] But instead of using surveillance to identify sources of scrap production, they have used it to punish those they find culpable of mistakes. This has the unintended effect that inspectors on the shop floor often turn a blind eye to the attempts of operators to push defective steel onto the next work point. They naturally sympathize with the operators' attempts to escape responsibility for what is not of their own doing, whether it be that steel arrives at their workplace already defective or that working conditions make substandard steel unavoidable if it is to be produced at all. The inspectors don't want to be party to punishing workers for mistakes they either did not make or had to make. In short, rather than solving the problem, the punitive system exacerbates it.

For example, there is a continual struggle between the primary rolling mill and the Combined Steel Works as to who is responsible for steel that cannot be rolled. The rolling mill blames the steel producers for not turning out steel according to specifications or for uneven surface on the ingots, while the Combined Steel Works blames the rolling mill for mistakes in reheating the ingots or poor rolling practices. Because of antiquated reheating equipment and poor measuring devices, and because of the sensitivity of quality steel to rolling practices, it is hard to distribute responsibility fairly. The difficulty of discovering the source of the problem is only exacerbated by the application of punitive sanctions, leading each side to cover up its own mistakes and spy on the other. Although the root cause of quality failures lies outside the control of operators, the correction of that which does lie within their control requires immediate cooperation between inspectors and producers. This will only take place in the absence of punitive and arbitrary interventions by middle managers. Centralization of quality control is another exception which proves the rule, that is, that technically efficient production depends on autonomous organization at the workplace.

Scrap Bay

Unaccustomed to the problem of shortages, the American experts had nothing to say about attempting to change critical supply conditions, in particular the situation at the scrap yard. Here supply uncertainties are so extreme that no amount of shop-floor autonomy can facilitate adjustment. The history of the scrap bay illustrates well the character and sources of shortage in a socialist economy.

When the Combined Steel Works was being planned, the government told LKM management that it would provide no more than ten billion forints to finance the project. The original estimate was twelve billion forints, so top management had to decide on cuts. The essential technology had to remain, they argued, and instead reductions should be at the expense of some peripheral part of the plant. Accordingly, in order to reduce the size and therefore the cost of the scrap bay, management inflated figures for the density of scrap they would be receiving. They estimated that the scrap density would be between 1.4 and 1.8 tons per cubic meter, whereas the real figure should have been between 0.6 and 0.8 tons per cubic meter. In this way they pushed the responsibility for higher-density scrap onto the enterprise which collects and distributes the scrap. This, they knew, would only be possible if there would be capital investment in scrap-processing equipment—a very unlikely event. So the scrap bay was built much too small for the voluminous loose scrap, and as a result it is impossible to sort the scrap into different grades, as is done in many capitalist steel plants. Instead it is simply dumped into one huge disorganized mound. From there the scrap master has to organize deliveries to the UHP and the converter. Both sets of demands are usually urgent, but the cranes are slow in collecting the scrap because they were designed to gather much heavier types. Moreover, when quality steel is being produced it is critical to know the alloy content of the scrap, but with only a small electronic device at their disposal such a sorting operation is beyond the capability of the work crew.

The consequences are obvious. The scrap master and his work crew have a great deal of autonomy but little control over their work. They are cynical and frustrated and feel the hopelessness of their task. Here autonomy is antithetical to efficient production because the shortages are simply too great in relation to production needs. The original attempt to save on what appeared to be a peripheral operation becomes a major obstacle to the production of quality steel, for which the Combined Steel Works was explicitly designed.

Conclusion

We have opposed the common argument that modern technology requires the return of control to the shop floor. Technology by itself is not determinant: Its condition of effective deployment, in particular the most effective work organization, depends on the form of the wider political economy. We highlighted the link between a centralized economy and the character of work organization in a state socialist enterprise using the most up-to-date capitalist technology. More important, we took issue with another variant of the reskilling argument: the prognosis of Piore and Sabel that the future of capitalist society heralds increased worker control over production through flexible specialization. They do not argue from technological determinism, but give precedence to market factors: the need to cater to a multifaceted consumer demand. On the basis of what we know about the mini-mills and integrated steel plants in the United States, demand pressures lead to centralization and coercive managerial strategies rather than, as Piore and Sabel claim, the resurrection of the craft paradigm.[8]

Our own case study suggests that it is in state socialism, where supply constraints are the more significant force shaping development, that some form of shop-floor self-organization holds the greatest potential. Fluctuations in the quality and availability of raw materials, machinery, and labor power require some form of autonomous and flexible workshop organization for technical efficiency.[9] We have seen how, on the one hand, there developed dual systems of management and of incentives. In order to adapt to supply constraints in the context of tightly interdependent work sites, shop-floor management had to be given the room to make decisions spontaneously and elaborate a set of plant norms that governed lateral coordination. The centrally controlled computer system was mainly useful as a source of information, not as a means of prescription, for which it was originally intended. On the other hand, when middle management sought to interfere in the direction of day-to-day operations, crises and work stoppages were the frequent result.

Shop-floor autonomy need not necessarily revolve around a few key figures who direct production. In some situations, such as the machine shop we studied at Bánki (chapters 2 and 3), workers themselves became the central figures in organizing work. Managers were fewer and acted as the emissaries or agents of workers. At LKM, on the other hand, the character of the technology and tightly coupled production involved key leaders at the different work sites, who work out deals among themselves, developing social ties and a sense of joint responsibility. The workers under them undertake a multiplicity of tasks, and in this sense they engage in a form of flexible specialization, but they don't exercise any guiding control over the process of production. Instead they are its agents.[10]

In its strongest form the claim of this chapter is that the promotion of technical efficiency, that is, the realization of a firm's production possibilities, requires centralization in advanced capitalism and shop-floor autonomy in state socialism. How then do we explain cases of shop-floor autonomy in advanced capitalism and centralization in state socialism?

National economies are constrained not solely by demand or by supply but also by some combination of the two. First, and most simply, within capitalism, shop-floor autonomy springs up precisely where factors of production cannot be controlled—for example, in the construction industry or coal mining—just as, within state socialism, pressures for centralization are most intense where there are stringent demand constraints—for example, in military production. Second, supply constraints may become more critical in capitalist societies as profitability becomes less salient. Within a large corporation, divisions may be bound into a political center much as socialist enterprises are bound to the state, leading to insatiable investment demands and shortages. On the other hand, market competition may develop among divisions within a socialist enterprise so that demand rather than supply becomes the salient constraint.

Third, and even more generally, we argue that too categorical a distinction between supply-constrained economies and demand-constrained economies tends to overlook the mutual determination of supply and demand. That is to say, the more specific and variable the demand, the more significant becomes any variation in the quality and availability of factors of production. Inasmuch as the intensification of demand constraints leads to supply problems, so shop-floor autonomy may emerge under capitalism. Equally under socialism, shortages may so adversely affect the quality of the product that the enterprise will find difficulty selling the product and thereby invite centralization.

We can also explain countertendencies to our model in terms of class struggle. Namely, in advanced capitalism workers have sometimes successfully resisted the expropriation of skill or centralization of control, just as in state socialism shop-floor operators and workers are often defenseless against the concerted efforts of trade union, party, and management to control production. While such economic and social factors explain variations both over time and between places within advanced capitalism and within state socialism, in no way do such variations refute the contention of this chapter that for the survival of these societies, the tendencies must be stronger than the countertendencies.

Finally, we don't want our conclusion to be misunderstood. We are not saying that autonomy on the shop floor will by itself resolve the dilemmas of socialist economies. Their fate hangs elsewhere, namely in the hierarchical relations between state and enterprises—relations which create the very problems to which self-organization is one adaptive response.

5   Painting Socialism

"New Evolutionism" is based on faith in the power of the working class, which, with a steady and unyielding stand, has on several occasions forced the government to make spectacular concessions. It is difficult to foresee developments in the working class, but there is no question that the power elite fears this social group most. Pressure from the working classes is a necessary condition for the evolution of public life toward democracy.

Adam Michnik, 1976

Following Marx, classical Marxism retained a boundless faith in the working class as deliverer of revolutionary promise. By virtue of its objective position in capitalist production, the working class bears the chains of all oppressed classes. Its revolutionary mission is to burst those chains by overthrowing capitalism and inaugurating the classless society of communism. In emancipating itself, the proletariat emancipates the entire human race. This mythology of an inevitable, teleological movement from class in itself to class for itself rides on two theses.

The first is the *polarization* thesis. Capitalism combines private ownership of the means of production with socialized organization of work. While capitalists dispose of their capital, workers—with only their labor power to dispose of—are brought together into the factory, where the division of labor establishes their unity through interdependence. Here they form a collective worker, capable of running production independent of their employer. Driven by market competition to reduce the costs of production, individual capitalists cut wages, intensify work, and introduce new technology which deskills some workers, reducing them to appendages of machines, while throwing others into the reserve army of unemployed. The pursuit of profit impoverishes workers so that capitalists cannot find consumers for their products. Recurrent crises of overproduction lead to the bankruptcy of the weaker and smaller capitalists, who descend into the proletariat. The concentration and centralization of capital proceeds along with the disappearance of intermediate strata. Wealth accumulates at one pole of society and poverty at the other pole.

The polarization thesis only accounts for the objective conditions of the working class, the rise of a class *in* itself. Workers form a class *for* itself when they combine first into trade unions and then into a political party in order to pursue their interests in the political arena. According to the *class struggle* thesis, conflict between classes counters the isolating and atomizing effects of competition among firms and among workers. Class conflict not only builds solidarity but demystifies class relations. Workers recognize that their own interests are irreconcilable with those of capital and that, as a collective worker, they can autonomously set the means of production in motion. In short, class struggle begets class struggle, intensifying until workers expropriate the means of production through revolution and establish the kingdom of socialism.

Recent theorizing about class in advanced capitalist society takes as point of departure one or the other of these theses. There are those, such as Erik Wright, who contest the polarization thesis with theories of the generation of class positions outside as well as between capital and labor.[1] With these new categories Wright endeavors to explain variations in the distribution of class identity, class consciousness, and income inequality within and between capitalist societies. In pushing toward class consciousness he introduces class alliances and family relations as mediating social forms.[2] He *assumes* that the objective material interests of workers lie in socialism, and so his task is to redefine the working class—within a theoretically consistent scheme—to obtain the best fit between class position and class consciousness. He does not confront the problem of the revolutionary passivity of the working class, however defined, in all capitalist societies.

Whereas Wright works from class in itself toward class for itself, there are those who move in the opposite direction in order to challenge Marx's class-struggle thesis. According to Adam Przeworski, for example, because workers are able to advance their material interests within capitalism, class struggle—rather than developing in an intensifying spiral—leads to concessions, class compromise, and demobilization.[3] Residual mobilization is orchestrated by macro-actors, in particular parties and trade unions, strategizing within capitalist democracy, thereby shaping the class identities of different occupations and assembling them into social forces. In this way Przeworski explains variations in class formation both over time and between countries. But such "class formation" is no longer rooted in any relationship to production.[4]

Starting from class for itself, Przeworski loses sight of class in itself just as Wright, starting from class in itself, loses sight of class for itself. They both fail to supply the link between class position and class formation because neither develops any microfoundations of class. They ignore the lived experience of class. In connecting class location to class consciousness, Wright leaps over the ideological and political institutions of production. Przeworski's analysis of class compromise is only concerned with the distribution of profits, while his examination of class formation turns workers into dupes of macro-actors. The experience of production is simply left out of account.

In my own studies of the microfoundations of working-class formation I have argued that it is impossible to read forward from class position to class subjectivity (Wright) or read backward from class actor to class position (Przeworski) without reference to the mediating political and ideological apparatuses of production.[5] Because these apparatuses of production vary independently of production, and because production in turn varies independently of class structure, there is no one-to-one relationship between class position and class formation.[6] In other words, the link between class in itself and class for itself depends on the lived experience in production, that is, on the organization of work and its regulation, that is, on what I call the *regime of production*. The link between class in itself and class for itself depends on the character of the regime of production. Under advanced capitalism, *hegemonic* regimes engender consent to capitalism by constituting workers as individuals and by coordinating their interests with those of managers and owners. This organization of consent takes place independently of the identities and consciousness forged outside work. We need go no further than the workplace to understand why the working class in advanced capitalism does not become a revolutionary force *if* we examine the political and ideological institutions of production and the lived experience they generate.

In this chapter I turn to state socialism and argue that the production regimes of state socialism engender *dissent*. Like the consent organized under capitalism, dissent toward state socialism is not simply a mental orientation but is embedded in distinctive and compulsory rituals of everyday life. Moreover, under certain conditions, dissent leads workers to struggle for the transformation of state socialism toward a democratic socialism. This *negative* class consciousness produced by the state socialist regime of production provides the raw material for a *positive* class consciousness, a vision of an alternative order which can only be forged in class *mobilization*. If I am correct, then history has played an ironic trick on Marx. The polarization and class-struggle theses, which were supposed to demonstrate how proletarianization would give rise to a revolutionary working class under capitalism, in reality prove more relevant to state socialism. I hope to show that the reason for this lies in state socialism's creation of distinctive regimes of production.

Solidarity: A Workers' Revolt against a Workers' State

We begin with the most obvious instance of polarization and struggle in Eastern Europe: the origins and evolution of Solidarity. In 1980–81, for sixteen months, Polish workers attempted to construct a socialist society in their own image. Even in its temporary defeat this was a momentous victory: the first society-wide Marxian revolution in history. The working class gave Solidarity's ten million members its energy and determined its direction. Its leaders came from the working class, hardened by experiences in the earlier revolts of 1956, 1970, and 1976. Intellectuals expressed and often inspired the strategy of revolution, but they were not its directing force. Indeed, they played a rearguard role, containing working-class impulses to radicalization and deflating the movement's utopian aspirations.[7] Initially Solidarity insisted on its trade union status, but the unfolding crisis drove it from a movement for the self-defense of society toward a self-governing republic.

If Solidarity was Marxian in its class basis and its goals, its context, its idiom, and its form violated all conventional Marxian norms. The movement did not arise in an advanced capitalist society but in a society that claimed to be socialist. The self-proclaimed vanguard of the working class, the Polish United Workers' party, found itself confronted by the organized representatives of the working class. At the same time, although the members of Solidarity acted as a class, they did not label themselves as a class. Solidarity was not bound by a commitment to Marxism or even socialism but was profoundly anti-Marxist, driven by nationalist and democratic sentiment expressed in religious symbolism.[8] Finally, this was a revolution in which no one was killed, a revolution that was as much moral as it was social and political. Yet, despite itself, Solidarity, inasmuch as it can be regarded as a homogeneous movement, aspired to socialist goals, a self-organized society in which the freedom of workers became the vehicle for the freedom of all. A nation stood united behind a workers' movement for the democratic transformation of state socialism.[9]

But Solidarity was not simply playing out a nineteenth-century vision; it invented a new form of revolution, the "self-limiting revolution." At one level its self-limiting character was tactical. It sought to avoid a repetition of the Soviet invasions of 1956 and 1968 by not challenging either the "leading role of party" or established international alliances. It always drew back from confrontation, sought common ground and compromise with the "authorities," and held down trade unionist demands that would plunge the country into a destabilizing economic crisis. However, self-limitation was more than a pragmatic response to the obdurate economic and geopolitical realities. It had its own raison d'être. Solidarity repudiated the Bolshevik model of "frontal assault" and substituted a "war of position." It sought to conquer the trenches of civil society rather than seize state power, to self-organize society while keeping its political shell intact.[10] In 1970, Kuron, one of the intellectual architects of this "evolutionary revolution," advised irate workers who had been brutalized by the police: "Don't burn down [Party] Committees: found your own." Aspiring to political power not only invites Soviet tanks, it also sets in motion the logic of repression, reproducing the oppressive order it seeks to destroy.

Solidarity is the twentieth century's response to the Paris Commune, symbolizing a new type of prefigurative revolution. Its evolution refused the classical opposition of reform and revolution. It began as a social movement for the defense of society against the state, withdrawing from responsibility for the administration of society. After nine months the economic crisis assumed such proportions that Solidarity was compelled to move from self-defense to self-government, from a self-limiting revolution to what Staniszkis calls an "institutional revolution." The state's refusal to enter into any social accord combined with acts of provocation to sow seeds of dissension within the Solidarity leadership and of despair among the people. Although self-limitation remained until the very end, mounting frustration eroded self-censorship in the autumn of 1981, a year after the government had signed the Gdansk accord. Despite Solidarity's massive, disciplined, and enthusiastic support, without compromise from the regime it could not close the gap between aspiration and reality. Public attacks on the party apparatus and its leading personnel, fraternal messages to the "working people of Eastern Europe and all the nations of the Soviet Union," and continuing demonstrations and strikes greeted the regime's turn to the offensive after the July party congress. Solidarity was set on an inevitable collision course with the authorities. Here struggle and polarization fed one another in an ever-expanding and ever-deepening spiral of conflagration.

Was this convulsion a purely Polish phenomenon, one more in a long history of national insurrections, or did it betray a general tendency of state socialism? Historians have stressed the heritage of an ancient culture which has enabled an underground society to develop and persist for almost two centuries of occupation with brief and partial respites in the last century and for twenty-five years of disenchanting independence between the two world wars this century. They give special attention to the Roman Catholic church as protector of the national conscience, to the legacy of noble democracy, and to a rich spiritual and literary heritage which fed and consoled the political frustrations of an oppressed nation. Solidarity is but the most recent of a series of uprisings—1733, 1768, 1791, 1794, 1830, 1863, 1905, 1920, 1944—against foreign and in particular Russian occupation. These are the pegs upon which the Polish collective consciousness is hung. Timothy Garton Ash writes of the Polish revolution: "But there was no society in eastern Europe *less* prepared voluntarily to accept *Soviet* socialism, imposed by Russian bayonets. Soviet socialism did not start from scratch in Poland; it started with a huge political and moral debit. Stalin himself said that introducing communism to Poland was like putting a saddle on a cow; the Poles thought it was like putting a yoke on a stallion. This fundamental historic opposition and incompatibility is the most basic cause of the Polish revolt against Yalta and Soviet socialism in 1980."[11]

Social scientists, on the other hand, have tried to subsume the rise of Solidarity under more universal rubrics. Inevitably there are those who argue that Solidarity was the result of deprivation—declining living standards, longer queues for basic goods, denial of political freedoms, and so on. Because there is always deprivation and because people experience relative rather than absolute deprivation, other commentators have dwelt on the frustration of rising expectations, the false promises of the Gierek decade accentuated by economic bungling, corruption, and increasing inequality. Those who regard relative deprivation as always present among the oppressed turn to theories of "resource mobilization" to explain Solidarity's success, such as it was. The Roman Catholic church, intellectuals organized for the defense of workers, and binding ties between workers and peasants, white-collar and blue-collar workers, provided the basis for Solidarity.[12]

Others pay more attention to the movement itself. For those who view Poland as a form of state capitalism, Solidarity is an example of a revolutionary working-class struggle that inevitably afflicts all capitalist societies. Although he sheds much light on Solidarity's continuing blindness to the realities of state power, to the importance of the police and military, Colin Barker makes little attempt to explain the occurrence of Solidarity.[13] Applying his ideas of the development of collective identity and the "self-production" of society, Alain Touraine and his collaborators undertake a detailed analysis of Solidarity as an evolving social movement. They explore the changing balance of trade union, national, and democratic interests in relation to tensions between Solidarity's identity as an upsurge of social will and as a force for the reconstruction of society, between its defensive and counteroffensive impulses. However, when it comes to explaining its appearance they too fall short, appealing alternately to the category of totalitarianism and to a shopping list of factors—economic stagnation, blocked social mobility, migration of workers from rural areas to cities with different cultural traditions, and the illegitimacy of the regime.[14]

Those who focus on the character of Poland's political regime have more adequate explanations for the rise and form of Solidarity. Andrew Arato, for example, analyzes the Polish situation in terms of the opposition of state and civil society.[15] He considers the concept of "corporatism" (as opposed to pluralism and totalitarianism) as most appropriate to understand the dynamics of the Polish regime.[16] Yet others, such as Bronislaw Misztal, have drawn parallels between the rise of social movements in capitalist and state socialist societies due to growing state intervention in social life.[17] Always careful to examine both sides of the conflict, the dynamics of both regime and movement, Jadwiga Staniszkis argues that Solidarity springs from the combination of two forms of protest absorption: corporatist attempts to segment the population into groups with greater or lesser access to the state, and populist status inversion, in which top officials plead with workers to accept compromise.[18] While they are sensitive to the discourse of Solidarity, these excellent analyses do not plumb the depths of the lived experience that drove the Polish working class to invent a new type of revolution.

All these explanations either emphasize Poland's unique history or adduce the working-out of some general principle. In both tendencies, working-class revolt against state socialism becomes an expression of something more fundamental—Poland's long history of resistance to foreign domination, civil society versus the state, the oppressed rising up against totalitarianism, authoritarianism, corporatism. Comparisons with previous uprisings in postwar Eastern Europe cast light on what is unique to Solidarity and what may be more general. Adam Michnik, for example, considers the revolts of 1956, 1968, and 1980 as a learning process in which successive strategies for transforming society are abandoned. The Hungarian and Czechoslovakian catastrophes demonstrated the failure of revolt from below and of reform from above, leaving Solidarity to experiment with reform from below.[19] Touraine and his coauthors see the evolution of struggles against the regimes of Eastern Europe as a shift of initiative from intellectuals to workers, from divisions within the ruling circles to the unity of the working class. But this learning process, this teleology, goes unexplained. Moreover, it overlooks the remarkable fact that even in 1956 and 1968 the defense of the uprising very quickly shifted to workers and the alternative institutions they created. Why should workers play such a central role in challenging a regime that claims to represent their interests?[20]

Rather than treat Solidarity as an oasis of struggle, a model to be upheld or refuted, approved or condemned, I am concerned to explore its roots in specific working-class experiences of state socialism. I try to understand in what ways Solidarity typified working-class opposition to state socialism and in what ways it was unique. Why should the first Marxian revolution take place in state socialism rather than advanced capitalism and why, of all state socialist societies, in Poland? This was the project that took me into Hungarian factories.

Hungary is a particularly apt comparison since, like Poland, it too has suffered national humiliation at the hands of surrounding powers, it too experienced working-class revolt in 1956, and it too has had a relatively open civil society. But there the parallels stop. For in the 1980s, Hungary possessed none of those characteristics that made the rise of Solidarity so distinctive. Instead of a collective memory inspired by nationalism and Catholicism, binding society into a force hostile to the state, Hungary is a fragmented society, ambivalent about its past, driven by individualism and entrepreneurship. Hungarian workers have learned to maneuver within the socialist order rather than revolt against it. They are contemptuous of the Solidarity movement which plunged Poland into economic chaos. "They got what they deserved. Unlike we Hungarians, who work for our living, the Poles expect to have meat on their table by striking."[21] From being a land of brothers and sisters, overnight Poland became, in Hungarian eyes, a nation of loafers and hustlers. Their collective mobilization sent shivers down the Hungarian spine.[22] Surely Hungary points to the uniqueness of the Polish Solidarity movement?

As I shall argue, this is only partially correct. Despite their differences, Polish and Hungarian workers share a common class consciousness—one that is critical of socialism for failing to realize its own proclaimed goals of efficiency and equality. Precisely how this negative class consciousness emerges can be understood only by entering the daily life of workers, in particular by examining the distinctive features of the socialist factory. Of course, class consciousness implies class mobilization only under certain conditions: the development of collective interests and of the collective capacities to pursue those interests. So the possibilities of collective mobilization are undermined by channels for individual mobility and the absence of autonomous institutions operating in a relatively open civil society. In these latter respects, Poland, Hungary, and the Soviet Union differ markedly. But first let us turn to what these societies share by stepping once more into the hidden abode of production.

The October Revolution Socialist Brigade

Between 1985 and 1987 I worked three times in the Lenin Steel Works for about a year in all. Each time I was a furnaceman in the October Revolution Socialist Brigade. I had made my way into the heart of the socialist proletariat, the Hungarian equivalent of the Lenin Shipyards, the Ursus tractor factory, the coal mines of Upper Silesia, the steel plants of Huta Warszawa, Nowa Huta, and Huta Katowice. If an embryonic Solidarity was to be found anywhere, then it would be found here. In all socialist countries, steelworkers have been glorified as the heroic vanguard of the proletariat. Their Promethean struggle with nature provides the irreplaceable foundation for socialist development. Acclaimed in the monuments and placards of socialist realism, they were the home of Stakhanovites and their mythological feats of socialist emulation. But now in the Hungary of reform, with the period of heroic socialism long since past, what has happened to the glamorous steel-worker? What marks him as a socialist worker?

Certainly I had arrived in a proletarian city. With a quarter of a million inhabitants, Miskolc is Hungary's second biggest town and industrial center. Its pulse is ruled by the factory siren. Chimneys belch smoke and dust into a polluted atmosphere; at the turn of the shifts, buses spread through the city—jam-packed with the silence of the weary; housing projects are cramped and overflowing; bars bulge on payday; and tiny weekend homes, planted next to one another in the surrounding hills, provide an eagerly sought refuge when work, weather, and family permit. The city's character is engraved in the rhythm of its time and its distribution in space. Although quite a distance from the center and not easily visible from the main street running from one end of town to the other, the Lenin Steel Works and the Diósgyör Machine Factory are the directing forces of city life. The symbols of heroic socialism may have been painted out, but the hard life remains.

The Lenin Steel Works is the oldest of three integrated steel mills in Hungary, having celebrated the end of its second century of production in 1970. In 1985, out of the total 3.8 million tons of steel produced in Hungary, the sixteen thousand workers at the Lenin Steel Works produced around 1.2 million tons.[23] I was given a job in the new Combined Steel Works, constructed in 1980 and 1981 with the most advanced technology imported from Sweden, Germany, and Japan. It contains a mixer, which holds the pig iron coming from the old blast furnaces, as well as a scrap bay. Both feed the spectacular eighty-ton DEMAG basic oxygen converter which gradually replaced the eight antiquated Siemens-Martin furnaces. There is also an eighty-ton electric arc furnace which melts down scrap steel, after which it is further purified in a vacuum degasser. From the converter and electric arc furnace the molten steel is taken either to the new five-strand continuous caster or to the casting bay where it is solidified into ingots. In both cases the steel then proceeds out of the Combined Steel Works to the rolling mills, somewhat outdated with the exception of an East German finishing mill.

To get to my workplace I join the crowds passing through the number one gate. On top of the gate they have fixed Lenin's head. Like the red star that hovers over the largest blast furnace, Lenin escapes our notice as we flash our passes at the attendants and hurry on to our work stations. The Combined Steel Works is a brisk twelve-minute walk away

along a main thoroughfare. It's a walk into the past as I pass the old
foundry, various warehouses, the antiquated primary mill, the small
electric arc furnaces hidden from view but noisily pulverizing scrap
steel into a molten bath, and the old Martins with only their eight tow-
ering chimneys still erect. Steelworkers fondly refer to their plant as an
industrial museum. All along are the disorderly scrap yards—mounds
of wasted steel and rubbish to be deposited in one of the furnaces. Away
in the distance the three blast furnaces face what looks like a huge petro-
chemical works but is in fact the Combined Steel Works. On a bridge
overhead I can just make out the lettering of a slogan from yesteryear:
"With increases in the quantity and quality of steel let us struggle for
peace." Here too the trappings of socialism have faded. So it seems from
the outside.

I work as a furnaceman around the huge barrel-shaped vessel that is
the basic oxygen converter. Inside, molten pig iron and scrap steel combine under a high-pressure injection of oxygen to form steel and slag in
batches of eight tons, called "heats." I am one of eight members of the
October Revolution Socialist Brigade—six furnacemen, a steel maker,
and his assistant, the "operator." As furnacemen we tend to the converter's needs as it goes through its cycle of production. We begin by opening the huge steel doors in front of the converter, and then guide the
two overhead crane drivers barely visible through the dust a hundred
feet above. The first rests the beaked tip of a scrap car on the lip of the
converter's mouth. Slowly raising the back of the car, he sends twenty
tons of scrap crashing into the vessel. We signal the second crane driver,
and a ladle with some sixty tons of pig iron sails in overhead. As the pig
iron is teemed (poured) into the vessel, the entire podium is lit up by
huge flames leaping up out of its mouth. We close the doors and run
away from the screaming whistle of the oxygen lance as it passes down
into the now upright converter. A departing Boeing couldn't make more
noise.

For fifteen minutes we take refuge in our cubbyhole—"the eating
room"—away from hostile eyes and ears. Here I listen to endless remi-
niscences from the past, when steelworkers were steelworkers. Gyuri,
our lead furnaceman and winner of innumerable medals and honorific
titles, recounts the good old days at the Martin furnaces when there
were no computers to dictate the amount of scrap, pig iron, carbon,
fluorspar, and lime, or fancy sampling devices or electronic thermocouples. "We had to use our judgment. Experience really counted. Now
any untrained peasant from a cooperative can be a furnaceman." Józsi,
at forty-five the oldest in the brigade, whose father had been a big shot

at the rolling mills, says he would never let his son follow in his footsteps: "There's no future in steel anymore." He too appreciates the Martin, where he could work in peace, take a rest when the furnace was filled and being fired, without interference from incompetent bosses. He was his own man with a specific job to do. True to his word, before I left in 1985, he returned to one of the two Martins still in operation.

But haven't conditions improved? Isn't it safer, less hot, less exhausting? Csaba, from a younger generation, is the first to agree. But others are more ambivalent about losing old skills even when working conditions improve. They miss the challenge of the old furnaces, unplugging the taphole in excruciating heat, shoveling away at the alloys, and arguing about the steel maker's judgment. And none like the nervousness which surrounds the converter. When there were eight Martin furnaces, if one broke down there were seven others. But if the converter stops production it's a catastrophe. Everyone goes crazy. Never the heroes they were painted, the furnacemen nevertheless retain a nostalgia for a work rhythm that they controlled. Life was harder but more human. From the way they talk, even the furnaces were human. Now they are chained to a charmless monster. We hear the oxygen infusion reach its final roar as the lance is withdrawn. We file or stagger out.

Gyuri, using the controls at the side, turns the converter horizontally to pour off slag. We take up our stations in front of the steel doors separating us from the fiery mouth and the steel bubbling away inside at sixteen hundred or even seventeen hundred degrees. Peering through the windows in the doors or, if the converter is still vertical, examining the flame leaping upward out of the mouth, the experienced eye of the steel maker can tell immediately whether the oxygen blow was successful. Clad in our fireproof clothing and squinting through our filtered lenses attached to our hard hats, we thrust thermocouples on long steel lances into the turbulent bath. With a long heavy spoon we take out samples. The podium in front of the steel doors is a sea of activity, people running backward and forward with flaming torches, thumping cardboard tubes against the floor, plunging glass tubes into spoons of sparkling steel, and then bringing those spoons down with a resounding crash to remove the steel shell stuck inside.

All along, Béla, the steel maker, curses when there's the slightest delay. Every second is precious. It takes five minutes to get the chemical analysis back from the laboratory, by which time the steel can cool fifty degrees. Bandi flicks a switch in the control room and the alloys come crashing down the chute from the bunkers overhead, plunging into the swirling steel. Gyuri swings the vessel over to the other side so that steel flows out of its underbelly through the taphole in a silver arc into the ladle waiting below. Ten minutes later, eighty tons of steel are ready for casting. We take a final temperature and Béla signals us to toss in a number of bags of carbon or girders of cold steel as a last adjustment to its chemical composition or temperature. If we are on a run then already some of us will be preparing for the next heat, taking a sample of the pig iron, beckoning the scrap-yard supervisor to get a move on, while Gyuri teems out the slag remaining in the bottom of the vessel.

The cycle for a single heat is about thirty-five minutes; if things go according to plan we should produce thirteen heats a shift. But things don't go according to plan and we are doing well if we complete seven or eight heats; the average is about five.[24] To fill the time we are saddled with a panoply of dreaded auxiliary tasks, such as repairing the taphole of the converter if it becomes too large or too small. A platform carries us right to the edge of the converter, where it may be fifty or even sixty degrees centigrade. There we melt away slag with an oxygen torch or reline the hole with cement. When the vessel's brick lining thins after about five hundred heats, we have to regularly repair the weak patches by spraying special refractory material through a long thin pipe.[25] Sometimes we have to clean the trolley that moves the slag dish backward and forward on the lower level. We have to crowbar off the still-warm lava that has accumulated all over its base—not to mention the cleaning operations at the end of every shift, hosing down the podium and bulldozing the rubble below.

Flexible specialization this may well be, but the restoration of craft control it is certainly not. Here there's nothing to distinguish state socialism from advanced capitalism. But where furnacemen at the Lenin Steel Works greet the closure of the Martin furnaces with ambivalent nostalgia or smoldering resentment, depending on how they are affected, for their confreres in Pittsburgh, South Chicago, or Gary such technological innovation creates a double bind. On the one hand it accelerates unemployment and thus anger and despair; on the other hand, to resist could court the even greater catastrophe of irrevocable plant closure. Their situation is desperate, yet still they find little fault with capitalism. Paradoxically, the furnacemen of the October Revolution Brigade, although more or less insulated from the ravages of the world market and unable to comprehend what it means to be without a job, nevertheless know only too well how to criticize their system. From where comes their perspicacity?

"The Prime Minister Is Coming"

In fieldwork the meaning of an event depends on what follows and not on what precedes it.[26] *Manufacturing Consent* emerged from the continual interpretation and reinterpretation of what perplexed me when I first entered my South Chicago machine shop: the furious rate at which people worked for no apparent reason. Similarly, I have been and continue to be riveted by the drama which unfolded during my first two weeks at the Lenin Steel Works.

It was a freezing February morning in 1985 when I began my first shift. There was a lull in production and I was casually talking to Feri, whose job was to clean the oxygen lance, when Stegermajer, the plant superintendent, came up yelling at us to get on with sweeping the place clean. The look of disgust on Feri's face made it clear what he thought of the idea. Who'd ever heard of keeping a steel mill clean? And anyway it was not his job. But there was no arguing with the menacing look on Stegermajer's face, so we lazily took up our brooms and began brushing away at the railings, creating clouds of dust and graphite that would descend elsewhere to be swept up again by someone else's broom. Aggressiveness and shouting seemed a way of life here at the Lenin Steel Works. The bosses were always on edge. What were they so nervous about? How different from Bánki, the auto plant where I had worked before. There we were left to our own devices to make out on our machines or not, to take a walk, visit a mate as we pleased. There was no make-work.

No sooner had we brushed the railings to reveal a dull green and yellow than painters appeared, brightening up the surroundings at least for a few minutes until the dust and graphite descended once more. "Was this normal?" I wondered. The next day the painting continued and I heard that some delegation would be visiting, but no one cared who, why, or when. As became clear in succeeding days, this was to be no ordinary visit. No less a person than the prime minister himself would be coming. The automatic chute, broken now for many weeks, that sends alloys from the bunkers overhead down into the ladle below, was being repaired. We would no longer have to shovel the alloys into a wheelbarrow and tip them down the chute ourselves, choking in the clouds of silicosis-producing dust as we did so. Thank God for the prime minister.

On the Friday before the Tuesday coming of the prime minister, production had come to a standstill. Welders were out in force with their tanks of acetylene, resting uncomfortably near to the converter. New silver doors threaded by water pipes to prevent warping were being erected to fence off the vessel. Hordes of young lads from neighboring cooperatives were swarming around to give the converter and its surroundings a final touch. Preparations were as elaborate as for a satellite going into orbit. Soldiers were shoveling the snow away from the entrances below and cleaning up the debris that they uncovered. It seemed that the entire land had been mobilized for the visit of the prime minister.

I found Józsi swearing in our eating room. "This is a steel mill, not a pharmacy." He'd just been told to change into new overalls, with a new hat and gloves. I looked at him in disbelief, assuming I had not understood him properly. "You won't even be working when the prime minister comes," I said. He looked at me as though I'd come from the moon. "What's that to do with anything? Everybody has to conform. This is window-dressing politics." So we all trooped off to get our new outfits, and came back mockingly giving our hard hats a final polish. Five minutes later, let alone next Tuesday, we would be filthy again.

Today was our turn for a communist shift. In aid of charity, such as support for a children's hospital or the National Theatre, we work an extra shift. It's a socialist form of taxation. We were assigned to paint the "slag drawer" yellow and green. It is a huge machine which skims off slag from the pig iron as it passes on its way to the converter. There were not enough paint brushes to go around. I could only find a black one. What could I paint black? What better than the most treasured of the furnaceman's tools—his shovel? I had hardly begun this critical task when Stegermajer came storming over, with his hand behind his back and his hard hat bobbing, his head bowed for combat. "What the hell are you doing?" "Painting the shovels black," I replied as innocently as I could. But he was not amused, so I quickly added, "Haven't you got any more brushes so I can help the others?" No, there weren't any. "So I can't help build socialism?" I continued, somewhat riskily. My mates cracked up, amused at the thought of their "kefir furnaceman" building socialism. Even Stegermajer caved in when Józsi interceded, "Misi, Misi, you don't understand anything. You are not *building* socialism, you are *painting* socialism. And *black* at that."[27]

The "painting" continued on Monday when we hauled out the always-ascending graphs demonstrating the superiority of the converter over the old Siemens-Martin furnaces. Party slogans and directives for the forthcoming party congress as well as photographs of earlier visits by dignitaries were displayed at resting points on Tuesday's scenic tour. At noon on Monday, Stegermajer came over to me with an embarrassed look. "You know the prime minister is coming tomorrow." I nodded and smiled. "Well, why don't you take a holiday." They surely didn't want their yogurt furnaceman upsetting the visit.

I assume the prime minister came. I saw his picture in the newspaper, peering into the wondrous converter. When I returned on Wednesday, the flags were down and the graphs were returned to their storeroom together with the party directives and photos. The filming was over. Once more we were a steel mill, at least until the next painting.

Workers looked upon this cabaret as just another instance of socialist waste and deception. On seeing workers melting ice with a gas flame, Gyuri shakes his head in dismay. "Money doesn't count, the prime minister is coming." Socialism, it seems, can only conjure up an image of efficiency by calling on its workers to collaborate in a desperate and farcical cover-up. But are all irrationalities of a piece, as they appear to the workers? Is there a rationality behind the irrationality, a deeper meaning to the painting? What interests parade behind the facade? Is this any more than a ritual affirmation of state power, having little to do with Hungary's political economy?

Bureaucratic Competition

The growth of a capitalist enterprise depends on its profitability; growth of a state socialist enterprise depends on state-dispensed investment funds. There are three steel mills in Hungary. Their common interest in expanding the resources available to the steel industry is broken up by an intense rivalry over the distribution of what is available. The rivalry is made all the more intense by the unequal efficiency of the mills. Dunaújváros, built after the war with modern Soviet technology, is the most profitable of the three. The Lenin Steel Works and the smaller Ózd, both much older and in places operating with last century's technology, barely break even. Just as critical is the production profile of the different enterprises. In an economy driven by shortage, the enterprise that produces a relatively homogeneous product is able to plan ahead its material requirements and is in a much better position than a company which produces a wide variety of products and whose material supplies fluctuate correspondingly. This makes Dunaújváros with its sheet-steel production a more efficient enterprise than the Lenin Steel Works, which produces diverse high-quality steels for the machine industry. Furthermore, quality being less important at Dunaújváros, it is less vulnerable to supply constraints, further heightening its image of greater efficiency. Their distinctive products lead to a corresponding distribution of influence: Dunaújváros with the Ministry of Finance, Ózd and the Lenin Steel Works with the Ministry of Industry. Competition between enterprises becomes competition between government bodies.

In theory, the production of steel in Hungary could be all located at Dunaújváros. Certainly the capacity and space is available, and indeed, such was the proposal of a secret Soviet report. At the Lenin Steel Works they are skeptical that Dunaújváros has the expertise to produce the high-quality steel it specializes in. In any event, the plan came to nothing simply because it is impossible to close down steel plants in a state socialist society. Miskolc society would be decimated if the Lenin Steel Works closed down. A management proposal to reduce employment by just eight hundred workers met with instant rejection by party authorities.[28] The balance of political forces leads, therefore, to a roughly equal distribution of resources among the three enterprises: The Lenin Steel Works gets its Combined Steel Works, Ózd receives new rolling mills, and Dunaújváros receives a coking plant and two 120-ton Soviet basic oxygen converters. Rather than being concentrated in one enterprise, investment is distributed among all three, where its effectiveness is drowned in the surrounding obsolete technology. Thus, the new Combined Steel Works is marooned among antiquated rolling mills and blast furnaces. The distribution of resources through political bargaining in a hierarchical order leads not only to a characteristic uneven development of technology but also to widespread shortages in raw materials and machinery. Since there are no hard budget constraints, enterprises have an insatiable hunger for resources—insatiable because the success of enterprises, and thus of the careers of their managers, depends on garnering resources for expansion.[29] And that explains the seemingly absurd preparations for the visit of the prime minister. As a very influential person, he had to be convinced that the Lenin Steel Works was at the forefront of the building of socialism.

Thus, by its own logic, building socialism turns into its painting, reminding all of the gap between what is and what should be, deepening the critical consciousness of workers and managers alike. This ritual juxtaposition of the real and the imaginary is not confined to the exceptional. It is part and parcel of factory life: the union elections, the production conferences, competition among socialist brigades and the communist shifts. Because it is embedded in real practices, the pretense unwittingly assumes a life of its own, a spontaneous critique of existing society and a potential force for an alternative society.[30]

Nor is critique confined to economic rationality. It extends to the principles of social justice that socialism proclaims. "Money doesn't count, the prime minister is coming" expresses the powerful resentment toward the Red Barons who direct society, whom we have to entertain with these charades. Furnacemen are fond of the joke about the contribution to socialism of three men. "The first receives five thousand forints a month. He builds socialism. The second receives fifteen thousand forints a month. He directs the building of socialism. The third receives fifty thousand forints a month. For him, socialism is built."

Csaba, who is neither a member of the party nor a member of the trade union, says all the best jobs go to the party people. Thus, I am told how "connections" dictate membership of the famous inside contracting systems—self-selected, self-organized "economic work partnerships" (VGMKs) which receive specific lump-sum payments for the completion of specific tasks outside normal working hours.[31] Pay can be three or four times the normal wage, which could easily double the pay a worker receives each month. Karcsi related the story of the VGMK assigned to clean up the roof of the Combined Steel Works—it contained the party secretary, the trade union secretary, and the communist youth secretary. How often did we berate Hegedüs, the day foreman, for being more concerned about his VGMK work than his formal duties. When we were on afternoon shift we would see him wandering around, sometimes supervising, sometimes even opening bags of cement for his mates in the VGMK which rebuilt the walls of the ladles.

Resentment is not leveled at inequality per se, since everyone wants to be rich, but against undeserved wealth accumulated through the exploitation of contacts or scarce skills without corresponding effort. Moreover, there are those who "deserve" to be poor. These are the half million Gypsies who, I am forever being told, despite government assistance continue to malinger and steal, live in a cesspool of poverty because they know no better, and thereby heap disrepute onto a nation of honest, decent, and hardworking people.

Many workers hold up East Germany as their model. Many have worked there and come back impressed by its egalitarianism as well as its efficiency. Béla, the steel maker and a party member, when production had stopped, often entered into heated arguments about the merits of the East German society, where the cleaning lady and the enterprise director received the same pension, where inflation was insignificant and you could survive on a single wage. "If there's socialism anywhere, it's in East Germany," Béla concluded. For Kálmán, a young ambitious furnaceman, on the other hand, NDK (East Germany) is "too political," you can't travel abroad so easily, and to move up you need to be a party member. Even though he is married to an East German woman, he wouldn't consider living there permanently. He's interested in getting ahead. "To hell with socialism."[32]

But socialism is all around, even in Hungary, compelling compliance with its rituals of affirmation. Painting *over* the sordid realities of socialism is simultaneously the painting *of* an appearance of brightness, efficiency, and justice. Socialism becomes an elaborate game of pretense which everyone sees through but which everyone is compelled to play.[33] It is an intermingling of a desultory reality and fabricated appearance in which the appearance takes on a reality of its own. The pretense becomes a basis against which to assess reality. If we have to paint a world of efficiency and equality—as we do in our production meetings, our brigade competitions, elections—we become more sensitive to and outraged by inefficiency and inequality.

Very different is the capitalist game through which workers spontaneously consent to its directing classes by *obscuring from themselves* its *system* of domination and inefficiency. We don't paint *over* the system of capitalism but rather paint it *out*. Socialism *calls on us to cover up* injustice and irrationality and to paint a vision of equality and efficiency. The very conditions that are hidden through participation in capitalist production, in socialist production become the focal concern of the players. The compulsion to participate in the socialist game is potentially explosive—the pretense becomes an alternative turned against reality.[34]

The Contradictory Imperatives of Control and Autonomy

Doesn't public compliance with the rituals of affirmation mask a private indifference or rejection of the ideals of socialism? As Csaba would remind me, "Socialism is fine in principle, but in practice it doesn't work." Socialism is at odds with human nature, so let's forget about it. To be sure, there is no self-conscious embrace of socialism, just as there is equally no embrace of capitalism. The class consciousness that emerges is of a negative character, opposed to hierarchy, bureaucracy, injustice, inequality, and inefficiency. It recognizes the systemic and class origins of pathologies. By itself this critique of state socialism does not carry with it a positive program. Rather, the potentiality of this negativity to become a positive program is determined by the lived experience that goes along with it, the distinctive routines of production and its regulation.[35]

Czeslaw Milosz draws on the Islamic practice of *ketman* to describe the schizophrenic adaptation of Polish intellectuals to the state's demand for public conformity. Writers and artists find ways of retaining an inner integrity while complying with the ritualized demands of the regime. But he too recognizes that *ketman* "brings comfort, fostering dreams of what might be . . ." Still more important, *ketman* means "self-realization *against* something." Intellectuals in the West are suffocated by their freedoms; they have nothing against which to define themselves, unlike in the East, where battering against a wall gives life its meaning.[36] But Milosz is writing about intellectuals who adapt by constructing an inner sanctuary. Poets, novelists, artists, by the very nature of their work, adopt *individual* solutions. It is otherwise with workers who have to paint socialism. They too realize themselves against something, but it is a collective realization, a realization that is shaped by the *social* character of production.[37]

The ritual affirmation of socialism has ideological effects according to the lived experience in which it is embedded. We must turn, therefore, from the spiritual migration of the intellectual to the earthly realities of work and its regulation. An alternative vision of the possible originates first in the technical imperatives of a shortage economy, which calls forth worker self-organization, and second in the class imperatives of state appropriation and redistribution of products, which requires legitimation.

Let us begin with issues of technical efficiency. We noted earlier that the transition from the open-hearth furnaces to the basic oxygen converter involved deskilling. At the Martin the furnacemen were flexibly organized to improvise in the face of shortages. Now they have lost that capacity, falling victim to the caprice of the converter. There is not much we can do about its sensitivity to the chemical composition of pig iron and scrap, or to temperature fluctuations arising from uncontrollable oxidation processes. As furnacemen, we carry out out routines but take little responsibility for the final result. That resides with the steel maker, Béla. Accustomed to the Martin, where he could nurse the process along through the eight-hour cycle, he never adjusted to the converter's forty-minute cycle. Critical judgments had to be made instantaneously without time for calculation or discussion. And he had to live with the consequences.

But what about the Japanese computer system, publicly boasted as state-of-the-art technology, designed to eliminate human judgment and thus human error—the secret of quality steel? Its flashing panels light up the walls of the control room; its monitors pour out information, calculating exactly what has to be done next. But there's a snag; the calculations assume a Japanese economy in which the quality and quantity of all inputs can be calibrated exactly and ahead of time. It assumes that variables can be held constant—an impossibility in a shortage economy. To follow the directions of the computer would be to ruin three heats out of four. Béla never ceased to curse those half-billion forints down the drain. But it's worse than useless. The steel maker can't just ignore the computer, for it relentlessly monitors and records everything he does, pointing an accusing finger at any deviation. Those above have ready ammunition, if they need any, for disciplinary action should a heat go wrong. Supposedly his aid, the computer becomes his enemy. He is compelled to protect himself by deceiving it, to strategize against his tormenter. It all drove Béla insane—rushing frantically between the converter and the control room, screaming at us on the way, beads of sweat pouring from his brow.

Béla's career as a steel maker came to a tragic end. While helping to clean up the debris below he got trapped under a steel pipe as it bent under the pressure of being caught between two approaching carriages. His leg was sawn in two. The inexperienced Gabi, fresh from technical college, succeeded him. Like Béla, he lives in fear of imminent catastrophe—a simple miscalculation of alloys or carbon can ruin a heat. A leaky ladle that goes undetected can spread a carpet of steel onto the floor below and hold up production for days. As nervous as Béla, Gabi is too young to scream orders to the men in charge of the casting bay, the continuous caster, or the scrap bay, or yell at us. He has to use more subtle methods if he is to get his way and survive daily interrogation by the bosses. They and the bigger bosses, who have staked their reputations and careers on this modern capitalist technology, can only interfere and disrupt production, or fine for purported negligence. The steel maker is left to organize production as best he can under their punitive threats.

Confronted with shortages, management has no alternative but to concede shop-floor self-management—that is, if management wants production to be efficient. But such efficiency always threatens to slide into self-organization independent of management, which threatens the self-interest of management. Management responds with a repressive order, buttressed by trade union and party. As our chief steward said, "The trade union is good for one thing. Keeping your mouth shut." It collects our dues, 1 percent of our earnings, sending half upstairs to headquarters and redistributing the rest as assistance in times of need:

when members are ill for an extended period, have a child, or face funeral expenses. The union officers distribute places in the holiday homes. It is a bureaucratized friendly (or should I say unfriendly) society with little or no power to fight for workers' rights. To the contrary, it withholds assistance from members with bad disciplinary records. An x or two (absence without permission) means no benefits. Józsi, always a victim of x's, shows me his pile of old trade union books at home and expresses his disgust by wiping them on his bottom. Long since he gave up his membership. Recognizing where its interests lie, management threatens to withdraw premiums from workers who are not union members or who haven't paid up all their dues.[38]

The party and communist youth organization (KISZ) are the second arm of managerial domination. KISZ and then party membership is the way up, Gabi assured me, when he was still struggling to find the two party references necessary for entry. He points to Bandi, who, he says, will have nothing to do with the party and will be stuck in his present job as "operator"—the steel maker's assistant. But the party is losing its grip as credentialing, seniority and experience, and to a lesser extent patronage (protekció) become more important. The new steel makers are from the Miskolc Technical University or the Dunaújváros technical college, and Péter proudly tells me that he managed to get into a VGMK, which had excluded one of his friends, a party member. Karcsi, ambitious though he is, doesn't see the point in joining the party. But eventually, after being promoted to "operator," he succumbs to pressure and resigns himself to giving up 240 forints a month in party and trade union fees—"fifteen liters of benzene," as he sourly reminds me.

This tension between organizational imperatives (self-organization in the face of shortages) and class imperatives (the concerted hierarchical domination of union, party, and management) governs life in the mill.[39] The tension was the source of a tragedy which occurred at the converter a week before I began work in 1987. For each heat, the slag that forms on top of the steel has to be poured out of the converter and into the huge slag dish waiting below. Every two or three heats, the dish is full of slag. The crane driver then lifts the dish off its cradle and transports it out of the steelworks. It was a Sunday early in May. As the dish was being raised it swung dangerously from side to side, slopping molten slag over the side. Standing nearby was Pista, recently transferred to the Combined Steel Works from the closed-down Martin furnaces where he had been a furnaceman for thirty years. His reactions were slowed by his rheumatism, and as he jumped away he tripped and molten slag splashed over his back. He was rushed to the hospital, where he died two days later.

Management determined that two people in particular were responsible for this fatality: the person who directs the crane driver and Gyuri, the lead furnaceman, who had overfilled the slag dish. Gyuri was told that his pay would be cut by four forints an hour for six months for fatal negligence. But all accidents have to be investigated by a safety committee and responsibility apportioned before any such fine can be imposed. Gyuri, himself a chief steward and a worker with an outstanding record of almost thirty years' service, went to the secretary of the enterprise trade union, but didn't get any satisfaction there. He quickly realized he would be on his own. He didn't see any point in fighting the case at the enterprise level, since management's definition of what happened would undoubtedly prevail. So he appealed to the city labor court. Here management tried to convince the judge that Gyuri had violated some work rule, so they produced a page photocopied from the handbook of "technical instructions" which set limits on how full the "ladle" should be. Fortunately for him, Gyuri had a copy of the manual too, and immediately saw that management was trying to hide the absence of any rules about handling the slag dish by substituting a rule applying to the very different ladle into which steel was poured.

Since the enterprise lawyer did not understand the technicalities of steel production, he couldn't defend management's interpretation, and a second meeting was called. Later on, recognizing the attempted deception, the lawyer resigned and refused to continue management's "dirty work." At the second meeting the judge threw the case out and Gyuri was exonerated. Suspicion was already raised long before any court case that management was in trouble when, a few months after the accident, they nominated Gyuri—their supposedly negligent furnaceman—for one of the highest "government honors." It was widely suspected that he was being bought off—a quid pro quo for bearing responsibility for the accident.[40] But he would not participate in what he viewed as a cover-up. As far as he was concerned, management was at fault. Not only were there no rules about filling the slag dish, but the root of the problem lay with the continual pressure on workers to get the heats out, no matter what. Empty dishes are often a long time in coming, so rather than wait, furnacemen overfill them. They know that management will not accept the excuse that there were no slag dishes if, for example, a run of heats going to the continuous caster is broken. In order to avoid being bawled out or fined, they risk overfilling the dish rather than wait for an empty one. Annoyed at the lack of support he got from the enterprise trade union, Gyuri resigned his chief steward-ship. His resignation wasn't accepted, but he refused to sign any docu-ments in his official capacity.[41] Gyuri's experience as a union official stood him in good stead as he fought his case through the courts. With-out any collective support, others would have found themselves de-fenseless.

Pista's death was at least in part the consequence of tensions that build up when workers try to adapt to the inadequate supply of materi-als and unreliable machinery in the face of intense pressure from their bosses to produce quality steel. That Gyuri won his case highlights management's increasing frustration as it became harder to discipline and intimidate the work force.[42] Fewer and fewer men attend the tech-nical high school for steelworkers. Among the entering cohort, the ma-jority are now women. Once aristocrats and heroes of labor, the steel-workers now lag behind electricians and mechanics who can ply their skills in the "private sector" (maszek) as well as in the state sector. Who wants to work on continuous shifts the rest of their lives at a salary not much better than the average? Belatedly, management began to com-pensate its core workers with places in VGMKs, but these disrupt pro-duction as workers (so management claims) devote less energy to their normal daily tasks. Just as important, the VGMKs act like secret soci-eties, becoming potential nuclei of solidarity and self-organization. Not surprisingly, they are already being phased out.

In Marx's theory of history, the forces of production can only ad-vance under private property by engendering a revolutionary working class. Marx was wrong: Capitalism continues to expand and its working class remains effectively incorporated within capitalism's limits. His ar-gument works much better for state socialism. First, the central appro-priation of surplus engenders a shortage economy so that the expansion of the forces of production requires worker self-management. Second, the central appropriation of the surplus is managed directly and visibly by organs of the state at the point of production. Workers all over the country define themselves in relation to a common exploiter. Third, be-cause it is visible, the extraction of surplus has to be legitimated, but as we have seen, this only heightens the contrast between what is and what could be. The ritual affirmation of socialism, the painting of socialism, generates an immanent critique because it combines with a lived expe-rience which places a premium on self-organization and makes the source of oppression transparent. Here then are the economic, political, and ideological bases for the development of a negative class consciousness, potentially threatening to the existing order.

The Political Effects of Economic Reform

But what turns the potentiality into reality, class consciousness into class mobilization? Here we must forsake the contrast between capitalism and state socialism and turn to the comparison of Hungary and Poland. From the standpoint of 1956, one would be hard-pressed to argue that Poland rather than Hungary would experience revolutionary turmoil twenty-five years later. Why has history turned out that way? Why has the strength and radicalism of the working class followed an ascending arc in Poland and a descending arc in Hungary?

The class consciousness of state socialist workers begets struggle under the following conditions. First, individual mobility is blocked so that advancement can only take place through group mobilization. Second, there exist political spaces and the organization of resources for collective mobilization. It is not difficult to fit Poland into this scheme. The economic crisis of the late Gierek years and an end to the rapid upward mobility of the fifties and sixties dramatically curtailed the opportunity for individual advancement. At the same time there was a convergence and deepening of opposition movements outside the party. This began after 1968, when the Polish state unleashed its fury on intellectuals and students and when the Soviet tanks rolled into Czechoslovakia to crush the last attempt at renewal of society from above. Oppositional intellectuals lost any ambivalence they had for working outside the party and finally came together in defense of workers arrested following the strikes at Radom and Poznan in 1976. The Catholic church also broadened its appeal by championing human rights for all, not just rights to freedom of worship but rights to free expression and to organization, culminating in the papal visit of June 1979. When strikes broke out in July 1980 over price increases, several workers' organizations had already been firmly established through the communications network set up by church, KOR, and such newspapers as *Robotnik*. The "sociological vacuum" between primary groups and the nation had been filled by the rise of civil society.

This is the conventional story of Poland's exceptionalism, stressing autonomous developments in the political sphere. Turning to Hungary, however, and asking how its working class has been pacified and demobilized since 1956, leads once more to a focus on how the economic substructure shapes politics and organization in civil society. From the standpoint of economic development the Hungarian reforms have had at best mixed success, but from the standpoint of political stabilization they have so far been very effective. Looking at them from the perspective of their political implications, we can discern three dimensions of the reforms: first, the greater autonomy of enterprises in determining what to produce and where to sell it; second, the growth of market forces in consumer goods; and third, the development of a second economy, whether as the direct production of domestic goods and services or as the provision of income from private production.

The relaxation of the central direction of the economy has weakened the role within the enterprise of the party, which together with the trade union is effectively subordinated to management. At the same time, the consumer goods and services at the disposal of the enterprise have also fallen as the sphere of consumption assumed greater autonomy. This compounds the decline of the party and trade union as they no longer can compel the old dependence on the enterprise based on their influence in the distribution of housing, education, day care, plots of land, and miscellaneous goods. The erosion of the foundation of bureaucratic despotism has given way to a regime of bureaucratic hegemony.

Housing, for example, is now distributed independently of place of work or work references. There is a long waiting list for council flats, but the relevant criteria are family size, income, and present accommodation, not political credentials and supervisory reports. There is also cooperative housing distributed through the National Savings Bank. Here *protekció* may count, but more critical is the ability to pay. To receive sick benefits, pensions, and maternity payments it is necessary for one to be employed, but one is not tied to employment in a specific enterprise. Neither management, trade union, nor party has the power to withdraw such benefits.

As market forces gain ascendancy, so income becomes more important. And there are multiple sources of income. Not one but two wage earners are necessary to maintain a family of four, and even then this is usually supplemented by some *maszek* work in the second economy, whether it be market gardening or selling a service. Furnacemen are doubly handicapped in this respect. Shift work makes a regular second job impossible, and the skills they learn are not generalizable. So Tamás, Laci, and Józsi, before he left in disgust for the Martin, sought out "supplementary work," which is the equivalent of overtime. But it is not easy to obtain, depending on management's beneficence. Csaba, recently divorced with heavy child support, lives with his parents but does no extra work. Gyuri, who lives in a village about an hour away, cultivates a big garden for home consumption. Karcsi is the entrepreneur. His rabbit business brought him enough money to take a honeymoon in Italy. Helped by his family, he was able to buy a two-and-a-half-room flat in the Diósgyör housing estate. More recently his pig business brought in some twenty thousand forints, which took him to Germany, where he bought a music center and an electronic game, selling each at great profit back home. With a little capital, ingenuity, and entrepreneurial spirit, it is still possible to make quite a handsome sum of money.[43]

Moreover, it is worth making money. Unlike in other Eastern European countries, you can buy pretty well anything from specialty foods to computers and videos, all for local currency, provided you have enough. Budapest is the consumer paradise of Eastern Europe, a bustling city attracting more and more tourists. There are no special shops for the apparatchiks. Instead the market rules, at least in consumer goods. Like Poland in the 1970s, Hungary has used some of its foreign currency to make imported luxury goods available to all, holding out rewards for those prepared to work hard or find other routes to riches. For the working class, day-to-day life is ruled by the almighty forint, not the queue or the party.

Facing a mounting economic crisis and increasing debt to Western banks, the state brandishes another instrument from its capitalist tool kit. Workers face a barrage of hostile propaganda in newspapers, on the radio, and on television as lazy, shiftless, and only interested in their GMK work. They must be disciplined with a little unemployment. Inefficient enterprises can declare bankruptcy or lay off workers. In 1987 the state's new hero is Ede Horvat, the Red Baron of Raba, acclaimed for the tough discipline he exercises over his work force and for closing down one of his plants. In 1988 the government is preparing plans to drastically curtail steel production at the Lenin Steel Works and at Özd. Unemployment is regarded as unavoidable if the country is to recover from its economic crisis.

Harnessing capitalism to state socialism has rising human costs. The state tries to compensate for wages falling behind inflation by simultaneously creating more openings for private entrepreneurship. The assumption is that the work capacity of the Hungarian family is inexhaustible. Life is ordered according to a giant piece-rate system. As workers struggle to make ends meet, they have to exceed the norm, which justifies norm revision. Socialism has a long history of organizing production in this way, but now it is extended to the sphere of consumption. Workers are helpless as they clamber up the down escalator, whose downward speed increases every year.

To celebrate the new year in 1988 the government introduced a two-pronged austerity measure—first, a personal income tax that would immediately penalize "extra work" whether in the private or in the state sector, and second, a value-added tax which in combination with the withdrawal of price subsidies led to about a 30 percent inflation overnight. Particularly galling was the almost fourfold increase in the price of children's clothes. The state exploits the family's desire for autonomy by multiplying the ways it can manage an ever-increasing burden. The costs of social security, care for the young, the elderly, and the emerging unemployed, are externalized to the family—the expanding welfare agency. The results are not difficult to foresee. Many collapse exhausted with heart attacks; some commit suicide, while others take to drink. Most of the working class is trapped in huge housing projects such as the Avas, where I used to live. Here eighty thousand workers struggle to make ends meet. In this maze of identical concrete blocks, families pressed into one-or two-room panel apartments crack at their seams. Divorce rates increase along with violence.

An increasing few, usually with the helping hand of others, manage to perch themselves on top of the escalator, building fancy houses in the Buda Hills or Tapolca, trying to remove themselves from the scramble below. Although inequality becomes more visible as it intensifies, workers are, so far, more intent on keeping up rather than combining to stop or slow the escalator.

As a mechanism of distribution, the market offers opportunities to all, though more to some than to others. Here individualism pays, providing one can obtain the materials and equipment necessary for participating in the private sector, and providing there is something to purchase with any profits that are made. This is still the case in Hungary. But in Poland, where shortages prevail, entrepreneurship is more difficult to sustain and an enormous amount of time is spent obtaining scarce goods. Well-being depends on networks based on ties of family, friendship, religion, profession, or work. Whom one knows and what one has to offer decide one's fate. If such patronage is further concentrated in a party elite and its hangers-on, then individual striving can prove frustrating and collective solutions become more attractive. Always a potentiality, such a solution becomes a reality when the state is not just illegitimate but shows itself to be weak, when there is an alternative institution such as the Roman Catholic church commanding the allegiance of the population, when powerful national sentiments galvanize into a vibrant collective memory, and when there are rudimentary channels for conveying information and engaging in public discussion.

But this is only half the explanation for the Polish trajectory. The other half comes from the spontaneous negative class consciousness which became the switch track that guided Solidarity along its ascendant but temporarily aborted path from independent trade union to self-organized society. In Hungary this same negative class consciousness combines with extra work in the second economy, with gardening and the VGMK work. However, if these opportunities become the preserve of a new class of entrepreneurs, if workers find the taxation rates on extra work too high to make it worthwhile, then Hungary could easily become another Poland.

Ideology, Interests, and Consciousness

I embarked on this study assuming that ideology, being externally constructed and imposed on day-to-day life, was unimportant. Least of all did I expect to find that a socialist ideology, one in which neither rulers nor ruled believe, would have significant effects. Paradoxically, not only despite but also because of their disbelief, rulers and ruled partake in rituals which underline all that the world could be, yet isn't. Out of this divergence of ideology and reality there develops a distinctive working-class consciousness. State socialism becomes the brunt of critique for failing to live up to its own pretensions, pretensions that assume an independent force because they are repeatedly enacted in orchestrated, compulsory rituals and because they correspond to unrealized aims and aspirations embedded in the lived experience of work.

Capitalism is different. Workers are not called on to build capitalism, they are exhorted to pursue their own interests and in so doing deny themselves a critical systemic understanding of the world—an understanding so natural to their socialist colleagues. Instead of painting capitalism, they manufacture consent. Far from being unimportant, capitalist ideology insinuates itself unnoticed into microstructures of power. It does not announce itself through rituals of affirmation, clashing with the routines of lived experience, but silently merges with everyday life. Capitalist ideology has none of the coherence or monolithic character of socialist ideology. Its heterogeneity and ubiquity, not its absence, are what make it so powerful. It acts without agents, behind our backs, so to speak.[44]

In my analysis of the South Chicago machine shop, I dissolved ideology, interests, and consciousness into a single lived experience. In showing how consent was organized on the shop floor, I missed what made this process specific to advanced capitalism. I missed not only the possibility but, more important, the significance of the separation of ideological lived experience and material lived experience—a separation which produces that spontaneous critical consciousness I have already described. Ironically, in the name of uniting appearance and reality, state socialism digs an unbridgeable chasm between the two, inciting workers to recognize how the world could be but isn't.[45] Moreover, I was too hasty in universalizing a correspondence between spontaneous consciousness and the interests that guide responses to structures of opportunity. Consciousness and interests do not necessarily coincide—one can be critical of state socialism but at the same time maneuver one's way through its labyrinth.

I now realize that collapsing these different categories prevented me from understanding the emergence of radical social movements outside the realm of private production. In contemporary capitalist society there are spheres in which rituals of ideology disengage from and become opposed to reality, generating a more critical consciousness. As one might expect, this takes place in the public sphere. Thus, the ideology of social justice and social service has often radicalized the struggles of state workers, leading them beyond purely economistic demands.[46] The so-called new social movements can be understood in a similar way. Here in the United States, for example, the rituals of democracy incite a comparison between ideals and reality, leading to the women's, civil rights, and green movements. Although one should not underestimate their importance as challenges to capitalist democracy, they are nowhere near as widespread, well entrenched, and fundamental as the challenges to state socialism.[47] This, I would argue, is because the language of individual rights is not as well entrenched in the lived experience of capitalism as socialist ideals are entrenched in the working-class experience of state socialism.

In this respect one should not, of course, view capitalist societies as identical. Just as the critique of socialism is more developed and sustained in some state socialist societies than in others, so the same is true of capitalist societies. Just as one has to distinguish the Soviet Union from Eastern Europe, so too one must distinguish the United States from Western Europe. From the standpoint of their satellites, both central powers command an almost inexplicable legitimacy over their own working classes. To be sure, among certain privileged strata there is a material basis to that consent, backed up by an impressive coercive apparatus. Perhaps just as important is the identification of nationalism with socialism in the case of the Soviet Union and with capitalism in the case of the United States. In Eastern Europe and, of course, in many of the non-Russian republics in the Soviet Union itself, nationalist traditions are generally hostile to the center and therefore to state socialism, just as in Western Europe anticapitalist traditions have historical roots absent in the United States.

These differences notwithstanding, here I wish to stress what state socialist societies have in common, what distinguishes them from capitalism, namely, the generation of tendencies toward their usurpation in favor of workers' socialism. The following steelworkers' joke, recounted to me in 1985, says it all. "The Soviet locomotive cannot go any further because there are no more rails. The socialist train comes to a stop. Brezhnev instructs the steel industry to make more rails. It is done and the socialist train continues until once more it comes to the end of the track. Andropov is now general secretary of the party and discovers there is no more steel to be had. So he orders the track behind the train to be put in front of it. The socialist locomotive continues until once more it comes to a standstill. Now there is no track either in front of or behind the train. Chernyenko has assumed leadership, but there is neither steel nor rails. So he instructs all the communists to get out of the train and rock it backward and forward so that the passengers inside will think that the socialist locomotive is once more on its way." We see here how the endemic shortages generated by a hierarchical economy lead to arbitrary but very visible interventions from on high, exacerbating rather than solving the problem. Mobilizing efforts are geared to maintaining appearances rather than changing reality, digging an ever-widening chasm between the two. Workers are not deceived; they, after all, are telling the joke. The opposition of appearance and reality becomes the class opposition of planners and producers, conceivers and executors. The lived experience excites a critical consciousness, a vision of workers organizing their own society, free of political charades and deception. In Moscow (1988), the joke continues with the energetic Gorbachev leaping onto the engine, liberating the intellectuals, and telling the workers to get out and push. "We'll pay later," he promises.[48]

The Russian Revolution of 1917 remains undigested, always ready to take revenge on the body that swallowed it. Unlike the English, French, or American revolutions, which have been more or less, rightly or wrongly, assimilated into their respective national histories, the Soviet revolution has been repressed for at least sixty years. The process of assimilation, which was abruptly halted in 1927 and achieved only a brief respite in the immediate post-Stalin years, may now be entering a new phase. In the name of "reconstruction," Soviet society is being liberated from some of its most repressive legacies. A giant painting of socialism is in progress, a potentially explosive combination of openness for intellectuals and discipline for workers. It is difficult to predict outcomes, but we would do well to heed Trotsky's advice and not give a finished definition to an unfinished process.

CONCLUSION

6   The Radiant Future

Soviet placards and paintings, newspapers and novels, film and music, radio and television portrayed communism as the "radiant future of all humanity." Every Soviet child was fed a diet of dialectical materialism and taught that history was on the side of communism while capitalism was doomed. Soviet war heroics, scientific achievements, and economic progress were all hailed as part of a great march forward to a resplendent tomorrow—one that justified great sacrifices from workers and peasants. But "communism" has fallen on bad days. It has come begging for aid from the West as panic and chaos threaten to dissolve the Soviet Union. Market reform is touted as the universal panacea as the country plunges into economic disaster. Communism has ended up in a shambles.

In Eastern Europe this seemingly invincible order collapsed within the space of a year. Moreover, with the notable exception of Rumania, these collapses occurred with hardly a whimper. What was to be the radiant future became the radiant past. In a remarkable ideological about-turn, now it is capitalism that is proclaimed the radiant future of all mankind.[1] How did these communist or what we have called state socialist societies crumble? Will the putative capitalist future be any more radiant than the socialist past? Will the gap between ideology and reality remain as wide as it was under the old regime? And, if so, with what effects? What is the real future of what was state socialism? These are the questions we try to answer in this admittedly more speculative chapter.

The Collapse of Communism

Since the collapse of state socialism in Eastern Europe was so widespread, we require a general theory of its demise. How should we now understand these societies? In Lenin's vision, socialism is a society in transition between capitalism and communism. It has three components which distinguish it from capitalism. First, socialism is a rationally organized society in which production is for peoples' needs rather than for private profits. Second, it is a just society in which people are rewarded according to their contribution to society rather than according to their ownership of the means of production. Third, it is a radically democratic society which compels those who appropriate and redistribute surplus to be accountable to those who produce surplus.

This third, democratic component goes further than parliamentary democracy, which, according to Lenin, is the best shell for class domination. He valued democracy not for its protection of basic rights of individuals but as a means of preventing the emergence of a new bureaucratic class.[2] Thus he insisted that the new officials who would run society be subject to instant recall, that they receive an average worker's wage, and that the repressive apparatus be dismantled and placed under the control of workers. The very radicalism of this proposal reflected not so much Lenin's utopianism, but his realism, his fear that the central appropriation of surplus would lay the foundation for a new class.

We now know, of course, that his fears were well founded. A radical democracy was never installed and a new bureaucratic class, therefore, did emerge. The dictatorship of the proletariat became the dictatorship over the proletariat. Moreover, the rise of a bureaucratic class turned the first two elements of socialism into their opposite. On the one hand, rationality through planning became the irrationality of an intense bureaucratic competition within the dominant class. Enterprise directors and state managers bargained about prices, targets, and the distribution of investment over the heads of the direct producers, who exercised little direct control of the dominant class. On the other hand, justice based on reward according to contribution became the injustice of reward according to position. The dominant class secured for itself excessive bonuses, and privileged access to scarce goods and services. In short, state socialism arose instead of workers' socialism.

Capitalism appears natural and inevitable because the private appropriation of surplus is hidden. By contrast, under state socialism, the central appropriation of surplus is transparent and therefore has to be legitimated. Here the state is the self-declared appropriator of surplus. It is the transparent oppressor and exploiter, making its appearance in production as a triple alliance between managers, union, and party. The very visibility of the agents of state domination requires an ideology which justifies central appropriation. This has been the ideology of Marxism-Leninism, that is, official or Soviet Marxism—the ideology that declares central appropriation to be both just and rational, and to serve the interests of all.

This socialist ideology is not simply propagated through mass media but, as we have seen, more significantly, it is embedded in a constellation of rituals in the workplace, such as communist shifts, production conferences, brigade competitions, production campaigns, and so on. Precisely because workers have to act out the virtues of socialism, they become conscious of its failings. In painting socialism as just and rational they become critical of its irrationality and injustice. The necessity of an ideology to justify class domination leads to a critique of state socialism for failing to live up to its ideals. In this sense workers come to embrace the values of socialism. This negative class consciousness expressed itself positively in working-class movements such as the Hungarian workers'-council movement of 1956, in the Polish Solidarity movement of 1980–81, and indeed in the strike waves in the Soviet Union in 1989.[3]

For the most part, however, its critical consciousness notwithstanding, the working class has been effectively demobilized by state socialism, which denies it institutional representation through unions or party, separates it from intellectuals, and creates opportunities for individual advancement through upward mobility or participation in the second economy. Thus the working class emerges from state socialism as a weak and atomized force. For the most part, workers were passive onlookers during the regime's transition. Certainly, it would be hard to argue that the regimes of Eastern Europe were swept away through popular revolt. In Poland and Hungary the transition was the result of negotiations between opposition and government.[4] But even in Czechoslovakia and East Germany, where popular movements took to the streets, repression from the dominant class was notable for its absence.

There have been popular uprisings of much wider proportions before, which failed to dislodge state socialist regimes. Only in Rumania could it be said that revolt from below was the leading force in the collapse of the old regime. Rather, state socialism collapsed from above. To say that the ruling classes of Eastern Europe gave way so quickly because the Soviet Union withdrew its guarantee is only to transfer the question to the Soviet Union. In considering the transitions, Eastern Europe must be regarded as part of the Soviet Union, which was suffering from the same crisis.

The dominant class lost confidence in its capacity to rule in the name of socialism. First, despite repeated attempts to bring reality into conformity with ideology, whether through repression or economic reform, there remained a yawning gap.[5] Even such a degenerate form of Marxism as Marxism-Leninism proved subversive of the class society it was supposed to legitimate. Second, the Solidarity movement highlighted the sort of challenges to state socialism that could emerge from the gap between ideology and reality, heightening the failure of a worker's state to represent the interests of the working class. Third, the professionalization of the bureaucratic class and the rise of an educated elite meant less tolerance for the patent contradictions between ideology and reality. For them, painting socialism took on a ridiculous, embarrassing, and macabre form. The dominant class could no longer believe in its own ideology. Instead of trying to bring reality into conformity with ideology, it has, therefore, sought to reconstitute itself under a new ideology which embraces free enterprise rather than state regulation, the market rather than the plan. Instead of trying to make socialism work, instead of trying to give socialist claims a material basis, it turned to a new ideology.

However, changing ideology is one thing, changing reality is quite another. Does the celebration of privatization and democratization stand any better chance of closing the gap between ideology and reality? And if not, what will be the consequences?

The Politics of Privatization

If the state socialist economy was so hard to reform in the direction of socialist ideals, how easy is it to move in the direction of capitalism? Certainly it has been possible to make the transition from communist ideology to the ideology of free enterprise, and it has been surprisingly easy to turn one-party states into liberal democracies. But these are affairs of the superstructure. Can these reforms effect a transformation of the economic system?

If any of the Eastern European countries is in a good position to make such a transition, surely it is Hungary, where economic reforms had gone furthest toward the restoration of capitalism before 1989. Following the 1956 revolt, the Hungarian economy was restructured along lines that brought back elements of the old order. In agriculture, collectivization reinstalled many of the richer and more skilled peasants as leaders of the new cooperatives. Because members of the cooperative were offered opportunities for private farming and access to credit and marketing facilities, there developed a symbiosis between first and second economies.[6] The new economic mechanism of 1968 tried to do the same for industry. It pioneered the transition from a command economy, which attempted to dictate enterprise targets and the allocation of goods and services, to a more flexible system of fiscal planning, which introduced more open bargaining and gave enterprises more autonomy to decide what, how, and for whom to produce. Of course, these changes should not be exaggerated; the state still controlled an elaborate redistributive system. At the same time the government encouraged the development of a legal second economy which would supplement wages and at the same time counter the rigidities of the state sector. The second economy developed not only outside the first economy in private production but also within the first economy. Workers organized themselves into work partnerships, so that outside normal working hours they could enter into private contracts with their own enterprise.[7] How have changes in ideology and in politics furthered or retarded the continued transition to capitalism? Let us turn first to the political changes themselves.

The Politics of Anticommunism

The rapid and unexpected escalation of openings in the political regime began in May 1988 when the aging secretary general of the Communist party, János Kádár, was peacefully removed from power at the National Party Conference. At this time Imré Pozsgai assumed notoriety as a reform communist calling for a multiparty system. "Pluralism" became a political buzzword and legislation was passed by parliament in 1988 that would recognize different parties and end the Communist party's forty-year monopoly on power.

Kádár was succeeded by Károly Grósz—who was very much cut out of the old party cloth, but who was soon overtaken by events as the party split into reformers and hard-liners. The reformers soon assumed control of the party until, at its historic conference in October 1989, the party transformed itself from the Hungarian Socialist Workers' party into the Hungarian Socialist party. In keeping with the times, particularly changes occurring in Poland, the Hungarian party tried to reconstitute itself within an openly declared multiparty system. The party apparatus at the workplace, together with the youth organization, which had already begun to crumble, was abolished. The exodus from the party accelerated. Finally, in the elections of April 1990 the Hungarian Democratic Forum (MDF), working from a nationalist and populist platform, defeated its main opponent, the League of Free Democrats (SZDSZ), who had adopted an openly liberal, procapitalist platform. The socialists, made up of reform communists, obtained only 11 percent of the vote, and the Social Democrats just 4 percent.[8]

Much of the political discourse—before, during, and after the election—was based on anticommunism: The MDF inclined toward blaming the erstwhile communist leadership, while the SZDSZ attacked the communist system. Each party sought to outdo the other in its anticommunist rhetoric, tainting its opponents with communist tendencies.[9] To defend the working class in this context was to risk accusations of Stalinism. Workers, as such, were consequently left out of the political process.[10] The SZDSZ fielded candidates more removed from local politics, and their greater radicalism was not as popular as the more moderate program of the MDF. Many workers had had enough of radicalism. The socialists were too discredited by the past to garner much support, but even they feared too-close association with the working class. When they formed themselves out of the Hungarian Socialist Workers' party they felt that the word *Workers'* was a bigger liability than the word *Socialist* in their new name. The Social Democrats were as caught up in rejecting the communist past as the others. Although the obvious party to defend the well-being of lower classes, it made little effort in that direction. As we shall argue below, leaving workers out in the cold prompted them to begin self-organization in the factories.

The anticommunist rhetoric had a second consequence, namely the rejection of all "plans," "visions," or even "programs" as a dangerous flirtation with the past. The future would look after itself so long as there was no central direction or intervention. Privatization had to be a spontaneous process, that is to say, the initiative had to come from below. In this vision, and it is a vision like any other despite its antivision rhetoric, democracy would release all the vital entrepreneurial energies of the Hungarian people—energies that had been imprisoned by the communist order. All that had to be done was to set up appropriate legislation and democracy would do the rest. So the election campaign paid little attention to the privatization process, how it might proceed and whom it might benefit. It simply did not matter who would be the owner, so long as it wasn't the state. Although it is true that some were perturbed about the possibility of foreign capital taking over the country, this distracted from questions about which Hungarians would gain from privatization.

Even before the election, the socialist government had been promulgating the rhetoric of spontaneity as eagerly as anyone. For behind the rhetoric stood the transformation of the class they represented—the class of state managers—into what Elemér Hankiss has called a political bourgeoisie. Ironically, the anticommunist rhetoric which all the parties shared served to conceal the very processes which enabled leading cadres of the old order to reestablish themselves as an economic power. To understand just how this was possible we must turn to the legislative process that promoted privatization.

Spontaneous Privatization

Since 1988 three pieces of new legislation on the pluralization of property forms have been enacted. The first to come into effect (January 1, 1989) was the Law on Economic Associations (Company Act), which had been prepared in seven months under the old regime. It made the formation of companies of limited liability (KFTs) and joint stock corporations (RTs) possible. The founding assets of a KFT had to be worth at least one million forints; of an RT, ten million forints.[11] The Foreign Investment Act was passed to encourage foreign companies to participate in the privatization program by supplying capital.

The creation of private enterprises can be understood as a far-reaching extension of previous legislation of 1982 which had established nine new types of independent small enterprise. Among them were the famous GMKs or economic work partnerships. The individual property of the members of a GMK is not protected against bankruptcy as it is in the new KFTs. On the other hand, much more capital is required for a KFT, putting it out of reach of many of those who had earlier participated in the GMK. Many KFTs have been formed with the support of foreign capital, since enterprises receive greater tax relief the higher the percentage of foreign ownership.

Just as the original GMK had a counterpart inside the state-owned enterprise—the VGMK—so the KFT also had its internal counterpart. The members of a VGMK contributed their skills and used enterprise property to carry out tasks assigned to them and paid for by management. This was a way for core workers or workers with connections to earn sometimes three or four times their normal rate outside their normal hours. The Company Act created entirely new opportunities for enterprise managers. They could carve out independent companies within a state enterprise so long as each such KFT was founded with a minimum 30 percent cash contribution. Nevertheless, managers could also invest their money in such companies both within their own enterprises and in KFTs created at other enterprises.

Not surprisingly, it wasn't long before directors of state enterprises realized that they could turn their most profitable divisions into KFTs while the state continued to bear the cost, indeed the increasing cost, of the loss-making divisions and overheads. Moreover, managers could be part owners of the KFT and at the same time receive managerial bonuses. Each KFT, being an independent company, established its own managerial hierarchy, so that there was also a multiplication of managers.

Furthermore, the taxation system encouraged managers, particularly the wealthy ones, to buy into the KFTs. All investment is tax deductible up to 30 percent of income, including any loans received to purchase assets in a state-owned company. If a manager is paying taxes at a rate of 50 percent on a substantial portion of his income, then he may well recoup the costs of his investment by paying less in taxes. He would, of course, have to pay interest on his loan, but there are now proposals to introduce very low-interest "privatization" loans which would make it even more lucrative for the already wealthy to buy up state property. The idea, so it was said, was to achieve the most rapid possible privatization. All evil rested with state property and all good with privatization.

The Company Act was only concerned with the creation of new enterprises. Thus, even when KFTs were created within the shell of a state enterprise, that shell still had to remain even if it was only a few individuals. The next step in the privatization legislation was the law for the transformation of state property, which came into effect on July 1, 1989. This explicitly established the following procedures for transforming a state enterprise into a private corporation. First, the founding capital of the state enterprise had to be expanded by a minimum of 20 percent (or one hundred million forints, whichever is less) by selling shares to an outside "entrepreneur." The law did not define who could be the outside "entrepreneur," but it was presumed to be another enterprise, Hungarian or foreign. Thus, a system of cross holdings was once more encouraged. Once the outside entrepreneur had been found, then shares amounting to 20 percent of the book value of the enterprise had to be given to the state and shares amounting to the value of the land given to the local council. The enterprise then tried to sell the remaining shares, keeping 20 percent of the proceeds and returning 80 percent to the state. Although it has yet to be accomplished, in principle the enterprise council can decide to give shares up to 20 percent of the book value of the company to voluntary associations, the local council, or a social security organization. These latter shares could be paid for out of future profits. The shares that still remain with the enterprise after three years revert to the state.

One of the more significant features of the transformation law is its recognition of multiple forms of property, including ownership by local councils, by mutual benefit associations, and potentially by employee and consumer associations. That is to say, the transformation act dispels the identity, usually upheld, between dismantling state property and privatization. Forms of social ownership which are not state ownership could be a vehicle for representing the interests of different groups in economic transformation. However, in the present anticommunist atmosphere all forms of social ownership are discredited as a dangerous flirtation with the past.

Another feature of the transformation law discourages its use, namely its attempt to incorporate the interests not just of managers but of all employees. With this in mind the enterprise council was given the responsibility for constructing a transformation plan for privatization. But what interests are represented there? Enterprise councils were created in a law of 1984 with the idea of granting enterprise autonomy and shifting ownership rights from ministries to self-governing bodies. On paper this represented a considerable change in the distribution of power, but in practice party and state limited the effectiveness of the enterprise council. In 1984 the political situation was such that the general director was able to fill almost all the positions with more-or-less loyal members. In any event, important decisions were unlikely to be made there. However, most of the enterprise councils were created in 1985, so that their five-year term of office was up in 1990, precisely at the time companies were planning their privatization. With the collapse of the party, the opening up of political processes, and the lodging of privatization plans with the enterprise council, elections to that body suddenly became a focus in the emerging production politics.[12] Once privatization has occurred the enterprise council dissolves itself, normally being replaced by a board of directors elected by the shareholders.

Their differences notwithstanding, both the Company Act and the transformation law leave plenty of scope for manipulation. One major source of abuse is the continuing absence of any commonly accepted method of evaluating the book value of enterprises. Parallel to the committee selected to prepare the Company Act, another committee was set up to propose legislation which would provide guidelines for the appraisal of the value of assets. But this committee never completed its work. The old socialist accounting system was meaningless, while a new accounting system based on the existence of a developed capital market had yet to appear. This made appraisal of the book value of an enterprise or part-enterprise a politically negotiated process, potentially serving the interests of both foreign capital and local management. By devaluing the physical assets of the KFT, managers could ensure that the cash holding became worth much more than the actual money contributed by the parties, be they Hungarian or foreign.

There were a number of controversial sales of undervalued Hungarian enterprises to foreign investors. In the case of the famous light bulb company, Tungsram, 50 percent was sold to a consortium led by the Austrian bank Girozentrale for $110 million, the remainder being bought by a Hungarian bank. Girozentrale then resold the consortium's shares to General Electric for $150 million. In another celebrated case, Hungarhotels, a chain of Hungary's best hotels and restaurants, decided to sell half its equity for the very low price of $110 million to a small Swedish firm acting as agent for an American chain. This became a national scandal until finally the Hungarian supreme court ruled the deal invalid on the basis of a technicality. The problem is not only how to evaluate the worth of enterprises but who actually owns them. Since state ownership was ubiquitous, rights of usage were more important. Now it is difficult to determine from whom an enterprise is to be bought—the state, the local council, or even the employees.[13]

The publicity given to such deals initiated the third phase of enterprise legislation, namely two amendments to the transformation act, taking effect on March 1, 1990. The first amendment stipulated that transactions amounting to more than thirty million forints by a single enterprise over the last two years should be approved by a state property agency (SPA). The second amendment created the state property agency to oversee transformations of state property. It was given almost unlimited powers to protect the interests of society and national economy. The powers of the SPA are so wide, unclear, and unregulated that its existence more or less supersedes the previous legislation.[14]

What started off as "spontaneous privatization" ends up with state regulation. How was this possible? The initial privatization legislation was developed in 1988, when the socialist order was still very much intact. Its introduction was a clear challenge to the monopoly of ownership by the state and faced obstacles on all sides—from the trade union, from the Ministry of Finance, and from the Ministry of Justice. Its advocates had their work cut out to get it through at all, let alone worry about the future consequences. They knew that other laws would have to be changed, but that would have taken them beyond their immediate task. At that time no one was anticipating the rapid collapse of state socialism and the new environment within which the law would function. No one anticipated how the legislation would offer opportunities for state managers to transform themselves into a political bourgeoisie. For a time the state closed its eyes to the abuse that took place in the name of "spontaneous privatization," but eventually public opinion compelled the establishment of state regulation. But it was done in the traditional manner of giving monopoly power to a single agency—the state property agency. There is not even a general law on privatization that would provide firm guidelines for such a body.

Spontaneous privatization began as an ideological assault on the past, but it ended up reproducing the class forces that dominated the past. In order to forestall the appropriation by state managers of the firms they had hitherto managed, the anticommunist bloc had to resurrect an anathema from the past, centralized control over the economy. Because central direction is ideologically unacceptable, this control had to be performed in private, unsupervised by democratic bodies such as parliament. The very instrument that was supposed to usher in a new era—liberal democracy—turned out to protect many features of the old regime. This happened not just at the level of the state but also at the level of the enterprise, as we see from the following case study of privatization.

The Lenin Steel Works—A Model Transformation

The transformation of the Lenin Steel Works (LKM) in January 1990 into a joint stock company was widely touted as a model of privatization. Let us see what actually occurred. Because LKM had been a loss-making company, it had been brought under direct state control. There was no enterprise council, and according to the transformation act there was no need to raise the founding capital by 20 percent, or one hundred million forints. Nevertheless, as we shall see, LKM did seek outside investment through the creation of internal KFTs. When it was turned into a joint stock company, the state became the major shareholder of its eleven billion forints in assets.

LKM faced seemingly impossible barriers to profitability under hard budget constraints. Raw materials had to be imported at increasing prices, much of its capital was antiquated, it suffered from considerable overmanning, and however hard it tried, it could not effectively enter Western markets because world competition was so intense. These constraints were real and operated quite independently of its management. The government had repeatedly bailed LKM out so that its management could present their operations as profitable. Nevertheless, at the beginning of 1990 the new corporation faced an accumulated debt on the order of two billion forints.

The company was essentially bankrupt, but desperately needed new capital for reconstruction. It had difficulty obtaining credit from national banks or government and so turned to the new source of finance provided by the privatization legislation, namely, foreign capital. It managed to attract about one billion forints' worth of investment from several companies, mainly Austrian and West German. However, partly because of political and economic uncertainties, these companies would only invest in particular parts of the enterprise, such as the continuous caster, the foundry, the electric arc furnace, and the rolling mills. By the middle of June (1990), the corporation contained twenty-six limited companies and joint stock companies.

Why were foreign enterprises prepared to invest in LKM? Surely there were more lucrative outlets for their capital? The foreign investors came in with strings attached. They were concerned not about the viability of LKM but with guaranteeing returns on their own investments. Some were able to exchange their investment for control over the distribution of LKM's products, lucrative price and trade agreements, while others extracted either guaranteed income returns on investment or guarantees on the profitability of the units in which they invested. The latter could be assured through the manipulation of internal transfer prices. Moreover, it was to the advantage of the central corporation to boost the profitability of internal companies with foreign investment, since that gave greater tax relief.

If some hoped that foreign investors would bring in new management who would reorganize LKM, then they were to be disappointed. They left the organization of steel production in the hands of the existing management. Two things, however, did change. First, there was a multiplication of managerial hierarchies, since each RT or KFT had its own general director and managerial structure. Moreover, they received very high incomes for their new positions. At the same time, layoffs still seemed to be unacceptable. Apart from natural attrition, management decided to cut the number of employees in the central organization— employees who were now clearly redundant. Instead of laying them off, however, they sent them to the various RTs and KFTs, boosting their already swollen administrative ranks with what came to be known as "parachutists." This was not a way of increasing profit but of redistributing losses.

The second change also intensified problems of the past. Creating internal companies based on profits increased tensions between units over the distribution of costs and the determination of internal prices. The old conflicts between, say, the rolling mills and steel production, or between the continuous caster and the converter, intensified. Struggles came to be focused on the manipulation of internal prices, determined by the bargaining strength of the different units. Pressures on internal prices were so great that a "price censorship committee" was created which regulated prices in the "interests of the company as a whole." Still, power relations and not market relations governed the relationship between the interdependent units within the steel mill. The introduction of profit centers did not and indeed cannot give rise to greater efficiency or reduce costs where the units are part of a single integrated production process.

LKM managers soon realized that the creation of KFTs exacerbated rather than diminished old problems. The units which top management had once controlled now assumed an autonomy that was legally based. Still, what could they have done? They were trapped by the logic of spontaneous privatization. They could obtain external financing only by seeking assistance from foreign capital, which entailed limiting market maneuverability, multiplying managers, and disrupting production. Short-term survival came at the cost of long-term viability. They were left to their own devices without any clear guidelines from above. There was no national industrial strategy, because that would be tantamount to planning—considered to be a dangerous regression toward communism.

In the case of the transformation of LKM, only about 10 percent of the shares are held by foreign enterprises—the remainder being held largely by the Ministry of Industry. An alternative solution has been to enter into a joint venture with foreign capital, such as is occurring at

Ózd. There the West German steel consortium, KORF, is buying out 60 percent of the Ózd steelworks. Ózd was probably the weakest steel complex, and if the takeover is successful will essentially lose control of its future.

There is another alternative which some enterprises, like the sinter plant supplying iron ore to LKM and Ózd, are pursuing. Rather than lose control of the enterprise to the state or to foreign capital, they are thinking of selling shares to their own employees. This is becoming an increasingly popular idea among managers, although no company has yet succeeded in completing it. There are a number of reasons for the interest in employee ownership. In the first place, it may help managers retain control of their enterprise when threatened with state or foreign direction. They would also stand to gain materially if shares are distributed to employees in accordance with their income and seniority in the company. In other instances, management uses employee ownership to solicit the support of workers. The collapse of the nomenclatura system, and thus of support from on high, has left managers vulnerable to organized workers. Managers can no longer appeal to the state, to the party, or even to the trade union to repress working-class struggles, so they appeal directly to workers with promises of shares in their own company.

In summary, we have seen how "privatization" was seized upon by managers to protect their interests, wherever possible, through collusion with foreign capital or the state. When this broke out into scandals, the state created the SPA, which recentralized control over privatization. There seemed no way out: Either strengthen the old managerial class or intensify state control over the economy. In either case the gap between ideology and reality remained as wide as ever, between eulogies to "free enterprise" and the persistence of a hierarchical economy. The struggles between enterprises and the state so characteristic of the past are being reproduced in the present.

Just as under the old regime, so now one obvious way to narrow the gap between ideology and reality would be to introduce genuine socialization of the means of production.[15] By distributing ownership of state property to different institutions, such as municipalities, consumer associations, mutual benefit societies, and (most obviously) workers' organizations, the grip of the old elites would be broken. Giving power to groups independent of the state may be the most effective road to a market economy. Not surprisingly, most government ministries and particularly the SPA, have been adamantly opposed to such institutional ownership, which they claim, but with little evidence, would be inefficient. They insist instead on natural or what they deem to be responsible ownership. Their reluctance to provide a genuine foundation for democracy by the dispersal of ownership, of course, reflects their class interests in becoming a state bourgeoisie.

In the final analysis, socialization of state property has not been realized because the social forces promoting it have been so weak and those opposing it so strong. To understand why this should have been the case, and particularly why demands for employee ownership have either not materialized or have failed, we have to turn to an analysis of the new regimes of production.

An Emergent Alternative: Workers' Councils

Rejection of the past and the mobilization of anticommunist ideology by all parties have been effectively used to prevent any form of collective organization by workers and to systematically exclude them from the political process. Unorganized before the present transition, the working class for the most part remains so. Mutual suspicions between intellectuals and workers have kept them apart so that workers have had to rely on their own resources. They have, therefore, been slow to take advantage of the political vacuum created by the withdrawal of the state and the collapse of the party, and to challenge the way privatization has been used to consolidate the preexisting power structure. The old Federation of Trade Unions continues in its old ways, claiming political neutrality in an attempt to recoup its lost legitimacy. At the enterprise, the old trade unions continue to forge an alliance with management as though nothing has happened. Despite this, the federation, as of July 1990, retains 3.5 million members, having lost only 800,000, mainly to a splinter group made up of technical, scientific, and other intellectual workers. The League for Independent Trade Unions, with loose links to the SZDSZ, has obtained a membership of only 50,000, which is itself far more than the Workers' Solidarity movement. Thus, the official trade unions continue to retain the allegiance of the overwhelming proportion of workers in industry.

Nevertheless, denial of any genuine representation for workers has also led to attempts at self-organization, which most naturally emerges in production—for that is where the destiny of workers is being determined, where the legacy of past class consciousness is most developed, where mobilizing power is most easily aggregated, and where the old trade union structures deny workers any self-defense. Workers' councils have sprung up around the country to seize the opportunities created by the autonomization of production politics.

Ellen Comisso has argued that trade unions protect workers as suppliers of labor power.[16] They are "extensively" organized and do not care about the fate of the individual enterprise. Workers' councils, on the other hand, respond to local conditions by defending the enterprise as a viable concern. Rather than being defensive in nature, workers' councils "include" all employees and perform a more entrepreneurial function. When trade unions fail to protect jobs and wages because they organize across firms, then workers are likely to turn to workers' councils. Thus, in contemporary Hungary, workers' councils are most likely to spring up where enterprises are being threatened with privatization, closure, or layoffs.

The following case studies confirm Comisso's hypotheses. In the first, a workers' council is established to combat layoffs and privatization. It fails because it is not inclusive of all employees. In the second case, management takes advantage of the new political order to create a workers' council to defend the interests of a division against enterprise headquarters. The division successfully establishes its independence and then disbands the workers' council. In the third case, a very successful handicraft firm establishes a workers' council and proposes employee ownership to counter threatened takeovers by foreign enterprises. Finally, we return to the Lenin Steel Works, where workers see the effects of the privatization described above. They create workers' councils to defend their present and future interests by demanding greater control over enterprise management.

A Workers' Council Aborted

Pét is essentially a one-enterprise town, with most of its inhabitants dependent on employment at the large chemical works, producing nitrogen products, mainly fertilizers. It is the biggest manufacturer of fertilizers in Hungary. The town itself is heavily polluted with the gaseous fumes from the plant, and employees have always lived in this unhealthy environment. But this became a secondary issue when the plant was threatened with partial closure.

It faced a shrinking market and falling prices. Heavily dependent on energy, it suffered a considerable setback when the Hungarian government decided to raise the price of natural gas, partially in response to the Soviet Union's withdrawal of subsidies for cheap energy. The company was caught in a pincer movement as costs increased at the same time that market prices for its products fell. It sustained heavy losses, and in 1989 the state took it over and the general director resigned. The emergency plan was to halve its three thousand employees. The union was closely connected to the old management and did nothing to resist the planned shrinkage.

Faced with layoffs, the workers rebelled against the trade union officials, and in August 1989 three hundred, mainly from the newest unit (NPK, built in the middle seventies), formed a workers' council. The background to the rebellion sheds light on the dilemmas of privatization and the legacy of the past. In the early 1970s the Ministry of Agriculture decided that it wanted to produce a new fertilizer specifically for Hungarian agriculture. Experts traveled the world to look for the best model for a new plant at Pét, and they decided to follow a more or less unique Norwegian enterprise. When the new unit, NPK, was finally finished in 1974, the energy crisis had already brought about dramatically rising costs of production. Moreover, the plant had been designed to produce a fertilizer for the average conditions of Hungarian agriculture, and it turned out that the average actually rarely pertained, so that demand was not as high as expected. In the most recent period, escalating costs of production, combined with an agriculture that cannot afford to pay for the fertilizer, have created a crisis for even this unit, the most modern in the enterprise.

To understand the unfolding events leading to the formation of the workers' council, we have to consider the specific production problems faced by the NPK plant. The new technology was very sensitive to changes in temperature and raw materials, and it took a number of years of experimentation before engineers finally knew how to bring it under control. Even then the operation of the plant depended on the expertise and experience of core workers and technicians to adapt very quickly to breakdowns. Because it was the last unit to be built at Pét, the workers there were less skilled and they were paid less, while the workplace environment was more dangerous and the work itself more exhausting than at the older units of the enterprise. Higher management was not interested in the specific problems experienced on the shop floor, and ruled, like at LKM, with a certain arbitrariness. Rumors were rife about corruption at higher levels, of managers stealing precious platinum or selling it cheaply to other enterprises for private returns. All these factors fueled discontent and higher turnover, disrupting production further. Management called for even greater efforts by those core workers who remained and upon whom the plant became increasingly dependent.

A strike was precipitated by the threatened departure of two of the three technical managers. In desperation, management increased their income by the very considerable amount of 250 forints a shift. This was the straw that broke the camel's back and workers walked out, disgusted with both management, who refused to recognize their increasing contributions under worsening conditions, and the trade unions, who were not concerned with their problems. It was at this point that a workers' council was formed, but it did not receive much support from the older units. In part this was due to a failure of leadership, but there were more important structural reasons. First, NPK was an independent unit and so there had been little communication between its workers and those in the other units. More important, the disciplinary regime was more despotic at the other units, where a powerful party apparatus instilled considerable fear among the workers. Workers were warned that if they joined the workers' council they would lose all their trade union benefits. This tempered the enthusiasm for the workers' council, which further lost credibility when it refused to participate in meetings with the trade union. In part because NPK was a newer unit and in part because management there depended upon an autonomous, self-organized work force, there was less fear and a greater political space within which to organize a workers' council. The workers' council still exists, but it is weak and concentrated in the NPK.

Receiving no support from management, the workers' council was simply unable to tackle the problems facing the enterprise. It was based in the NPK without the enterprise-wide support that was necessary for it to be effective. In particular, it had no response to the state's attempt to sell off the enterprise to a competitor for the ridiculously small sum of 100 million forints. Instead it was the creditors of Pét who refused to accept this bid. So the company was put up for auction after it had been appraised at 5 billion forints. The same competing enterprise offered to raise its bid to 600 million forints, but creditors again were not satisfied, and it was only in a second auction organized by the state holding agency that the bid went up to the more acceptable 1.75 billion forints. The workers' council offered no alternative to the sale, such as an employee buy-out, and so the company's fate was negotiated between the state holding agency and the creditors.

The Workers' Council as a Tool of Management

At Mosonmagyaróvár, the workers' council was more successful. In 1977 this profitable factory, which produced agricultural machinery, was taken over by the successful giant Rába company, internationally known for the parts it produced for Ikarusz buses, and for its agricultural and transportation equipment, trucks, and other large vehicles. After Mosonmagyaróvár had been taken over by Rába, its profits were drained away to Rába headquarters in Györ. The employees who were laid off by Rába top management as a result of deliberate shrinking of Mosonmagyaróvár's product range were asked to commute to Györ.

In 1989 a plant manager at Mosonmagyaróvár decided to stand up for the division's independence before it was too late. Despite the party's attempts to dissuade him, he called a meeting of the employees, at which they decided to form a workers' council. Horvát, the general director of Rába, known throughout Hungary as the Red Baron because of his dictatorial style of management, denounced the workers' council, which then called a strike, demanding that Mosonmagyaróvár be given back its autonomy with appropriate distribution of profits.

Horvát was due for reelection as general director by the enterprise council, which hitherto had been stacked with his own nominees. Realizing that in these new political times he would not control the elections of the new enterprise council, Horvát called an extraordinary meeting of the old enterprise council in order to get himself reelected. Legally, any decision of the enterprise council can be challenged within thirty days. So the president of the workers' council and two workers courageously filed a grievance against the legitimacy of Horvát's reelection. The court decided in favor of the workers' council, Horvát resigned, and Mosonmagyaróvár regained its independence.

It was a sign of the times that such a powerful figure as Horvát could be dislodged through legal channels by three employees taking out a grievance against him. However unpopular, Horvát had established himself as a pillar of the state managerial class. With the aid of the party he had built up Rába into a despotically run but efficient state enterprise. His workers and managers were relatively well paid so long as they did what they were told. Once the party apparatus crumbled, the emperor's power base was destroyed and a new general director was installed. The workers' council, deliberately constituted as independent of managerial, party, and trade union structures, was the most effective weapon against the incumbent power structure. Having achieved their goal, managers at Mosonmagyaróvár withdrew their support for the workers' council, which then collapsed because workers had not been effectively mobilized behind it, and also because it had no new goals.

But the story does not end here. In the summer of 1990, the company, now independent of Rába, was divided by new conflicts over its future. Leading forces within management wanted to enter into a joint venture with an Austrian company and close down all the "unprofitable" parts of the enterprise. This would entail massive layoffs. The workers' council was resurrected to fight against this plan in the interests of all employees. Whatever the immediate outcome of this struggle, the prospects for Mosonmagyaróvár and its workers' council are not bright, since for over a decade Rába made no substantial capital investment in the plant. Workers' councils have a better chance of survival where the enterprise is at least potentially economically viable without being dependent on external financing. We turn now to such an example.

A Workers' Council Pursues Employee Ownership

Herend is one of Hungary's oldest and most successful porcelain factories. It produces delicate hand-painted vases, bowls, dinner, tea, and coffee services, and small sculptures, 85 percent of which are sold abroad. There are about 2,100 workers at the factory, many of whom are highly skilled painters. Most of the workers actually live in the Herend village, so that making porcelain has become part of the community's tradition.

Herend has always been a profitable enterprise. The secret of its success lies with the inherited skills of its craft workers. Thus, in August 1989 management instigated a revolt when it awarded bonuses to itself amounting to over 150,000 forints while workers received only a few thousand. What incensed the workers most was that managers' bonuses went up while their own fell compared to the previous year. Perhaps in the past, management would have gotten away with it, but with the eclipse of the party, management, as in the case of Rába, was left undefended. One member of the enterprise council who heard about the bonuses began to organize a workers' council. This was viewed as an alternative to the trade union, which was entirely discredited by its past and continued association with top management. Rapidly the membership of the workers' council spread through the factory. Within three months 1,800 employees, about 85 percent, had joined the workers' council.

The question quickly emerged: What was the status of the workers' council? Whom did it represent, what rights did it have, what interests would it pursue? Although there was some interest in returning to the council idea of 1956, the leadership did not want to take over managerial functions, but rather wanted, first and foremost, to play the role of an effective trade union. With the help of an MDF lawyer they decided to fight the case for their legal recognition through the courts. They took advantage of the law of associations, passed at the beginning of 1988, which established the rules for creating new organizations and associations (although it was meant mainly for political parties). In September of 1989 the workers' council successfully gained rights to represent workers in bargaining with management and access to trade union property. Although they did not want to reduplicate the mistakes of the old trade union, still among their members could be found key members of management.

At this point the popularly elected workers' council wanted to play the role of a trade union with perhaps certain codetermination rights in management. They were not aware of nor interested in possibilities of privatization. Indeed, they wondered why they couldn't remain a state-owned enterprise. However, when it became clear that privatization was likely and that it would involve a foreign buy-out, the idea of employee ownership became more attractive as a means of exercising some control over management as well as distributing profits more equally. The workers' council effectively thwarted the general director's intentions to enter into a joint venture with a foreign buyer. A joint committee for planning the transformation of the company was formed with 50 percent managers and 50 percent from the workers' council. The general director's attempt to discredit the idea of an employee stock ownership plan (ESOP) only fueled his unpopularity, contributing to his final downfall.

In June the workers' council secured a huge representation in the enterprise council of Herend and ousted the general director. They became fully committed to a worker buy-out of the enterprise, although there was no legislation which would facilitate it. A transformation plan is being prepared that closely follows the guidelines of an ESOP wherein workers would be able to form a trust or foundation that would hold the shares, which would be paid for out of future profits. Herend is a best-case scenario for an employee buy-out, since the capital is mainly human capital, the company is rooted in the community, and it is profitable. The president of the workers' council was elected to parliament as an MDF candidate where he is promoting ESOP legislation. Last but not least, the workers' council has already established its legitimacy by first displacing the old trade union and then ousting the general director.

Workers' Councils at the Lenin Steel Works

The above three cases, but particularly the case of the Herend porcelain factory, were given considerable publicity by the MDF, which cautiously included workers' councils in its election platform. The idea spread so that by July 1990 there were over 150 officially registered workers' councils in the country. By November the figure was 600, involving ninety thousand members. Among them are the workers' councils at the blast furnace, the foundry, and the Combined Steel Works of what was the Lenin Steel Works. Hearing about Herend and helped by an MDF lawyer, an old-time leading operator began organizing a workers' council in the blast furnace. When we talked with him in June 1990, he recalled the importance of his experiences in the 1956 council movement when he was seventeen and a young employee at LKM. He and his fellow organizers had taken the constitution of the Herend workers' council as their own and presented it in court for registration in January 1990. Although the court was able to put up some obstruction, in the end it could not stop the formation of the workers' council, which was finally given legal approval in the middle of April. In June (1990), of the 300 workers in the blast furnace, 120 were members of the workers' council and 80 were still enrolled in the old trade union, while 100 were not members of either organization. From the blast furnace the idea has spread to the Combined Steel Works and the foundry. The struggle with management for extending the rights of workers is only just beginning.

What motivated the formation of the workers' council at LKM? As elsewhere, the most basic impetus was opposition to the old-style trade unions, who colluded with management to defend the interests of the enterprise rather than those of workers. The subordination of the trade union was symbolized by its automatic signature of any managerial decree, whether or not it was in the interests of workers. The workers' council vowed that it would defend individual workers against arbitrary managerial sanctions. Its most ardent supporters go further and want to see workers' councils exercising control over management and even organizing elections of managers. Finally, the leadership of the workers' council wanted to promote employee ownership, although they were not sure how this was to be accomplished. In this last regard they differed from the council ideas of 1956, which usually took for granted state ownership of the means of production.

Opposition to trade unions follows lines anticipated by Comisso. Rather than establish "extensive" organization across industry, the workers' council seeks to build up an "inclusive" worker organization from the shop floor. Membership dues will not be sent upstairs to cover the costs of union officials at the enterprise, branch, and national levels. Instead, they will be used locally for the membership: to employ lawyers to pursue grievances, to distribute benefits, and to create a strike fund. Since the movement tries to establish shop-floor democracy and restore dignity in the workplace, the two national organizations of workers' councils are still very weak.[17] Without institutional power, workers' councils are very vulnerable to state or managerial offensives.

The Significance of Workers' Councils

We are not saying that workers' councils are the wave of the future. Unless politically institutionalized (as in Yugoslavia) or based on collective ownership, they are bound to be weak and parochial. Nevertheless, they do reflect specific conditions of the transitional period: (1) hostility to trade union bureaucracy, which failed to defend the interests of workers at the level of the enterprise; (2) the legacy of working-class consciousness; (3) the continued exclusion of workers from the political process, both at the level of the enterprise and at the national level; (4) democratization, which in giving autonomy to parliament and legal institutions also gives autonomy to production politics; and (5) privatization, which on the one hand lodges crucial decisions at the level of a popularly elected enterprise council, and on the other hand creates despair by multiplying bureaucratic irrationalities.

What are the implications of workers' councils, and more generally the transformation of production politics, for working-class struggles? Liberal democracy has led to the withdrawal of the state from the enterprise as a visible organizer of exploitation and domination. Out of the fusion of production and state apparatuses it creates their relative autonomy, thereby bottling up conflicts within the enterprise. There are no longer the painting rituals that bring workers together to celebrate communism and demonstrate the gap between ideology and reality. Capitalism is celebrated in the commodity, not in the public ritual, and this has an atomizing, pacifying effect.

To be sure, the rituals of democracy will call attention to the gap between representation for all and the political exclusion of workers qua workers. You cannot build a new society out of the rejection of the old. Anticommunism cannot sustain the new regime for long and cannot be mobilized to continue the exclusion of workers. The logic of parliamentary democracy will lead to one or more of the major parties' explicitly defending the interests of workers, or to the formation of a labor party. If this were to happen, workers might be expected to break out of their current apathy and cynicism toward national politics. But such a possibility presumes the stability of democracy, to which we turn next.

The State Socialist Road to Capitalism

Social scientists have been searching for parallels and models with which to understand Eastern Europe and the Soviet Union. They have gravitated around theories of regime transition, developed to comprehend processes of democratization in Latin America.[18] This "transition school" calls attention to the indeterminacy of regime change and the fragility of newly formed democracies. Rather than argue that there are specific conditions—cultural, socioeconomic, educational, etc.—conducive to democratization, they consider regime transition as a game played within objective constraints but with uncertain outcomes. For the most part these models give scant attention to economics, and therefore miss the distinctiveness of the double transition that is being attempted in Eastern Europe.

Adam Przeworski is exceptional in his explicit attention to the mutual conditioning of economic and political orders. Based on the Latin American experience as well as studies of Western Europe, his argument is that liberal democracy conserves the existing economic order.[19] In their origin, democracies are the product of a compromise among classes, and in their effects they organize class compromise. Instead of being an instrument of economic transformation, liberal democracy depends upon a growing economy that can provide the economic basis for class compromise.

We have made a similar argument for Hungary. Far from being a threat to the old dominant classes, liberal democracy provides the screen behind which they continue to wield power and control the economy. The smoothness of the transition in Eastern Europe, particularly in Hungary, can be attributed to the way in which state managers have been able to endorse liberal democracy as being in the interests of all while reconstituting their own class power. Still, if the economy declines, so that giving to one class always means taking away from another, then the class compromise upon which democracy rests will collapse and democracy's life will be short.[20]

Counterpoint: The Transition from Capitalism to Socialism

We have to look elsewhere for models of economic change which illuminate the question of the transition to capitalism. What can we learn from theories of the transition from capitalism to socialism? Here too, many had expected that democracy would be the instrument of transition. According to the classical Marxist model the working class would become increasingly homogeneous, degraded, impoverished, and numerous. It would consolidate its power in the form of a party which would be voted into office with a mandate to expropriate control over the means of production and install socialism. The project failed for many reasons: Workers weren't interested in socialism; there weren't enough workers to vote socialist parties into office without the support of other classes; party and trade union leadership developed interests of their own which dovetailed with the perpetuation of capitalism; and when socialist parties did assume power and tried to introduce socialist measures they faced capital flight and economic decline, which either discredited their socialist goals or led to their removal by military coup. So socialist parties gave up trying to make the transition to socialism and instead tried to give capitalism a socialist character. Social democracy was the compromise between achievable but irrational capitalism and unachievable but rational socialism.

Just as liberal democracy cannot bring about a transition from capitalism to socialism, so now it is equally incapable of bringing about a transition from socialism to competitive capitalism. In endowing the enterprise with autonomy it only preserves its old institutional form. The socialist enterprise pursued strategies attuned to the hierarchical economy—strategies which gave rise to distinctive enterprise structures, as described here for Bánki and LKM. Preserving these structures in a capitalist environment can only intensify irrationalities, as we saw in the case of the privatization of LKM. It is naive to think that laissez-faire will introduce hard budget constraints, or that hard budget constraints will immaculately transform structures and wipe away resistance from managers within the enterprise. It is difficult enough to transform the United States corporation already adapted to the market, let alone the state socialist enterprise adapted to a state-regulated economy.

If there is no evolutionary road from capitalism to socialism, there also may be no evolutionary road from state socialism to capitalism. Just as bolshevik theory insisted on a revolutionary transition from capitalism to socialism, so now in that same country there is a growing lobby that argues for a Pinochet-type dictatorship to bring about the transition to capitalism. However, proponents of dictatorship don't show how such centralization could ever subsequently lead to decentralization. They ignore that even in Chile, Pinochet's radical privatizing free-market policies led his government to intervene in the economy as much as did the socialist government of the Unidad Popular.[21] That liberal democracy won't deliver capitalism doesn't mean dictatorship will.

The Ambiguous Role of International Capitalism

However, the transition from socialism to capitalism is favored by at least one factor absent in the reverse movement, and that is the hospitable world context. Socialism in one country may indeed be impossible, given the pressures of the surrounding capitalist world economy, but this is not a problem for a country seeking to make a transition away from socialism. Indeed, once a nation opens its economy to the world capitalist order, its development depends on its ability to compete with more advanced capitalist nations on terms defined by the latter. In this respect, Hungary is simply not in a position to compete with Western Europe, the United States, and Japan. The existing state enterprises adapted their organizational structure to a closed hierarchical economy, which makes adjustment to an open market economy difficult. We have already referred to the lucrative deals foreign investors have negotiated and at what costs to Hungarian development. We should also mention the huge international debt, estimated at $20 billion, which makes Hungary beholden to foreign banks and agencies such as the IMF and the World Bank. Finally, by relinquishing its imperial role, the Soviet Union deprives Eastern Europe of access to cheap energy and guaranteed markets for its goods. At the same time, Soviet withdrawal leaves Hungary vulnerable to economic pillage by capitalist nations, most obviously Germany—once it has set its own house in order. The international forces promoting capitalism in Hungary will also be responsible for its underdevelopment.

But there is another implication of the transition taking place within a world capitalist order. In the attempts at constructing socialism there were no concrete models which guided the transition. Socialism existed in the dreams of its protagonists and, to a sadly limited extent, in the minds of Marxist intellectuals. In the transition to capitalism, however, there do exist examples of successful capitalism, which Hungary and other Eastern European countries aspire to emulate. Here lies the seductiveness of capitalism, which holds out the possibility of achieving a Swedish welfare state or German industrial efficiency even though the vast majority of capitalist societies are poor and repressive. The ideologues of capitalism say that Hungary can move "from rags to riches" if Hungarians will only make sufficient sacrifices, if they will work hard and accept material deprivation today as the cost of a radiant future tomorrow.

The Hungarian dream of upward mobility in the global order is bolstered by the prevailing wisdom that Hungary's development was held back by its communist past, so that shedding that past will automatically bring development. This view simply fails to take into account the problems of late entry into a capitalist world system. No less than the transition to socialism, the transition to capitalism is based on an illusion, not on a radiant future that has not been achieved, but on one that has been achieved. It is based on the concrete and powerful fantasy that Hungary can become like Sweden or even South Korea rather than follow the path of Tanzania or Guatemala.

Realistic Possibilities

Just as in the past state policy was based on a single road to socialism, so now state policy veers toward a single road to capitalism. The illusion that somehow Hungary can escape the vice of international capitalism is the mirror image of the vehement denunciation of communism. Since communism was all evil, capitalism must be all beneficent. Such a view is, of course, nurtured by the emergent political bourgeoisie and its international creditors. Nevertheless, there are skeptics who recognize that Hungary cannot recapitulate the trajectory of the leading capitalist societies. Instead they explore the possibility of an ill-defined "Third Road," which is neither capitalist nor socialist. The Third Road has had a long history in Eastern Europe, and Iván Szelényi is one of its most articulate recent spokesmen.[22] Writing before the collapse of state socialism, he argued that the history of Hungary has been one of interrupted embourgeoisement, and distinctive to Hungary's contemporary trajectory is the return to a bourgeois road via an emergent petite bourgeoisie. His claims are supported by the continued efflorescence of the second economy and private accumulation in agriculture. However, he ignored the problems of the state sector upon which the private sector has depended, assuming that it can be slowly displaced by an indigenous bourgeoisie. While it is true that the petite bourgeoisie have developed considerable muscle, as witnessed in recent strikes by retail-outlet employees and taxi drivers, nevertheless they cannot provide the basis of a modern economy located in a capitalist world system.

A fear lurks, then, that the Third Road is not the one Szelényi is thinking of—but a Third Road to the Third World. If the first road to the Third World is the colonial road and the second is the road of dependency, the third is the socialist road. Such a pessimistic scenario is more likely to emerge from studies of the state sector. As we have seen, in this realm property relations are not easily changed and a plausible strategy would be to work within the limits of the public enterprise. Like the social democrats under capitalism, free marketeers under state socialism could make the best of a bad job by developing a form of state capitalism. In effect this is what János Kornai proposes.[23] Because he sees the dangers of trying to install capitalism overnight, because his goal is to return to a mythical past of perfect competition and hard budget constraints, and because of his profound understanding of the resilience of the state socialist economy, he accepts that the state sector will remain for some time to come. He proposes that in order to facilitate the transition, the state sector be made to work more efficiently and subsidize wherever possible the private sector.

The democratic state must be invoked to enforce hard budget constraints through political means, by denying enterprises the right to bargain over prices, subsidies, allocation of resources, access to foreign exchange, and so on. But even he doesn't explain how an anemic parliamentary democracy, itself fragile, can possibly regulate state enterprises. Parliamentary democracy exists precisely to deflect political attention from the extended reproduction of the centralized economy. If the state is to begin to regulate the economy more effectively, if it is to prevent the degeneration of planning into what David Stark has aptly called "clanning,"[24] then it will require a much more radical democracy than the trappings of liberal pluralism.

All roads seem to lead to the same economic and political impasse because they make no attempt to dislodge the incumbent dominant classes or to make them accountable to subordinate groups. A more promising prospect for meaningful democracy, not surprisingly opposed by the political bourgeoisie, would be to give different groups a stake in the Hungarian economy by dispersing ownership. It is said that private ownership is the necessary basis for democracy because it disperses power. In fact, private ownership concentrates power and turns liberal democracy into a mockery of its ideals. Institutional ownership would provide the basis for a more genuine participation of its citizenry in national life. When public bodies such as local councils, employee associations, and consumer associations own property, they will have both the capacity and the motivation to participate in politics. This could counter the massive political apathy in the country at large.

On the other hand, employee ownership is said to be inefficient because workers are not "responsible owners." However, workers are likely to be as responsible as the political bourgeoisie, whose credibility has evaporated in a trail of appalling scandals. With an ownership stake, employees would have an interest in making their enterprises more competitive. They would be more committed to the viability of their enterprises. We have already seen in earlier chapters just how astute workers are in their understanding of production and how managers are more often the source of economic irrationality. For workers to participate in management through some system of codetermination would only be building on one of the positive legacies of a shortage economy, namely the legacy of collective self-organization of work.

Finally, employee ownership would not only make significant contributions to democracy and enterprise efficiency, but it would also be more just. Workers bore the brunt of the past, and they will have to bear the brunt of any future transition, so it is only just that they be given a say in their own destiny through the extension of property rights. They, more than the emergent political bourgeoisie, deserve the fruits of their past labors in the form of ownership of their enterprises.

All of which is not to say that employee ownership is some universal panacea. Rather, given the array of alternatives in the present economic and political context, it is an appropriate avenue to be pursued, along with other strategies, on the road to capitalism.[25]

*

Lenin thought that imperialism was to be the last stage of capitalism. He was wrong. His successors thought that Soviet "communism" would mark the last stage of capitalism. They too were wrong. Like imperialism before it, state socialism unwittingly laid the basis for the development of capitalism on a world scale. As capitalism increasingly transcends national barriers it becomes, for the first time, truly global. But at the same time its irrationalities will become more palpable and irrevocable. So Marxism will once more come into its own as the major analytical tool with which to criticize these developments.

But will Marxism also be able to articulate a feasible alternative to capitalism? The Marxian repudiation of utopian socialism in favor of scientific socialism was a rhetorical device which left Marxism without concrete visions of a future beyond capitalism. Because socialism was "inevitable," classical Marxism regarded blueprints as unnecessary as well as undesirable. This fatal omission made it possible for the voices of Soviet Marxism to proclaim Stalinism as the realization of socialist ideals. Now, the death of Marxism-Leninism offers an opportunity to reexamine the history of the Soviet Union, whose tragedy was to place socialism on the agenda of world history at the same time that it faced conditions which guaranteed its failure. But this is not a call to dismiss the Soviet Union as a gigantic mistake. Its history is full of lessons for any future vision of socialism—visions that will return with a vengeance as capitalism, unleashed from restraint, brings such devastation and de-

struction as to threaten human existence. Inevitably, capitalism will re-
vive the struggle for a radiant future—a future in which history is reap-
propriated by its makers, in which material insecurity is abolished, and
in which individuals are allowed to develop their potentialities. When
that time comes, socialists must be better equipped with visions of what
they want and how it might work. In the meantime the epigones of
Adam Smith should make the most of their honeymoon, because it will
not last. And when the pendulum swings there will be no evil communism to blame. The struggle for socialism is at its dawn, not its dusk.

Notes

Preface

1. Chapters 2 and 3 are based on fieldwork conducted for two months at Bánki during the summer of 1984. Chapter 2 was authored by Burawoy as "Piece Rates, Hungarian Style," *Socialist Review* 79 (1985): 43–69. Chapter 3 was jointly authored by Burawoy and Lukács as "Mythologies of Work: A Comparison of Firms in State Socialism and Advanced Capitalism," *American Sociological Review* 50 (1985): 723–37. Chapters 4 and 5 were based on fieldwork conducted at the Lenin Steel Works during the period 1985–87. Chapter 4 was authored by Burawoy and Lukács as "What is Socialist about Socialist Production? Autonomy and Control in a Hungarian Steel Mill," in *The Transformation of Work*, ed. Stephen Wood (London: Hyman and Unwin, 1989), pp. 295–316, while chapter 5 was written by Burawoy as "Reflections on the Class Consciousness of Hungarian Steel Workers," *Politics and Society* 17 (1989): 1–34.

Chapter One: A Sociological Diary

1. Alexander Zinoviev, *The Radiant Future* (London: Bodley Head, 1981).

2. Michael Burawoy, *Manufacturing Consent: Changes in the Labor Process under Monopoly Capitalism* (Chicago: University of Chicago Press, 1979).

3. Miklós Haraszti, *A Worker in a Worker's State* (Harmondsworth, England: Penguin Books, 1977).

4. Michael Burawoy, *The Politics of Production: Factory Regimes under Capitalism and Socialism* (London: Verso, 1985).

5. We discuss these studies in chapter 3.

6. I discuss these factors in much greater detail in *The Politics of Production*, chapter 4.

7. Alfred Chandler, *Strategy and Structure: Chapters in the History of the American Industrial Enterprise* (Cambridge, Mass.: MIT. Press, 1962), and Jean-Charles Asselain, *Planning and Profits in Socialist Economies* (London: Routledge and Kegan Paul, 1981).

8. Harry Braverman, *Labor and Monopoly Capital* (New York: Monthly Review Press, 1974).

9. This is also an argument made in Vladimir Andrle, *Workers in Stalin's Russia* (New York: St. Martin's Press, 1988), particularly chapter 3. He argues that Taylorism works only under stable conditions of production, absent in the period of Stalinism.

10. It might be useful to distinguish between "functional flexibility," which refers to the reorganization of work to adapt to uncertainty of inputs, that is, shortages, and "numerical flexibility," which refers to the contraction and expansion of the labor force in response to changing levels of demand. Prototypically, state socialism requires functional flexibility whereas capitalism requires numerical flexibility. For an analysis of these two notions of flexibility as they apply to England, see Anna Pollert, "The 'Flexible Firm': Fixation or Fact?" *Work, Employment, and Society* 2 (1988): 281–317.

11. György Konrád and Iván Szelényi, *The Intellectuals on the Road to Class Power* (New York: Harcourt Brace Jovanovich, 1979).

12. See Alejandro Foxley, *Latin American Experiments in Neoconservative Economics* (Berkeley: University of California Press, 1983), and Karl Polanyi, *The Great Transformation* (New York: Rinehart, 1944).

Introduction to Part One

1. Konrád and Szelényi, *The Intellectuals on the Road to Class Power*.

2. Haraszti, *A Worker in a Worker's State*.

3. Reinhard Bendix, *Work and Authority in Industry* (New York: John Wiley, 1956), chapter 6.

4. Andrew Walder, *Communist Neo-Traditionalism* (Berkeley: University of California Press, 1986).

5. Ibid., p. 8. The idea of "communist neo-traditionalism" is developed most extensively by Kenneth Jowitt. See "An Organizational Approach to the Study of Political Culture in Marxist-Leninist Systems," *American Political Science Review* 68 (1974): 1171–91, and "Soviet Neo-Traditionalism: The Political Corruption of a Leninist Regime," *Soviet Studies* 35 (1983): 275–97.

6. David Stark and Victor Nee, "Toward an Institutional Analysis of State

Socialism," in *Remaking the Economic Institutions of Socialism: China and Eastern Europe*, ed. Victor Nee and David Stark (Stanford: Stanford University Press, 1989), pp. 1–31.

7. Andrle, *Workers in Stalin's Russia;* Lewis Siegelbaum, *Stakhanovism and the Politics of Productivity in the USSR, 1935–1941* (Cambridge: Cambridge University Press, 1988); Donald Filtzer, *Soviet Workers and Stalinist Industrialization* (Armonk, N.Y.: M. E. Sharpe, 1986).

8. In the Soviet Union the state created the distinction between "open" and "closed" enterprises. The "closed" enterprises were often part of the industrial military complex and offered material concessions to their workers in return for political loyalty. See Victor Zaslavsky, *The Neo-Stalinist State* (Armonk, N.Y.: M. E. Sharpe, 1982), particularly chapter 3.

Chapter Two: Piece Rates, Hungarian Style

1. The reference to the "white house" has multiple meanings. The head office of the enterprise was a "white" house, but "white house" also refers to the headquarters of the Central Committee of the party in Budapest. This in turn was an ironic commentary on the pretensions to power of the Hungarian Communist party.

Chapter Three: Mythologies of Industrial Work

1. D. M. Nuti, "Socialism on Earth," *Cambridge Journal of Economics* 5 (1981): 391–403.

2. Ernest Mandel, "Ten Theses on the Social and Economic Laws Governing the Society Transitional between Capitalism and Socialism," *Critique* 3 (1974): 5–22.

3. Charles Bettelheim, *Economic Calculation and Forms of Property* (London: Routledge and Kegan Paul, 1976).

4. Rudolf Bahro, *The Alternative in Eastern Europe* (London: Verso, 1978).

5. Typical is the frequently cited article by Gregory Grossman which emphasizes the difficulties that command economies face in achieving "microbalance" of supply and demand, while assuming that such a balance is more readily achieved in a market economy. ("Notes for a Theory of the Command Economy," *Soviet Studies* 15:2 [1963]: 101–23.) There are of course notable exceptions, such as Joseph Berliner's study of managerial incentives in the United States and the Soviet Union ("Managerial Incentives and Decision Making: A Comparison of the United States and the Soviet Union," in *Comparative Economic Systems*, ed. Morris Bornstein [Homewood, Ill.: Richard D. Irwin, 1974], pp. 396–427) and Abram Bergson's comparison of productivity between the two countries ("Comparative Productivity and Efficiency in the USA and the USSR," in *Comparison of Economic Systems*, ed. Alexander Eckstein [Berkeley: University of California Press, 1971], pp. 161–218).

6. Tamás Bauer, "Investment Cycles in Planned Economies," *Acta Oeco-*

nomica 21 (1978): 243–60; János Kornai, *The Economics of Shortage*, 2 vols. (Amsterdam: North Holland Publishing Company, 1980); Iván Szelényi, "The Intelligentsia in the Class Structure of State-Socialist Societies," in *Marxist Inquiries: Studies of Labor, Class, and States*, ed. Michael Burawoy and Theda Skocpol (Chicago: University of Chicago Press, 1982), pp. 287–326.

7. There are a number of studies that have shown that at a system level the productivity of the USSR is less than that of the United States. Needless to say, the computations are very complex and make many assumptions. Briefly, they involve comparing the output of one country with the output of the other if the second were to use the inputs of the first. According to Berliner's calculations ("Managerial Incentives and Decision Making") for 1960, if the United States uses Soviet inputs and if the outputs are calculated in Soviet prices, then the relative "efficiency" of the USSR nonfarm economy is between 36 and 39 percent of the United States. On the other hand, if the USSR uses American inputs and calculates output in U.S. dollars, the relative "efficiency" of the USSR nonfarm economy turns out to be between 87 and 98 percent of that of the United States. A similar but more elaborate analysis by Bergson ("Comparative Productivity and Efficiency in the USA and the USSR") arrives at a relative productivity of the Soviet Union between 39 and 59 percent of the United States's. The results raise many interesting questions of interpretation. Higher average productivity can be attributed to stage of economic development rather than "system efficiency." And if we attribute the difference to greater "efficiency," this does not imply greater technical efficiency of enterprises, but can be explained in terms of allocational efficiency. Finally, the figures only refer to efficiency as realization of production possibilities, not to optimal output, which would involve an evaluation of noneconomic objectives and costs.

8. See Harvey Liebenstein, "Allocative Efficiency vs. 'X-Efficiency,' " *American Economic Review* 56 (1966): 392–415, and Peter Wiles, *Economic Institutions Compared* (Oxford: Basil Blackwell, 1977), chapter 15.

9. First, we did not pick our two factories. Allied was the only place Burawoy was able to get a job, and he was helped by a close relation who was engineering manager. We stumbled onto Bánki as a result of a lecture Lukács gave at a conference attended by its director. Second, the distinctiveness of Hungary may lie as much in the freedom to conduct research and the relative openness of public discussion as in its industrial organization.

10. Konrád and Szelényi, *The Intellectuals on the Road to Class Power;* Szelényi, "The Intelligentsia in the Class Structure of State-Socialist Societies."

11. Szelényi, "The Intelligentsia in the Class Structure of State-Socialist Societies."

12. Kornai, *The Economics of Shortage*.

13. Ibid.

14. See, for example, Ernest Mandel, *Late Capitalism* (London: Verso, 1975), and David Gordon, Richard Edwards, and Michael Reich, *Segmented Work, Divided Workers* (Cambridge: Cambridge University Press, 1982).

15. Bauer, "Investment Cycles in Planned Economies."

16. See, for example, Michel Aglietta, *A Theory of Capitalist Regulation—The U.S. Experience* (London: Verso, 1979); Larry Griffin, Joel Devine, and Michael Wallace, "Monopoly Capital, Organized Labor, and Military Spending in the United States, 1949–1976," in *Marxist Inquiries: Studies of Labor, Class, and States*, ed. Michael Burawoy and Theda Skocpol (Chicago: University of Chicago Press, 1982), pp. 113–54; and James O'Connor, *The Fiscal Crisis of the State* (New York: St. Martin's Press, 1973).

17. Kalman Rupp, *Entrepreneurs in Red* (Albany: State University of New York Press, 1983).

18. David Granick, *Soviet Metal-Fabricating and Economic Development* (Madison: University of Wisconsin Press, 1967).

19. Braverman, *Labor and Monopoly Capital*.

20. For more detailed descriptions, the reader can consult Burawoy, *Manufacturing Consent*, for Allied, and the previous chapter of this book for Bánki.

21. Wiles, *Economic Institutions Compared*, p. 25.

22. M. Holubenko, "The Soviet Working Class," *Critique* 4 (1975): 22.

23. Wiles, *Economic Institutions Compared*, p. 25.

24. David Lane and Felicity O'Dell, *The Soviet Industrial Worker* (Oxford: Martin Robertson, 1978), p. 20.

25. Murray Seeger, "Eye-witness to Failure," in *The Soviet Worker*, ed. Leonard Schapiro and Joseph Godson (London: MacMillan, 1981), pp. 100–101.

26. Fyodor Turovsky, "Society without a Present," in *The Soviet Worker*, ed. Schapiro and Godson, pp. 161–62; István Gábor and Péter Galasi, "The Labour Market in Hungary since 1968," in *Hungary: A Decade of Economic Reform*, ed. Paul Hare, Hugo Radice, and Nigel Swain (London: Allen Unwin, 1981), pp. 41–53.

27. Other studies of Hungarian firms reinforce our observations. See, for example, Lajos Héthy and Csaba Makó, *A Munkásmagatartások és a Gazdasági Szervezet* [*Workers' Behavior and Business Enterprise*] (Budapest: Akadémiai, 1972); János Köllö, "Munkaeröhiány, munkaerö-allokáció és bérezés egy pamutszövödében [Labor Shortage, Labor Allocation, and Reward in a Cotton Mill]" in *Kereseti- és Bérviszonyaink* [*Our Income and Wage Relations*], ed. Károly Fazekas et al. (Budapest: Hungarian Academy of Sciences, Institute of Economics, paper 28, 1983), pp. 125–86; Zoltán Farkas, "Munkások érdek- és érdekeltségi viszonyai [Relations and Levels of Interest among Workers]," *Szociológia* 1–2 (1983): 27–52; Károly Fazekas, "Teljesitményhiány és teljesitménybérezés a vállalati gazdálkodásban [Restriction of Output and Payment by Results in the Enterprise]," in *Kereseti- és Bérviszonyaink* [*Our Income and Wage Relations*], ed. Fazekas et al., pp. 125–86. Mária Ladó and Ferenc Tóth describe in detail the extra tasks, above and beyond the formal requirements of the job, that workers have to complete if they are to make their piece rates ("A munkaráforditások elismertetésének mechanizmusa és társadalmi következményei a munkaszervezetekben [Mechanisms and Social Consequences of Recognition of Efforts in Labor Processes]" in *A Teljesitmény-növelés feltételei a mun-

kaszervezetben [Conditions of Productivity Growth in Work Organizations], ed. Ágnes Simonyi [Budapest: ABMH Munkaügyi Kutatóintézet, 1983], pp. 17–42).

28. In reality, of course, within a socialist firm the ease with which workers can make their basic wage varies just as employment insecurity is unevenly distributed within a capitalist firm.

29. Leonard Kirsch, *Soviet Wages: Changes in Structure and Administration since 1956* (Cambridge: MIT Press, 1972), p. 46.

30. Richard Edwards, *Contested Terrain* (New York: Basic Books, 1979).

31. Here are the figures from the last four years of proposed and accepted norm cuts. In 1981, 659 were proposed and 323 (49 percent) were accepted; in 1982, 837 were proposed and 465 (55.6 percent) were accepted; in 1983, 457 were proposed and 265 (58 percent) were accepted; and in 1984, 385 were proposed and 294 (76.4 percent) were accepted.

32. Ferenc Fehér, Agnes Heller, and György Márkus, *Dictatorship over Needs* (Oxford: Basil Blackwell, 1983), p. 36.

33. Joseph Berliner, *The Innovation Decision in Soviet Industry* (Cambridge: MIT Press, 1976), p. xi.

34. See Burawoy, *The Politics of Production*, part 4.

35. Thus, for example, we discovered an elaborate incentive structure in the Hungarian steel industry, according to which managers can more than double their income through sponsoring innovations. Highly rewarded innovation is a prerogative of management. If workers propose an innovation they can get paid only a nominal sum, but if they elicit the cooperation of their bosses and then of their bosses' bosses and so on, the amount of the reward increases commensurately. Ordinarily managers' incomes are little more and sometimes less than those of semiskilled workers, so that money from innovations can be critical to maintaining their life-style.

36. Hedrick Smith, *The Russians* (London: Sphere Books, 1976), p. 282.

37. See, for example, Granick, *Soviet Metal-Fabricating and Economic Development;* Alec Nove, *The Soviet Economy* (New York: Praeger, 1965); Joseph Berliner, *Factory and Manager in the USSR* (Cambridge: Harvard University Press, 1957); Seeger, "Eye-witness to Failure"; Hillel Ticktin, "The Contradictions of Soviet Society and Professor Bettelheim," *Critique* 6 (1976): 17–44; and H. Smith, *The Russians*.

38. We would tentatively suggest that rush work is most likely to occur when there are both supply and demand constraints. Thus Mária Ladó and Ferenc Tóth describe rush work in an electronics firm with workers living in the factory and laboring around the clock in certain periods, while in others staying at home and undertaking second jobs. The firm was subject to intensive shortage of materials on the one side and the demand for punctual delivery on the other. ("Egy ipari üzem munkaszervezete—a hiányjelzésre épülö munkaszervezet [Labor Organization in an Industrial Shop—A Labor Process Based on Shortages]," manuscript, Munkaügyi Kutatóintézet, Budapest, 1982.) Usually socialist firms face weak demand constraints, but here the customer placed ex-

acting and politically enforced demands on the firm. In one of the most systematic studies of arrhythmical work, Mihály Laki comes to similar conclusions, namely that arrhythmical work is the result of accountability to the state, which generates both shortages and ministerial pressures to increase profits and sales. Where the demand constraints are particularly rigid, as in production for exports and investment goods, rush work is more pronounced. Particularly relevant to the discussion here are Laki's figures which suggest that rush work is not much more prevalent in socialist than in capitalist countries, although Hungary has one of the worst records. ("End-year Rush-work in Hungarian Industry and Foreign Trade," *Acta Oeconomica* 25 [1980]:37–65.)

39. David Dyker, "Planning and the Worker," in *The Soviet Worker*, ed. Schapiro and Godson, p. 57.

40. Szelényi, cited in Fehér, Heller, and Márkus, *Dictatorship over Needs*, p. 34.

41. Peter Wiles, "Wages and Incomes Policies," in *The Soviet Worker*, ed. Schapiro and Godson, p. 17.

42. Dyker, "Planning and the Worker," pp. 40–41.

43. See, for example, Randy Hodson and Robert L. Kaufman, "Economic Dualism: A Critical Review," *American Sociological Review* 47 (1982): 727–39; James Baron and William Bielby, "Bringing Firms Back In: Stratification, Segmentation, and the Organization of Work," *American Sociological Review* 45 (1980): 737–65, and "The Organization of Work in a Segmented Economy," *American Sociological Review* 49 (1984): 454–73; Arne Kalleberg, Michael Wallace, and Robert Althauser, "Economic Segmentation, Worker Power, and Income Inequality," *American Journal of Sociology* 87 (1981): 651–83; and Ivar Berg, ed., *Sociological Perspectives on Labor Markets* (New York: Academic Press, 1981).

44. See David Stark, "Rethinking Internal Labor Markets: New Insights from a Comparative Perspective," *American Sociological Review* 51 (1986): 492–504.

45. Turovsky, "Society without a Present," pp. 162–65.

46. For an account of the free play of the external labor market in Hungary, see Gábor and Galasi, "The Labour Market in Hungary since 1968," and Péter Galasi and György Sziráczki, "State Regulation, Enterprise Behaviour, and the Labour Market in Hungary, 1968–83," *Cambridge Journal of Economics* 9 (1985): 203–19. György Kövári and György Sziráczki describe the dilemma of an enterprise seeking to both attract new workers and keep old ones. In 1979 its strategy was to increase the basic wage for newcomers so that it approached that of the old-timers, and at the same time to uncouple actual earnings from basic wages. In this way, key workers could earn two to three times their basic wage, mainly through overtime, while new arrivals would struggle to make their basic wage. Five years later, facing an even worse labor shortage, the company introduced VGMKs in an attempt to retain the allegiance of core workers. The VGMKs not only provided earnings for workers but proved to be cheaper than the two alternatives: importing Polish guest workers and contracting work out.

(Kövári and Sziráczki, "Old and New Forms of Wage Bargaining on the Shop Floor," in *Labour Market and Second Economy in Hungary*, ed. Péter Galasi and György Sziráczki [Frankfurt: Campus Verlag, 1985], pp. 264–92.)

47. Károly Fazekas and János Köllö, "Fluctuations of Labour Shortage and State Intervention," in *Labour Market and Second Economy in Hungary*, ed. Péter Galasi and György Sziráczki (Frankfurt: Campus Verlag, 1985), pp. 42–69.

48. Polanyi, *The Great Transformation*.

49. Fehér, Heller, and Márkus, *Dictatorship over Needs*, p. 76.

50. Seeger, "Eye-witness to Failure," p. 105.

51. Michel Crozier, *The Bureaucratic Phenomenon* (Chicago: University of Chicago Press, 1963).

52. It is widely believed that Hungarian foremen have lost considerable power during the last thirty years and that they are the weakest link in the managerial hierarchy. Lukács argues that this is far from being the case in reality and emphasizes the continuing strength and centrality of the foreman in Hungarian industry. (János Lukács, "A müvezetök helye és szerepe munkaszervezeteinkben [The Place and Role of Foremen in Our Labor Organization]." Manuscript, Hungarian Academy of Sciences, Institute of Sociology, 1984.)

53. Lajos Héthy and Csaba Makó, *Munkások, érdekek, érdekegyeztetés [Workers, Interests, Reconciliation of Interests]* (Budapest: Gondolat, 1978).

54. Farkas, "Munkások érdek- és érdekeltségi viszonyai [Relations and Levels of Interest among Workers]"; Kövári and Sziráczki, "Old and New Forms of Wage Bargaining on the Shop Floor."

55. Mária Ladó and Ferenc Tóth, "A munkaszervezet centrumában—A centrális helyzet kialakulásának, újratermelödésének feltételei és következményei [At the Core of the Labor Organization—Conditions and Consequences of Formation and Reproduction of Core Positions in the Labor Process]" (manuscript, 1985).

56. György Sziráczki, "The Development and Functioning of an Enterprise Labour Market in Hungary," *Économies et Sociétés* 3–4 (1983): 517–47.

57. Csaba Makó, *Munkafolyamat: A társadalmi viszonyok erötere [The Labor Process: An Arena of Social Struggle]* (Budapest: Közgazdasági és Jogi Könyvkiadó, 1985); Gábor Kertesi and György Sziráczki, "Worker Behaviour in the Labour Market," in *Labour Market and Second Economy in Hungary*, ed. Péter Galasi and György Sziráczki (Frankfurt: Campus Verlag, 1985), pp. 216–46.

58. Michael Burawoy and Anne Smith, "The Rise of Hegemonic Despotism in U.S. Industry," *Prokla* 58 (1985): 139–53.

59. Fehér, Heller, and Márkus, *Dictatorship over Needs*, p. 178.

60. Makó (*Munkafolyamat: A társadalmi viszonyok erötere*) has termed this situation "quasi-bureaucracy." There are bureaucratic rules, but shop-floor workers and managers, instead of following them, exhibit a certain autonomy necessary for adaptation to production exigencies.

61. See also Edwards, *Contested Terrain*.

62. László Bruszt, "Központositás vagy mühely autonómia [Centralization

or Workplace Autonomy]" (manuscript, Institute of Sociology, Hungarian Academy of Sciences, 1984).

63. Chandler, *Strategy and Structure.*

64. Oliver Williamson, *Markets and Hierarchies* (New York: Free Press, 1975), and "The Modern Corporation: Origins, Evolution, Attributes," *Journal of Economic Literature* 19 (1981): 1537–68.

Introduction to Part Two

1. See Joanna Goven, "The Anti-Politics of Anti-Feminism: State Socialism and Gender Conservation in Hungary, 1945–1990" (Ph.D. diss., University of California, Berkeley, 1992). Lynne Haney makes a similar argument in her fascinating paper, "Privatization and Female Autonomy: The Hungarian Woman's Experience" (manuscript, University of California, Berkeley, 1990).

2. Indeed, the Hungarian state has taken advantage of popular support for "the private sphere" by encouraging the autonomy of the family, burdening it with social insurance functions and making it the crucible of the second economy. By overloading the family, the state was able to pay lower wages and reduce its expenditures on welfare programs. Inevitably, this led to soaring divorce rates as compared to the 1950s, when the state tried to regulate the family. In the early period of state socialism the state tried to use women as its agents for establishing a new domestic division of labor and a new code of sexual conduct. At that time women and particularly their "emancipation" came to symbolize the encroachment of the state into the private sphere. See Goven, "The Anti-Politics of Anti-Feminism."

Chapter Four: Production in a Shortage Economy

1. János Kornai, *The Economics of Shortage.*

2. See Michael Piore and Charles Sabel, *The Second Industrial Divide* (New York: Basic Books, 1984). In our view it is not surprising, therefore, that capitalist firms facing demand-side fluctuations turn to more effective control of supplies, as in the Japanese "just in time" system (Schonberger, 1982; Sayer, 1985), since these mechanisms establish the conditions under which the greatest centralization of control can occur. See Andrew Sayer, "New Developments in Manufacturing and Their Spatial Implications" (Working Paper, Urban and Regional Studies, University of Sussex, 1985), and Richard Schonberger, *Japanese Manufacturing Techniques* (New York: Free Press, 1982). Needless to say, we don't share the conventional picture of the Japanese factory as the center of creative autonomous work groups, but rather we see the much more coercive system described by Satoshi Kamata, *Japan in the Passing Lane* (New York: Basic Books, 1983); Robert Cole, *Japanese Blue Collar* (Berkeley and Los Angeles: University of California Press, 1971), chap. 7; and Muto Ichiyo, "Class Struggle on the Shop Floor—The Japanese Case," *AMPCO—Japan-Asia Quarterly Review* 16:3 (1984): 38–49.

3. For an excellent analysis of the way corporate culture is used to obtain the participation of middle managers in their own elimination, see Vicki Smith, *Managing in the Corporate Interest* (Berkeley: University of California Press, 1990).

4. Here we have been very influenced by the work of Iván Szelényi on the character of central appropriation, by the work of Tamás Bauer on plan bargaining, and by the work of János Kornai on the shortage economy. While we accept Kornai's criticism of equilibrium theory and his description of capitalism and socialism as suction and shortage economies respectively, we find his explanation of the differences inadequate. Focusing on hard and soft budget constraints obscures precisely the contributions of Szelényi and Bauer, namely the importance of the logics of appropriation and distribution in the two systems. See Szelényi, "The Intelligentsia in the Class Structure of State-Socialist Societies"; Bauer, "Investment Cycles in Planned Economies"; and Kornai, *The Economics of Shortage*.

5. Originally the scrap yard was fitted out with a computer system that would automatically register the amount of both heavy and light scrap charged. The idea was that the front end of the car that delivers the scrap would be filled with light scrap to cushion the impact of the heavy scrap at the rear when both hit the converter walls. In this way the converter would have a longer life. But shortage of scrap and of time, particularly due to program changes when the amount of scrap would be changed abruptly, made this sorting-out process infeasible. So the computer control system doesn't work; all scrap is registered manually and therefore is easily subject to manipulation. Similar manipulations take place in the case of the hot metal. The crane driver is responsible for registering the amount of hot metal. He can turn his counter to zero after there is already a few tons of hot metal in the ladle.

6. These experts came from a consulting firm linked to one of the biggest United States steel corporations. They had been sent to LKM at the insistence of the Ministry of Industry as part of the conditions for loans from the World Bank.

7. The careful following of heats from the point of steel production to their departure from the factory as finished steel is still not possible. We found it impossible to trace what happened to a given heat after it left the Combined Steel Works. Part of the problem is that because there are so many different steels being produced, parts of the same heat may end up in different places. Another problem, we were told, is that the storage yard contains so many different types of steel that it would be virtually impossible to locate a particular heat. And then there doesn't seem to be a careful recording of steel that is scrapped and returned to steel production.

8. See Donald F. Barnett and Robert W. Crandall, *Up from the Ashes* (Washington, D.C.: Brookings Institution, 1986), and Harland Prechel, "Capital Accumulation and Corporate Rationality: Organizational Change in an American Steel Corporation" (Ph.D. diss., University of Kansas, Lawrence, 1986).

9. Of course, there is the important proviso that self-organization is ineffec-

tive and perhaps counterproductive in the context of intense shortage, most likely to occur in peripheral sectors of state socialist economies or in the early period of taut planning in the Soviet Union. But as state socialism develops and the problem of shortages, while remaining, becomes less severe, so self-organization becomes a possible way of increasing technical efficiency.

10. Here one might also refer to the emergence of worker collectives, known as VGMKs, which are essentially systems of internal subcontracting made up of self-selected, self-organized groups of workers and managers paid for the completion of specific tasks. VGMKs can be found at LKM, but in declining numbers. In a fascinating article, David Stark underlines their simulation of rudimentary markets adapted to uncertainties generated in bureaucratic environments, whereas we regard them as signifying the requirements of self-organization on the shop floor. See Stark, "Rethinking Internal Labor Markets."

Chapter Five: Painting Socialism

1. For his successive class maps see Erik Olin Wright, *Class, Crisis, and the State* (London: Verso, 1978), chapter 2; *Classes* (London: Verso, 1985); and, for his most recent scheme, *The Debate on Classes* (London: Verso, 1989), chapter 8.

2. See, for example, Erik Olin Wright, "Women in the Class Structure," *Politics and Society* 17 (1989): 35–66, and Erik Olin Wright, Carolyn Howe, and Donmoon Cho, "Class Structure and Class Formation: A Comparative Analysis of the United States and Sweden," in *Cross-National Research in Sociology,* ed. Melvin Kohn (New York: Sage Publications, 1989).

3. See Adam Przeworski, *Capitalism and Social Democracy* (Cambridge: Cambridge University Press, 1985), and Adam Przeworski and John Sprague, *Paper Stones: A History of Electoral Socialism* (Chicago: University of Chicago Press, 1986). I have critically examined these works in Burawoy, "Marxism without Microfoundations," *Socialist Review* 89: 2 (1989): 53–86. Adam Przeworski replies in "Class, Production, and Politics: A Reply to Burawoy," *Socialist Review* 89: 2 (1989): 87–111.

4. Of course Przeworski is not alone in this tendency, which has been inspired by Edward Thompson. Although Thompson's book *The Making of the English Working Class* (New York: Vintage Books, 1963) did pay attention to the material conditions of exploitation, his overriding focus was on the language of class as an independent force. Others, such as William Sewell in his *Work and Revolution in France* (Cambridge: Cambridge University Press, 1980) and Gareth Stedman Jones in his *Languages of Class* (Cambridge: Cambridge University Press, 1983), have taken Thompson's cultural analysis even further from the realm of material production. What distinguishes Przeworski's work from this now-fashionable industry of discourse is its theoretical self-consciousness.

5. Also reacting against the teleology of class in itself to class for itself, but nevertheless wishing to retain some connection between the two, Ira Katznel-

son introduces two levels of analysis between "structure" and "collective action": "ways of life" and "dispositions." However, by multiplying the range of mediating institutions and allowing lived experience and consciousness to vary independently of each other, he makes the link between class structure and class formation so contingent as to be virtually nonexistent. See Katznelson, "Working Class Formation: Constructing Cases and Comparisons," in *Working Class Formation*, ed. Ira Katznelson and Aristide Zolberg (Princeton: Princeton University Press, 1986), pp. 3–44.

6. I have learned a great deal from several Berkeley students who have worked along similar lines. Jeffrey Haydu's *Between Craft and Class: Skilled Workers and Factory Politics in the United States and Britain, 1890–1922* (Berkeley: University of California Press, 1988) shows how factory regimes shaped the different patterns of mobilization among metal workers in England and the United States before World War I. Richard Biernacki's study of the textile industries in England and Germany shows how different cultural definitions of the commodity labor come to be inscribed in different factory regimes, leading to different forms of protest and, by extension, to different national labor movements (Biernacki, "The Cultural Construction of Labor: A Comparison of Textile Mills in England and Germany" [Ph.D. diss., University of California, Berkeley, 1988]). Soon Kyoung Cho shows how despotic factory regimes in the electronics industry in South Korea tend to mobilize women workers into a collective force, whereas the hegemonic regimes of the Silicon Valley fragment and atomize the work force. See Cho, "The Labor Process and Capital Mobility: The Limits of the New International Division of Labor," *Politics and Society* 14: 2 (1985): 185–222. Linda Fuller has shown how factory regimes can change within state socialism, allowing greater autonomy from the central directing apparatuses and greater participation for workers. (Fuller, *The Politics of Workers' Control in Cuba, 1959–1983: The Work Center and the National Arena* [Philadelphia: Temple University Press, 1992].)

7. Jadwiga Staniszkis is one of the few analysts sensitive to the different interests of intellectuals and workers. Rather than arguing that self-limitation emerged spontaneously from the working class, she suggests that Solidarity's "expert" advisers, acting as conduits for governmental restraint, were responsible for retaining "the leading role of the party" in the preamble to the first agreement. More generally, they engineered the "shift from radical anti-bureaucratic and anti-hierarchical semantics . . . toward liberal semantics underlining human rights problems, but relatively less radical in relation to the political framework existing in Poland." (Staniszkis, *Poland's Self-Limiting Revolution* [Princeton: Princeton University Press, 1984], p. 49.) Her conclusion is that Solidarity, rather than forging an alliance with oppositional intellectuals or the Roman Catholic church, should have joined forces with the burgeoning antibureaucratic forces within the party, including the so-called "horizontalist" movement. This was never seriously entertained because of Solidarity's "fundamentalist" hostility to the party.

8. These themes are emphasized by most accounts of Solidarity. They come across forcibly in the recollections of worker activists and observers from the Baltic Coast region. A number of these reports appeared in English in *Sisyphus* 3 (1982): 252–309. They highlight the importance of the religious symbolism and above all religious rituals, such as the Mass, which maintained the confidence and faith of the workers through the difficult first two weeks of the strikes. The language of class had been appropriated by the dominant class and the party apparatus so that workers drew on their common historical culture but particularly on the language of religion to cement their solidarity. In addition, the reports describe the subjection of party secretaries and trade union officers to public humiliation while, at the same time, rank-and-file party members were often leading activists in Solidarity. Workers also expressed a suspicion of intellectuals, even members of KOR, the Committee in Defense of Workers. Not just critical of hierarchy and bureaucracy, workers set up the basis of democratic representation and participation, often taking them to obsessive lengths.

9. See, for example, Stanislaw Starski, *Class Struggle in Classless Poland* (Boston: South End Press, 1982), pp. 167–245. The socialist project comes out most clearly in the program adopted by the delegates to Solidarity's national congress at the beginning of October, 1981. Although there was no reference to socialism and although Solidarity's cultural platform was stridently nationalist rather than internationalist, the program nevertheless included the defense of working-class interests both in production and in consumption, a commitment to social policies which would ensure minimum standards of living and above all equality, and economic reforms which combined planning, self-management, and market. The overall objective was a self-governing republic based on institutions of self-management as well as of a liberal democracy. See *Labor Focus* 5: 1–2 (Spring 1982): 3–14.

10. Gramsci insisted that the occupation and transformation of trade unions, church, party, school, and press—that is, the institutions of civil society—was a necessary part of socialist strategy in capitalist societies of the twentieth century. But he never abandoned the idea that the conquest of civil society would have to be followed by the seizure of state power if any revolutionary transformation was to be successful. Given Poland's geopolitical situation, Solidarity leaders attempted to avoid this last phase at all costs, always insisting that they were not a party. See, for example, Jacek Kuron, "Not to Lure the Wolves out of the Woods: An Interview with Jacek Kuron," *Telos* 47 (Spring 1981): 93–97.

11. Timothy Garton Ash, *The Polish Revolution: Solidarity* (New York: Vintage Books, 1985), p. 4. See also Norman Davies's lucid attempt to read Solidarity back into Polish history, *Heart of Europe* (Oxford: Oxford University Press, 1986). Undoubtedly Polish oppositional intellectuals, such as Adam Michnik, publicly drew lessons from Polish collective memory in their political speeches. But the question remains, how is it that the Poles have been able to sustain and

deepen their collective national consciousness, whereas in other countries (such as Hungary) with similar histories, the national consciousness is less prominent and has failed to galvanize social movements?

12. For economic deprivation see Ian Shapiro, "Fiscal Crisis of the Polish State: Genesis of the 1980 Strikes," *Theory and Society* 10:4 (1981): 469–502, and for resource mobilization see Elisabeth Crighton, "Resource Mobilizaton and Solidarity: Comparing Social Movements across Regimes," in *Poland after Solidarity: Social Movements versus the State*, ed. Bronislaw Misztal (New Brunswick: Transaction Books, 1985), pp. 113–32.

13. Colin Barker, *Festival of the Oppressed: Solidarity, Reform, and Revolution in Poland, 1980–81* (London: Bookmarks, 1986). The same is true of the "state collectivist" view. Michael Szkolny, for example, argues that the regime has "conceptually embezzled" the essential ideological weapon that could be used by the working class to threaten the social order—socialism and Marxism. While the church has provided the basis for constructing Solidarity in the face of a totalitarian power, it has not created the language for overcoming conceptual embezzlement. So how can Szkolny account for the rise of such a powerful working-class movement in a "state collectivist" society? Here he substitutes historical narrative for sociological explanation. See Szkolny, "Revolution in Poland," *Monthly Review* 33:2 (June 1981): 1–21.

14. Alain Touraine, François Dubet, Michel Wieviorka, and Jan Strzelecki, *Solidarity: Poland, 1980–81* (Cambridge: Cambridge University Press, 1983). See also Grzegorz Bakuniak and Krzysztof Nowak, "The Creation of a Collective Identity in a Social Movement: The Case of 'Solidarność' in Poland," *Theory and Society* 16:3 (May 1987): 401–29.

15. Andrew Arato, "Civil Society vs. the State," *Telos* 47 (Spring 1981): 23–47 and "Empire vs. Civil Society," *Telos* 50 (Winter 1981–82): 19–48.

16. For a different use of the concept of corporatism, see Staniszkis, *Poland's Self-Limiting Revolution*, chapters 1 and 2.

17. Misztal, "Social Movements against the State: Theoretical Legacy of the Welfare State," in *Poland after Solidarity: Social Movements versus the State*, ed. Bronislaw Misztal (New Brunswick, N.J.: Transaction Books, 1985), pp. 143–64.

18. Staniszkis, *Poland's Self-Limiting Revolution*, chapter 1.

19. Adam Michnik, "A New Evolutionism," in *Letters from Prison and Other Essays* (Berkeley: University of California Press, 1985), pp. 135–48. See also Ivan Svitak, "Comparisons," *Telos* 47 (Spring 1981): 110–12. Much earlier, Leszek Kolakowski, in a famous and prophetic article, defended the possibility of reforming "bureaucratic socialism" from within and opposed those who saw real change as emerging only through revolution. He suggested how a movement for democratization might exploit the tensions and contradictions of the post-Stalinist regime. See Kolakowski, "Hope and Hopelessness," *Survey* 17:3 (Summer 1971): 37–52.

20. Two of the most influential accounts of the class character of state socialism deny the possibility of an independent workers' movement. In *The Alterna-*

tive in Eastern Europe, Rudolf Bahro goes so far as to dismiss the very concept of the working class: "The concept of the working class has no longer any definable object in our social system, and, what is far more important, it has no object that can appear as a unity in practical action. . . . Our society is no longer characterized by a 'horizontal' class division, but rather by a 'vertical' stratification. . . . Deprived of these associations which are adapted to their immediate interests, the workers are automatically atomized vis-à-vis the regime. They are in any case no longer a 'class for itself,' and not at all so in a political sense" (pp. 183–84, 190). In *The Intellectuals on the Road to Class Power*, György Konrád and Iván Szelényi, although far from denying the existence of a working class, regard class consciousness as unattainable without the aid of intellectuals: "Not only do they [intellectuals] refuse to foster the culture of other classes; their monopoly is even stricter than that, for they appropriate and absorb the culture of other classes and strata or, failing that, disparage them. In this way they prevent the working class (for example) from becoming conscious of its own identity in its present structural position" (p. 249). However, in his most recent book, *Socialist Entrepreneurs* (Madison: University of Wisconsin Press, 1988), Szelényi introduces what he calls a "praxis centered" notion of class in which class struggle refers to the ubiquitous everyday struggle for survival. Intellectuals are no longer central to the development of class struggle, but this new concept of class is too general to be of any analytical use.

21. Ironically, in July 1980 a joke actually circulated in Warsaw: "Those who do not strike do not eat meat." (Daniel Singer, *The Road to Gdansk* [New York: Monthly Review Press, 1982], p. 212.) At this point the regime was handing out wage increases to all who struck, fueling the militancy of the workers.

22. The perspective of oppositional intellectuals was more supportive of Solidarity. See Miklós Haraszti, "Hungarian Perspectives," *Telos* 47 (Spring 1981): 142–52.

23. The average number of man-hours worked per ton of finished steel in Hungary has remained relatively constant at about 25, compared with 8.6 in the United States (1978). The 1978 figures for other countries are as follows: Japan, 9.8; West Germany, 11.8; United Kingdom, 23.2; France, 14.2. See *Technology and Steel Industry Competitiveness* (Washington, D.C.: U.S. Department of Commerce, Office of Technology Assessment, 1980), p. 138. Since then figures have fallen even further so that in the United Kingdom the figure is 7.1 in 1984–85. See *Report and Accounts 1984–85* (London: British Steel Corporation, 1985), p. 6. One should note that labor costs per ton look very different since the hourly compensation of an American steelworker is thirty to forty times that of a Hungarian steelworker at official exchange rates.

24. In the fall of 1986 the last Martins were closed down and all the pig iron from the blast furnaces was directed to the Combined Steel Works. This led to more heats being produced per shift; we were averaging between nine and twelve in the summer of 1987. In 1988 the closure of one of the three blast furnaces, the shortage of iron ore and scrap, and the falling demand for steel led to a decline in the number of heats per shift.

25. In 1987, under pressure to reduce hard currency expenditures (the bricks came from Austria), a few experiments were made to try to extend the life of the lining. By following what is standard practice in other plants, that is, by adding magnesium oxide to the fluxing agents, it was possible to protect the wall. The number of heats per lining rose from six or seven hundred to twelve or thirteen hundred.

26. Paul Rabinow, *Reflections on Fieldwork in Morocco* (Berkeley: University of California Press, 1977), p. 6.

27. I didn't realize that I was following in the footsteps of the steelworkers of Huta Warszawa, who defied martial law by painting the red star above their gate black (Ash, *The Polish Revolution*, p. 304).

28. The situation has changed quite dramatically since 1985. When I first worked at the Lenin Steel Works, Hungary was still being touted as the economic miracle of Eastern Europe. Now its economic situation is viewed more as a disaster, saddled as it is with an international debt that is said to be over fifteen billion dollars. In 1988 the dramatic turnover of personnel in the Central Committee and Politburo, the replacement of Kádár by Grósz as first party secretary, and *perestroika* in the Soviet Union have launched a new phase of economic reform in Hungary which further elevates market forces within the state sector. So there are now plans to drastically cut down production at Ózd and consolidate it with the Lenin Steel Works. At the time of writing (1988), the most widely rumored plan would cost six thousand workers their jobs at Ózd, with little hope of gaining new employment there or elsewhere. In the words of an official from the Hungarian Chamber of Commerce, this would create unprecedented social tensions.

29. I am here borrowing from János Kornai, *The Economics of Shortage*. Kornai argues against equilibrium theory, in which supply balances demand. Instead he distinguishes hierarchical economies in which demand exceeds supply and market economies where supply exceeds demand. In the former, what he calls the shortage economy, enterprises do not confront stringent or "hard" budget constraints but "soft" budget constraints. The state adopts a paternalistic policy toward enterprises, protecting them against bankruptcy. On the other hand, in the surplus or market economies, enterprises face hard budget constraints and their survival depends on their profitability, defined by prices.

30. Mine is not a conventional understanding of the effects of ritual. In the Durkheimian tradition, rituals are viewed as building solidarity, inculcating the norms of society. See, for example, Victor Turner, *The Ritual Process: Structure and Anti-Structure* (London: Routledge and Kegan Paul, 1969). More recently, following Foucault, anthropologists have focused on ritual as the exercise of power. From this viewpoint E. M. Simmonds-Duke undertakes a fascinating analysis of the Rumanian bicentennial celebrations of a peasant uprising in Transylvania. The bicentennial becomes the occasion for a public debate, ostensibly about the uprising itself but more profoundly a struggle over competing definitions of national identity and socialism. As in the painting of socialism, the elaborate festivities were orchestrated by local officials for their own instru-

mental interests, and not imposed from above. But in Simmonds-Duke's account the regime elicits willing and enthusiastic participation at all levels of society. This makes the public ceremony more effective as a display of power in a weak state. By embodying a hierarchy of levels of participation in the debates, the ritual inculcates the experience of subordination. In Foucault's analysis, however, as in painting socialism, such ritual affirmation could and actually did become the occasion for collective resistance to the sovereign's power. This suggests that the ideological effects of ritual depend on the contexts in which they are enacted. While people may consent to the monopoly of intellectuals and party ideologues over pronouncements on the interpretation of history, the inspection of the steelworks by the prime minister only elicited dissent. In Hungary's more open and permissive political atmosphere, such public rituals excite greater resistance than in a country where repression is both more intensive and more extensive. The manifest message of the ritual itself might also be important. This was, after all, a nationalist celebration of a local hero rather than a proclamation of the virtues of socialism. See E. M. Simmonds-Duke, "Was the Peasant Uprising a Revolution? The Meanings of a Struggle over the Past," *East European Politics and Societies* 1 (1987): 187–224.

31. See the fascinating work of David Stark on these VGMKs. He sees them as the counterpart to internal labor markets in the capitalist firm, as forms of market adaptation to the exigencies of state socialist production. See Stark, "Rethinking Internal Labor Markets," and Stark, "Coexisting Organizational Forms in Hungary's Emerging Mixed Economy," in *Remaking the Economic Institutions of Socialism*, ed. Victor Nee and David Stark (Stanford: Stanford University Press, 1989), pp. 137–68.

32. This was in 1986. In 1987 he was promoted to operator, but early in 1988 he left with his wife for East Germany to seek work there. Notwithstanding the relatively high pay he received, he couldn't find any reasonable accommodation in Miskolc and didn't think he had much future in the steel mill.

33. One is reminded of Václav Havel's wonderful essay "The Power of the Powerless," wherein he asks why a greengrocer would place in his shop window the slogan "Workers of the World Unite!" See Václav Havel et al., *The Power of the Powerless* (London: Hutchinson, 1985), pp. 23–96. He describes the greengrocer's act as a token of subordination, a lie in which each has to participate, but in participating makes it possible for the lie to go on. Everyone is simultaneously victim and supporter of the system. As an expression of ideology within a system of power, the ritual allows individuals a minimal dignity. Ideology becomes the dictatorship of the ritual. The world of appearances tries to pass for reality, but in the process disengages itself from reality. This very imposition of ideology establishes the ground for an alternative; the lie produces the truth: "Living the truth is thus woven directly into the texture of living a lie. It is the repressed alternative, the authentic aim to which living a lie is an inauthentic response. Only against this background does living a lie make any sense: it exists *because* of that background" (p. 41). Havel's "truth" is an intellectual's. It is revealed in the dissident's refusal to accept the tissue of lies, in upholding

the law and cracking its facade, and in the second culture. The life aims of workers, on the other hand, tend toward an alternative vision of truth, equality, self-organization, and liberation from work.

34. After the strikes of 1976 the Polish government sought to elicit loyalty to itself and condemnation of strikers and their supporters by organizing mass rallies. These public rituals effectively consolidated the negative class consciousness of workers, laying the foundation for the positive class consciousness that developed during 1980 and 1981. See Bakuniak and Nowak, "The Creation of a Collective Identity in a Social Movement," p. 410.

35. In the United States there is also the juxtaposition of what Brian Powers calls "rituals" and "routines." In his analysis of a working-class high school he shows how students cling to the ideology of success, celebrated in such rituals as the graduation ceremony, while knowing that their chances of upward mobility are bleak. He shows how, even after they leave, they continue to cling to the possibility of making it, even as they fail. I am reminded of Czeslaw Milosz' account (see n. 36 below) of how Polish intellectuals after World War II were prepared to embrace the "Soviet" road to socialism, to participate in the painting of socialism even as they recognized its denial in reality. Thus, it is significant that the early opposition movements, led by intellectuals, always sought to work through the party. It was only in 1968 with the repression of students and intellectuals in Poland and the invasion of Czechoslovakia that many intellectuals finally lost faith in the revisionist route. Workers, on the other hand, with very different class experiences from the very beginning of state socialism, must have always found it much more difficult to bridge the chasm between what is and what was supposed to be, between their ideological status as "ruling class" and their real status as "subordinate class." For them the painting of socialism is a much more profound lie than is the ideology of success for working-class kids in the United States. See Brian Powers, "Second Class Finish: The Effects of Rituals and Routines in a Working Class High School" (Ph.D. diss., University of California, Berkeley, 1987).

36. Czeslaw Milosz, *The Captive Mind* (Harmondsworth, England: Penguin Books, 1985), pp. 79–82.

37. Milosz claims that the experiences of intellectuals can be generalized to the entire population: "Since the fate of millions is often most apparent in those who by profession note changes in themselves and in others, i.e. writers, a few portraits of typical Eastern European writers may serve as concrete examples of what is happening within the Imperium" (*The Captive Mind*, p. 82). Similarly, Kenneth Jowitt's analysis of adaptive responses generated by and subversive of Soviet regimes does not distinguish between classes. He stresses the development of instrumental, calculative, and often dissimulative approaches to the official sphere of life, undermining the values of equality, democracy, methodical economic action based on scientific planning, etc. It is clear that such individualistic responses are by no means universal, and the responses of intellectuals can be very different from those of workers. See Kenneth Jowitt, "An Organizational Approach to the Study of Political Culture in Marxist-Leninist

Systems," and "Soviet Neotraditionalism: The Political Corruption of a Leninist Regime."

38. Again in 1988, union and management agreed to introduce an automatic checkoff system whereby union dues were deducted directly from a person's pay. So now the union is even less responsive to the rank and file, since shop stewards no longer have to cajole and persuade their members to make their monthly contribution. This dovetails well with the renewed offensive against labor.

39. A more detailed analysis of these tensions can be found in chapter 4.

40. I don't want to suggest that management was unconcerned about accidents. Quite the contrary. A fatal accident was a major blemish on a manager's record and could eat away his bonus, a major part of his income. But given the pressure workers are under and the conditions of work, accidents are inevitable.

41. Gyuri would never again have anything to do with the official union. He would spearhead the drive to establish workers' councils in the Combined Steel Works.

42. Management's attitude is captured by a slogan plastered on the wall in the plant superintendent's office: "At work—dictatorship; in public life—democracy."

43. In 1988 Karcsi was finding it much more difficult to make a lot of money. Buying damaged piglets and raising them was no longer so remunerative. Feed had become more expensive, and there was more competition as more and more people entered all lines of business. And then on top of that he would now have to pay taxes on any profits he made. In 1988 he again went on his three-yearly trip to Western Europe. He brought back with him today's status symbol, a videocassette player. Since, after customs duties, the price difference between goods bought abroad and those bought at home is much less than it was even three years ago, there is not much profit to be gained from reselling articles purchased in Germany. Competition has created a new class of entrepreneurs who increasingly dominate the private sector, while workers find it more and more difficult to make money on the side. As Iván Szelényi has argued for the case of housing, opening up the market initially operates to the advantage of workers, countering the inequalities of administrative allocation, but subsequently the distributional inequalities of state and market tend to reinforce each another. See Iván Szelényi, *Urban Social Inequalities under State Socialism* (Oxford: Oxford University Press, 1985).

44. Some might argue that the rituals of the Japanese factory constitute a painting of capitalism. This would excite an imminent critique of Japanese capitalism for not being sufficiently capitalist. It would counteract any tendencies, always weak in capitalism, for the lived experience of work to generate an interest in socialism.

45. I have borrowed this formulation from Martha Lampland, "Working through History: Ideologies of Work and Agricultural Production in a Hungarian Village, 1918–1983" (Ph.D. diss., University of Chicago, 1987), chapter 3.

46. Here I have been very influenced by the work of Paul Johnston. See his "Politics of Public Work" (Ph.D. diss., University of California, Berkeley, 1988).

47. See Burawoy, "Should We Give Up on Socialism? Reflections on Bowles and Gintis' *Democracy and Capitalism,*" *Socialist Review* 89:1 (1989): 59–76. For Sam Bowles and Herb Gintis's reply, see "Democratic Demands and Radical Rights," *Socialist Review* 89:4 (1989): 57–72.

48. That jokes are such a pervasive form of communication is itself testimony to the gulf between appearances and reality. Jokes are the most effective way of capturing the double existence of workers: the opposition between ideological and real experiences. In capitalism, ideology is more diffuse and enjoined to reality more smoothly, so jokes are not so central to the discourse of daily life. See, for example, the preponderance of jokes about socialism in Steven Lukes and Itzhak Galnoor, *No Laughing Matter* (London: Routledge and Kegan Paul, 1985).

Chapter Six: The Radiant Future

1. I say *mankind* advisedly, since much of the anticommunist agitation has gone along with an equally vehement endorsement of the patriarchal family.

2. It has become a cliché to criticize Lenin for his neglect of individual rights. One of his earliest and most eloquent critics was Rosa Luxemburg, who argued that there can be no radical democracy without the protection of bourgeois rights. See Rosa Luxemburg, "The Russian Revolution" (1918), in *Rosa Luxemburg Speaks,* ed. Alice Waters (New York: Pathfinder, 1970). For more contemporary criticisms, see A. J. Polan, *Lenin and the End of Politics* (Berkeley: University of California Press, 1984), and Steven Lukes, *Marxism and Morality* (Oxford: Oxford University Press, 1985).

3. For an excellent description and analysis of the miners' strikes in the Ukraine, see Theodore Friedgut and Lewis Siegelbaum, "Perestroika from Below: The Soviet Miners' Strike and Its Aftermath," *New Left Review* 181 (May–June 1990): 5–32.

4. See László Bruszt, "1989: The Negotiated Revolution in Hungary," *Social Research* 57 (1990): 365–87. Ellen Comisso argues that the difference between Poland's and Hungary's negotiated transitions lay in the presence of Solidarity—an established alternative to the Communist party which was absent in Hungary. "It is this that perhaps explains why the PUWP [Polish United Workers' Party] stood firm for so long in the face of mass opposition while the Hungarian party, confronted with the demands of a few thousand intellectuals, conceded virtually everything" (Comisso, "Crisis in Socialism or Crisis of Socialism," *World Politics* 42 [1990]: 570).

5. Many writers believe that the socialist economy is inherently unreformable. János Kornai, for example, argues that the root of the problem lies in soft budget constraints, and that any attempt to harden them without changing ownership relations is doomed to failure. See Kornai, *The Economics of Short-*

age, and "The Hungarian Reform Process: Visions, Hopes, and Reality," *Journal of Economic Literature* 24 (1986): 1687–1737. Ellen Comisso argues similarly that the obstacles to the economic reform of state socialism lie not in politics but in the economy itself, which generates allocational inefficiencies, cannot create an effective capital market, suffers from principal-agent problems in the relationship of the state to enterprise managers, and fails to effectively increase productivity. See Comisso, "Market Failures and Market Socialism: Economic Problems of the Transition," *Eastern European Politics and Societies* 2 (1988): 433–65. This may be true, but all economic systems—capitalism just as much as state socialism—suffer from distinctive irrationalities. Commentators on state socialism have always preferred to emphasize the irrationality of socialism, as though the alternative was a rational capitalism. Adam Przeworski ("Can We Feed the World? The Irrationality of Capitalism and the Infeasibility of Socialism," *Politics and Society* 19:1 [1991]: 1–38) recognizes the fallacy of such arguments and instead contrasts the irrationality of capitalism with the infeasibility of socialism. But if we are talking about blueprints, then capitalism is no more feasible than socialism, and if we are talking about models, socialism is no less irrational than capitalism. Either we develop serious parallel models which highlight the irrationalities of each, or we dispense with such static models and build dynamic models of state socialism. Some of the most interesting work in this area is being done by Péter Galasi and Gábor Kertesi. They show that bribery is inherent in a shortage economy and results in declining quality of goods and services for nonbribers. Once bribery begins, it is, therefore, in the interests of everyone to bribe, but only up to a limiting point, namely, when nonbribers no longer receive a minimal level of quality. At this point there is no advantage to bribing and one might say (although they don't) that the system is on the verge of collapse. Galasi and Kertesi apply their models with some success to health services and housing construction. See "Corruption and Ownership: A Study in Property Rights Theory" and "Side Payment and Selective Advantages in an Economy Dominated by the State" (manuscripts, Department of Labor Economics, Karl Marx University, Budapest, 1990).

6. See Rupp, *Entrepreneurs in Red;* Nigel Swain, *Collective Farms Which Work?* (Cambridge: Cambridge University Press, 1985); and Szelényi, *Socialist Entrepreneurs.*

7. See David Stark, "Rethinking Internal Labor Markets," and László Neumann, "A VGMK és az intézményes érdekegyeztetés [The VGMK and the Institutional Coordination of Interests]," *Közgazdasági Szemle* 10 (1987): 1217–228.

8. There were over forty parties competing in the elections. In the end, only six received seats in parliament: the Democratic Forum with 25 percent of the vote and 165 seats; the Free Democrats with 21 percent of the vote but only 92 seats; the Independent Smallholders with 12 percent of the vote and 43 seats; the Socialists (reform communists) with 11 percent of the vote and 33 seats; the Young Democrats (allies of SZDSZ) with 9 percent of the vote and 21 seats; and the Christian Democrats with 7 percent of the vote and 21 seats. Once parlia-

ment opened, the parties organized themselves into two major coalitions, one around the governing party (MDF) and the other around the opposition party (SZDSZ). Within the two major parties there are, of course, different tendencies. Within the SZDSZ, for example, there is an important social democratic wing.

9. This was, of course, not the only issue that divided the two parties. The SZDSZ accused the MDF of endangering relations with neighboring countries by their nationalist fervor, while the MDF accused the SZDSZ of bolshevism in the way they wanted to impose their vision of the capitalist future on Hungary. In this accusation the MDF was also referring to the communist past of some of the leading members of the SZDSZ.

10. One analysis of voting based on opinion polls taken after the elections argues that the high rates of nonvoting (35 percent in the first round and 55 percent in the second round) were in part the result of working-class abstention, which in turn pointed to the absence of a viable social democratic platform. See Tamás Kolosi, Iván Szelényi, Szonja Szelényi, and Bruce Western, "The Making of Political Fields in the Post-Communist Transition: Dynamics of Class and Party in Hungarian Politics, 1989–1990" (paper presented at the annual meeting of the American Sociological Association, Washington, D.C., 1990).

11. The official exchange rate rose from about forty-five forints to the dollar in 1988 to sixty forints to the dollar in 1990.

12. A new law came into effect in 1990 which slightly changed the composition of the enterprise council. Originally, 50 percent of its members were elected by employees and 50 percent were appointed by the general director, who was not a voting member. Now 50 percent plus one of its members are to be elected while the majority of the remaining slots are automatically filled by top managers, leaving only a minority appointed by the general director. In the elections of 1990 an unexpectedly low number (about 15 percent) of enterprise directors lost their jobs. Since certain ownership rights are still invested in the enterprise council, many have been arguing for "renationalization," bringing state enterprises under stronger central control so as to coordinate privatization. Others see the enterprise council as a temporary management body which will cease to exist as soon as privatization has occurred. See Vedat Milor, "Hungary: The Political Economy of Ownership Reform" (manuscript, World Bank, 1990); and *Hungary Today* 2:9 (September 1990): 2–3.

13. Ellen Comisso has argued that one of the most important obstacles to the transition to capitalism is the legacy of communal ownership in which individuals and groups had the right to freely use property as they wished. In this system of property rights, might determined right, and the party state through its monopoly of coercion was able to dictate the appropriate use of property. The collapse of the party state and the installation of democracy does not itself hand over property rights to actors with purely economic responsibilities, which is the basis of capitalism. Indeed, without a transition to private property, Comisso argues, many of the pathologies of the old regime are exacerbated under the new regime. See Ellen Comisso, "Property Rights, Liberalism, and

the Transition from 'Actually Existing' Socialism," *East European Politics and Societies* (forthcoming).

14. Originally the SPA was to have an executive director and a board of eleven directors. Six of these would be elected by parliament and five nominated by the following interest groups—employers' associations, trade unions, environmental protection agencies, social security agencies, and state holding companies. This was changed by the new government so that the eleven members are made up of seven government officials, three selected by the opposition parties, and one independent. The board is now less representative of different interests in society. More important, even though the board meets once every two weeks, the transactions it is supposed to examine are so full of technical details that most of the power resides with the staff of the SPA, and particularly its director. In September 1990, the transformation law was further altered to give even more control to the SPA. Originally, the shares owned by the state in enterprises undergoing privatization were nonvoting shares. These have been changed to voting shares, giving the SPA much greater power over the transformation process. Second, the SPA decides autonomously whether to accept or reject a transformation plan submitted by the enterprise council. If it rejects the plan then it tenders offers from other bidders for the privatization of the company. In its attempt to reduce the power of enterprise managers, the state has strengthened its hold over the transformation of the economy.

15. See, for example, Erzsébert Szalai, "Systemic or Elitist Change" (manuscript, Budapest, 1990).

16. Ellen Comisso, "Workers' Councils and Labor Unions: Some Objective Trade-Offs," *Politics and Society* 10 (1981): 251–79.

17. Originally, there were three national organizations: one which traced itself back to the 1956 workers' councils, another which was linked to the political grouping known as the "Left Alternative," and a third linked to the MDF. At the end of 1990 only the last two continued to exist.

18. The locus classicus of this literature is Guillermo O'Donnell and Philippe C. Schmitter, *Transitions from Authoritarian Rule: Tentative Conclusions about Uncertain Democracies* (Baltimore: Johns Hopkins University Press, 1986).

19. See Adam Przeworski, "Some Problems in the Study of the Transition to Democracy," in *Transitions from Authoritarian Rule: Comparative Perspectives*, vol. 3, ed. Guillermo O'Donnell, Philippe Schmitter, and Laurence Whitehead (Baltimore: Johns Hopkins University Press, 1986), and "The Games of Transition" (manuscript, University of Chicago, 1990).

20. For studies of such collapse which stress the failure of dominant classes to constitute a hegemonic bloc with a hegemonic project, see David Abraham, *The Collapse of the Weimar* (Princeton: Princeton University Press, 1981), and Kathleen Schwartzman, *The Social Origins of Democratic Collapse* (Lawrence: University of Kansas Press, 1989).

21. See Alejandro Foxley, "After Authoritarianism: Political Alternatives," in *Development Democracy and the Art of Trespassing*, ed. Alejandro Foxley, Mi-

chael McPherson, and Guillermo O'Donnell (Notre Dame, Ind.: Notre Dame University Press, 1986), pp. 191–216.

22. See Szelényi, *Socialist Entrepreneurs*.

23. János Kornai, *The Road to the Free Economy: Shifting from a Socialist System, the Example of Hungary* (New York: W. W. Norton, 1990).

24. David Stark, "Privatization in Hungary: From Plan to Market or from Plan to Clan?" *East European Politics and Societies* 4 (1990): 351–392.

25. There are, of course, all sorts of problems with employee ownership, if only because of the irrationality of the capitalist order in which it operates. Pointing to its specific inefficiencies does not by itself detract from its value, since all solutions have their inefficiencies. Too often the argument against employee ownership is based on an illusory model of capitalism that exists nowhere but in the head of an economist. For a discussion of the various alternative strategies of transition, including employee ownership, see Stark, "Privatization in Hungary," and Milor, "Hungary: The Political Economy of Ownership Reform." For a detailed proposal for implementing an employee stock ownership plan for Hungary, see János Lukács, "Employee Stock Ownership Programme: Basic Principles of the Concept of Regulation" (manuscript, Rész-Vétel, November 1990).

Bibliography

Abraham, David. *The Collapse of the Weimar*. Princeton: Princeton University Press, 1981.

Aglietta, Michel. *A Theory of Capitalist Regulation—The U.S. Experience*. London: Verso, 1979.

Andrle, Vladimir. *Workers in Stalin's Russia*. New York: St. Martin's Press, 1988.

Arato, Andrew. "Civil Society vs. the State." *Telos* 47 (Spring 1981): 23–47.

———. "Empire vs. Civil Society." *Telos* 50 (Winter 1981–82): 19–48.

Ash, Timothy Garton. *The Polish Revolution: Solidarity*. New York: Vintage Books, 1985.

Asselain, Jean-Charles. *Planning and Profits in Socialist Economies*. London: Routledge and Kegan Paul, 1981.

Bahro, Rudolf. *The Alternative in Eastern Europe*. London: Verso, 1978.

Bakuniak, Grzegorz, and Krzysztof Nowak. "The Creation of a Collective Identity in a Social Movement: The Case of Solidarność' in Poland." *Theory and Society* 16:3 (May 1987): 401–29.

Barker, Colin. *Festival of the Oppressed: Solidarity, Reform, and Revolution in Poland, 1980–81*. London: Bookmarks, 1986.

Barnett, Donald F., and Robert W. Crandall. *Up from the Ashes*. Washington, D.C.: Brookings Institution, 1986.

199

Barnett, Donald, and Louis Schorsch. *Steel: Upheaval in a Basic Industry.* Cambridge, Mass.: Ballinger, 1983.

Baron, James, and William Bielby. "Bringing Firms Back In: Stratification, Segmentation, and the Organization of Work." *American Sociological Review* 45 (1980): 737–65.

———. "The Organization of Work in a Segmented Economy." *American Sociological Review* 49 (1984): 454–73.

Bauer, Tamás. "Investment Cycles in Planned Economies." *Acta Oeconomica* 21 (1978): 243–60.

Bendix, Reinhard. *Work and Authority in Industry.* New York: John Wiley, 1956.

Berg, Ivar, ed. *Sociological Perspectives on Labor Markets.* New York: Academic Press, 1981.

Bergson, Abram. "Comparative Productivity and Efficiency in the USA and the USSR." In *Comparison of Economic Systems,* edited by Alexander Eckstein. Berkeley: University of California Press, 1971.

Berliner, Joseph. *Factory and Manager in the USSR.* Cambridge: Harvard University Press, 1957.

———. *The Innovation Decision in Soviet Industry.* Cambridge: MIT Press, 1976.

———. "Managerial Incentives and Decision Making: A Comparison of the United States and the Soviet Union." In *Comparative Economic Systems,* edited by Morris Bornstein. Homewood, Ill.: Richard D. Irwin, 1974.

Bettelheim, Charles. *Economic Calculation and Forms of Property.* London: Routledge and Kegan Paul, 1976.

Biernacki, Richard. "The Cultural Construction of Labor: A Comparison of Textile Mills in England and Germany." Ph.D. diss., University of California, Berkeley, 1988.

Bowles, Samuel, and Herbert Gintis. "Democratic Demands and Radical Rights." *Socialist Review* 89:4 (1989): 57–72.

Braverman, Harry. *Labor and Monopoly Capital.* New York: Monthly Review Press, 1974.

British Steel Corporation. *Report and Accounts 1984–85.* London: British Steel Corporation, 1985.

Bruszt, László. "Központosítás vagy műhely autonómia [Centralization or Workplace Autonomy]." Manuscript, Institute of Sociology, Hungarian Academy of Sciences, 1984.

———. "1989: The Negotiated Revolution in Hungary." *Social Research* 57 (1990): 365–87.

Burawoy, Michael. *Manufacturing Consent: Changes in the Labor Process under Monopoly Capitalism.* Chicago: University of Chicago Press, 1979.

———. "Marxism without Microfoundations." *Socialist Review* 89:2 (1989): 53–86.

———. *The Politics of Production: Factory Regimes under Capitalism and Socialism.* London: Verso, 1985.

———. "Should We Give Up on Socialism? Reflections on Bowles and Gintis' *Democracy and Capitalism.*" *Socialist Review* 89:1 (1989): 59–76.

Burawoy, Michael, and Anne Smith. "The Rise of Hegemonic Despotism in U.S. Industry." *Prokla* 58 (1985): 139–53.

Chandler, Alfred. *Strategy and Structure: Chapters in the History of the American Industrial Enterprise.* Cambridge, Mass.: MIT Press, 1962.

Cho, Soon Kyoung. "The Labor Process and Capital Mobility: The Limits of the New International Division of Labor." *Politics and Society* 14:2 (1985): 185–222.

Cole, Robert. *Japanese Blue Collar.* Berkeley and Los Angeles: University of California Press, 1971.

Comisso, Ellen. "Crisis in Socialism or Crisis of Socialism." *World Politics* 42 (1990): 563–96.

———. "Market Failures and Market Socialism: Economic Problems of the Transition." *East European Politics and Societies* 2 (1988): 433–65.

———. "Property Rights, Liberalism, and the Transition from 'Actually Existing' Socialism." *East European Politics and Societies* (forthcoming).

———. "Workers' Councils and Labor Unions: Some Objective Trade-Offs." *Politics and Society* 10 (1981): 251–79.

Crighton, Elisabeth. "Resource Mobilization and Solidarity: Comparing Social Movements across Regimes." In *Poland after Solidarity: Social Movements versus the State,* edited by Bronislaw Misztal. New Brunswick: Transaction Books, 1985.

Crozier, Michel. *The Bureaucratic Phenomenon.* Chicago: University of Chicago Press, 1963.

Davies, Norman. *Heart of Europe.* Oxford: Oxford University Press, 1986.

Dyker, David. "Planning and the Worker." In *The Soviet Worker,* edited by Schapiro and Godson. London: MacMillan, 1981.

Edwards, Richard. *Contested Terrain.* New York: Basic Books, 1979.

Farkas, Zoltán. "Munkások érdek- és érdekeltségi viszonyai [Relations and Levels of Interest among Workers]." *Szociológia* 1–2 (1983): 27–52.

Fazekas, Károly. "Teljesítményhiány és teljesítménybérezés a vállalati gazdálkodásban [Restriction of Output and Payment by Results in the Enterprise]." In *Kereseti- és Bérviszonyaink [Our Income and Wage Relations],* edited by Károly Fazekas et al. Hungarian Academy of Sciences, Institute of Economics, paper 28, 1983.

Fazekas, Károly, and János Köllö. "Fluctuations of Labour Shortage and State Intervention." In *Labour Market and Second Economy in Hungary,* edited by Péter Galasi and György Sziráczki. Frankfurt: Campus Verlag, 1985.

Fehér, Ferenc, Agnes Heller, and György Márkus. *Dictatorship over Needs.* Oxford: Basil Blackwell, 1983.

Filtzer, Donald. *Soviet Workers and Stalinist Industralization.* Armonk, N.Y.: M. E. Sharpe, 1986.

Foxley, Alejandro. "After Authoritarianism: Political Alternatives." In *Development Democracy and the Art of Trespassing*, edited by Alejandro Foxley, Michael McPherson, and Guillermo O'Donnell. Notre Dame, Ind.: Notre Dame University Press, 1986.

————. *Latin American Experiments in Neoconservative Economics*. Berkeley: University of California Press, 1983.

Friedgut, Theodore, and Lewis Siegelbaum. "Perestroika from Below: The Soviet Miners' Strike and Its Aftermath." *New Left Review* 181 (May–June 1990): 5–32.

Fuller, Linda. *The Politics of Workers' Control in Cuba, 1959–1983: The Work Center and the National Arena*. Philadelphia: Temple University Press, 1992.

Gábor, István, and Péter Galasi. "The Labour Market in Hungary since 1968." In *Hungary: A Decade of Economic Reform*, edited by Paul Hare, Hugo Radice, and Nigel Swain. London: Allen Unwin, 1981.

Galasi, Péter, and Gábor Kertesi. "Corruption and Ownership: A Study in Property Rights Theory." Manuscript, Department of Labor Economics, Karl Marx University, Budapest, 1990.

————. "Side Payment and Selective Advantages in an Economy Dominated by the State." Manuscript, Department of Labor Economics, Karl Marx University, Budapest, 1990.

Galasi, Péter, and György Sziráczki. "State Regulation, Enterprise Behaviour, and the Labour Market in Hungary, 1968–83." *Cambridge Journal of Economics* 9 (1985): 203–19.

Gordon, David, Richard Edwards, and Michael Reich. *Segmented Work, Divided Workers*. Cambridge: Cambridge University Press, 1982.

Goven, Joanna. "The Anti-Politics of Anti-Feminism: State Socialism and Gender Conservatism in Hungary, 1945–1990." Ph.D. diss., University of California, Berkeley, 1992.

Granick, David. *Soviet Metal-Fabricating and Economic Development*. Madison: University of Wisconsin Press, 1967.

Griffin, Larry, Joel Devine, and Michael Wallace. "Monopoly Capital, Organized Labor, and Military Spending in the United States, 1949–1976." In *Marxist Inquiries: Studies of Labor, Class, and States*, edited by Michael Burawoy and Theda Skocpol. Chicago: University of Chicago Press, 1982.

Grossman, Gregory. "Notes for a Theory of the Command Economy." *Soviet Studies* 15:2 (1963): 101–23.

Haney, Lynne. "Privatization and Female Autonomy: The Hungarian Woman's Experience." Manuscript, University of California, Berkeley, 1990.

Haraszti, Miklós. *A Worker in a Worker's State*. Harmondsworth, England: Penguin Books, 1977.

Haraszti, Miklós, interviewer. "Hungarian Perspectives." *Telos* 47 (Spring 1981): 142–52.

Havel, Václav. "The Power of the Powerless." In Václav Havel et al., *The Power of the Powerless*. London: Hutchinson, 1985.

Haydu, Jeffrey. *Between Craft and Class: Skilled Workers and Factory Politics in the United States and Britain, 1890–1922*. Berkeley: University of California Press, 1988.

Héthy, Lajos, and Csaba Makó. *A Munkásmagatartások és a Gazdasági Szervezet* [*Workers' Behavior and Business Enterprise*]. Budapest: Akadémiai, 1972.

——. *Munkások, érdekek, érdekegyeztetés* [*Workers, Interests, Reconciliation of Interests*]. Budapest: Gondolat, 1978.

Hodson, Randy, and Robert L. Kaufman. "Economic Dualism: A Critical Review." *American Sociological Review* 47 (1982): 727–39.

Holubenko, M. "The Soviet Working Class." *Critique* 4 (1975): 5–26.

Ichiyo, Muto. "Class Struggle on the Shop Floor—The Japanese Case." *AMPCO—Japan-Asia Quarterly Review* 16:3 (1984): 38–49.

Johnston, Paul. "Politics of Public Work." Ph.D. diss., University of California, Berkeley, 1988.

Jones, Gareth Stedman. *Languages of Class*. Cambridge: Cambridge University Press, 1983.

Jowitt, Kenneth. "An Organizational Approach to the Study of Political Culture in Marxist-Leninist Systems." *American Political Science Review* 68 (1974): 1171–91.

——. "Soviet Neo-Traditionalism: The Political Corruption of a Leninist Regime." *Soviet Studies* 35 (1983): 275–97.

Kalleberg, Arne, Michael Wallace, and Robert Althauser. "Economic Segmentation, Worker Power, and Income Inequality." *American Journal of Sociology* 87 (1981): 651–83.

Kamata, Satoshi. *Japan in the Passing Lane*. New York: Basic Books, 1983.

Katznelson, Ira. "Working Class Formation: Constructing Cases and Comparisons." In *Working Class Formation*, edited by Ira Katznelson and Aristide Zolberg. Princeton: Princeton University Press, 1986.

Kertesi, Gábor, and György Sziráczki. "Worker Behaviour in the Labour Market." In *Labour Market and Second Economy in Hungary*, edited by Péter Galasi and György Sziráczki. Frankfurt: Campus Verlag, 1985.

Kirsch, Leonard. *Soviet Wages: Changes in Structure and Administration since 1956*. Cambridge: MIT Press, 1972.

Kolakowski, Leszek. "Hope and Hopelessness." *Survey* 17:3 (Summer 1971): 37–52.

Köllö, János. "Munkaeröhiány, munkaerö-allokáció és bérezés egy pamutszövödében [Labor Shortage, Labor Allocation, and Reward in a Cotton Mill]." In *Kereseti- és Bérviszonyaink* [*Our Income and Wage Relations*], edited by Károly Fazekas et al. Budapest: Hungarian Academy of Sciences, Institute of Economics, paper 28, 1983.

Kolosi, Tamás, Iván Szelényi, Szonja Szelényi, and Bruce Western. "The Making of Political Fields in the Post-Communist Transition: Dynamics of Class and Party in Hungarian Politics, 1989–1990." Paper presented at the annual meeting of the American Sociological Association, Washington, D.C., 1990.

Konrád, György, and Iván Szelényi. *The Intellectuals on the Road to Class Power.* New York: Harcourt Brace Jovanovich, 1979.

Kornai, János. *The Economics of Shortage.* 2 vols. Amsterdam: North Holland Publishing Company, 1980.

————. "The Hungarian Reform Process: Visions, Hopes, and Reality." *Journal of Economic Literature* 24 (1986): 1687–1737.

————. *The Road to the Free Economy: Shifting from a Socialist System, the Example of Hungary.* New York: W. W. Norton, 1990.

Kövári, György, and György Sziráczki. "Old and New Forms of Wage Bargaining on the Shop Floor." In *Labour Market and Second Economy in Hungary*, edited by Péter Galasi and György Sziráczki. Frankfurt: Campus Verlag, 1985.

Kuron, Jacek. "Not to Lure the Wolves out of the Woods: An Interview with Jacek Kuron." *Telos* 47 (Spring 1981): 93–97.

Ladó, Mária, and Ferenc Tóth. "Egy ipari üzem munkaszervezete—a hiányjelzésre épülö munkaszervezet [Labor Organization in an Industrial Shop—A Labor Process Based on Shortages]." Manuscript, Munkaügyi Kutatóintézet, Budapest, 1982.

————. "A munkaráforditások elismertetésének mechanizmusa és társadalmi következményei a munkaszervezetekben [Mechanisms and Social Consequences of Recognition of Efforts in Labor Processes]." In *A Teljesitménynövelés feltételei a munkaszervezetben* [Conditions of Productivity Growth in Work Organizations], edited by Ágnes Simonyi. Budapest: ABMH Munkaügyi Kutatóintézet, 1983.

————. "A munkaszervezet centrumában—A centrális helyzet kialakulásának, újratermelödésének feltételei és következményei [At the Core of the Labor Organization—Conditions and Consequences of Formation and Reproduction of Core Positions in the Labor Process]." Manuscript, 1985.

Laki, Mihály. "End-year Rush-work in Hungarian Industry and Foreign Trade." *Acta Oeconomica* 25 (1980): 37–65.

Lampland, Martha. "Working through History: Ideologies of Work and Agricultural Production in a Hungarian Village, 1918–1983." Ph.D. diss. University of Chicago, 1987.

Lane, David, and Felicity O'Dell. *The Soviet Industrial Worker.* Oxford: Martin Robertson, 1978.

Liebenstein, Harvey. "Allocative Efficiency vs. 'X-Efficiency.'" *American Economic Review* 56 (1966): 392–415.

Lukács, János. "A müvezetök helye és szerepe munkaszervezeteinkben [The Place and Role of Foremen in Our Labor Organization]." Manuscript, Hungarian Academy of Sciences, Institute of Sociology, 1984.

————. "Employee Stock Ownership Programme: Basic Principles of the Concept of Regulation." Manuscript, Rész-Vétel, November 1990.

Lukes, Steven. *Marxism and Morality.* Oxford: Oxford University Press, 1985.

Lukes, Steven, and Itzhak Galnoor. *No Laughing Matter.* London: Routledge and Kegan Paul, 1985.

Luxemburg, Rosa. "The Russian Revolution." In *Rosa Luxemburg Speaks*, edited by Alice Waters. New York: Pathfinder, 1970.

Makó, Csaba. *Munkafolyamat: A társadalmi viszonyok erötere* [*The Labor Process: An Arena of Social Struggle*]. Budapest: Közgazdasági és Jogi Könyvkiadó, 1985.

Mandel, Ernest. *Late Capitalism*. London: Verso, 1975.

————. "Ten Theses on the Social and Economic Laws Governing the Society Transitional between Capitalism and Socialism." *Critique* 3 (1974): 5–22.

Michnik, Adam. "A New Evolutionism." In *Letters from Prison and Other Essays*. Berkeley: University of California Press, 1985.

Milor, Vedat. "Hungary: The Political Economy of Ownership Reform." Manuscript, World Bank, 1990.

Milosz, Czeslaw. *The Captive Mind*. Harmondsworth, England: Penguin Books, 1985.

Misztal, Bronislaw. "Social Movements against the State: Theoretical Legacy of the Welfare State." In *Poland after Solidarity: Social Movements versus the State*, edited by Bronislaw Misztal. New Brunswick, N.J.: Transaction Books, 1985.

Neumann, László. "A VGMK és az intézményes érdekegyeztetés [The VGMK and the Institutional Coordination of Interests]." *Közgazdasági Szemle* 10 (1987): 1217–228.

Nove, Alec. *The Soviet Economy*. New York: Praeger, 1965.

Nuti, D. M. "Socialism on Earth." *Cambridge Journal of Economics* 5 (1981): 391–403.

O'Connor, James. *The Fiscal Crisis of the State*. New York: St. Martin's Press, 1973.

O'Donnell, Guillermo, and Philippe C. Schmitter, *Transitions from Authoritarian Rule: Tentative Conclusions about Uncertain Democracies*. Baltimore: Johns Hopkins University Press, 1986.

Piore, Michael, and Charles Sabel. *The Second Industrial Divide*. New York: Basic Books, 1984.

Polan, A. J. *Lenin and the End of Politics*. Berkeley: University of California Press, 1984.

Polanyi, Karl. *The Great Transformation*. New York: Rinehart, 1944.

Pollert, Anna. "The 'Flexible Firm': Fixation or Fact?" *Work, Employment, and Society* 2 (1988): 281–317.

Powers, Brian. "Second Class Finish: The Effects of Rituals and Routines in a Working Class High School." Ph.D. diss., University of California, Berkeley, 1987.

Prechel, Harland. "Capital Accumulation and Corporate Rationality: Organizational Change in an American Steel Corporation." Ph.D. diss., University of Kansas, Lawrence, 1986.

Przeworski, Adam. "Can We Feed the World? The Irrationality of Capitalism and the Infeasibility of Socialism." *Politics and Society* 19:1 (1991): 1–38.

———. *Capitalism and Social Democracy*. Cambridge: Cambridge University Press, 1985.

———. "Class, Production, and Politics: A Reply to Burawoy." *Socialist Review* 89:2 (1989): 87–111.

———. "The Games of Transition." Manuscript, University of Chicago, 1990.

———. "Some Problems in the Study of the Transition to Democracy." In *Transitions from Authoritarian Rule: Comparative Perspectives*, vol. 3, edited by Guillermo O'Donnell, Philippe Schmitter, and Laurence Whitehead. Baltimore: Johns Hopkins University, Press, 1986.

Przeworski, Adam, and John Sprague. *Paper Stones: A History of Electoral Socialism*. Chicago: University of Chicago Press, 1986.

Rabinow, Paul. *Reflections on Fieldwork in Morocco*. Berkeley: University of California Press, 1977.

Rupp, Kalman. *Entrepreneurs in Red*. Albany: State University of New York Press, 1983.

Sayer, Andrew. "New Developments in Manufacturing and Their Spatial Implications." Working Paper, Urban and Regional Studies, University of Sussex, 1985.

Schapiro, Leonard, and Joseph Godson, eds. *The Soviet Worker*. London: MacMillan, 1981.

Schonberger, Richard. *Japanese Manufacturing Techniques*. New York: Free Press, 1982.

Schwartzman, Kathleen. *The Social Origins of Democratic Collapse*. Lawrence: University of Kansas Press, 1989.

Seeger, Murray. "Eye-witness to Failure." In *The Soviet Worker*, edited by Leonard Schapiro and Joseph Godson. London: MacMillan, 1981.

Sewell, William. *Work and Revolution in France*. Cambridge: Cambridge University Press, 1980.

Shapiro, Ian. "Fiscal Crisis of the Polish State: Genesis of the 1980 Strikes." *Theory and Society* 10:4 (1981): 469–502.

Siegelbaum, Lewis. *Stakhanovism and the Politics of Productivity in the USSR, 1935–1941*. Cambridge: Cambridge University Press, 1988.

Simmonds-Duke, E. M. "Was the Peasant Uprising a Revolution? The Meanings of a Struggle over the Past." *East European Politics and Societies* 1 (1987): 187–224.

Singer, Daniel. *The Road to Gdansk*. New York: Monthly Review Press, 1982.

Smith, Hedrick. *The Russians*. London: Sphere Books, 1976.

Smith, Vicki. *Managing in the Corporate Interest*. Berkeley: University of California Press, 1990.

Staniszkis, Jadwiga. *Poland's Self-Limiting Revolution*. Princeton: Princeton University Press, 1984.

Stark, David. "Coexisting Organizational Forms in Hungary's Emerging Mixed Economy." In *Remaking the Economic Institutions of Socialism*, edited by Victor Nee and David Stark (Stanford: Stanford University Press, 1989).

————. "Privatization in Hungary: From Plan to Market or from Plan to Clan?" *East European Politics and Societies* 4 (1990): 351–392.

————. "Rethinking Internal Labor Markets: New Insights from a Comparative Perspective." *American Sociological Review* 51 (1986): 492–504.

Stark, David, and Victor Nee. "Toward an Institutional Analysis of State Socialism." In *Remaking the Economic Institutions of Socialism: China and Eastern Europe*, edited by Victor Nee and David Stark. Stanford: Stanford University Press, 1989.

Starski, Stanislaw. *Class Struggle in Classless Poland*. Boston: South End Press, 1982.

Svitak, Ivan. "Comparisons." *Telos* 47 (Spring 1981): 110–12.

Swain, Nigel. *Collective Farms Which Work?* Cambridge: Cambridge University Press, 1985.

Szalai, Erzsébert. "Systemic or Elitist Change." Manuscript, Budapest, 1990.

Szelényi, Iván. "The Intelligentsia in the Class Structure of State-Socialist Societies." In *Marxist Inquiries: Studies of Labor, Class, and States*, edited by Michael Burawoy and Theda Skocpol. Chicago: University of Chicago Press, 1982.

————. *Socialist Entrepreneurs*. Madison: University of Wisconsin Press, 1988.

————. *Urban Social Inequalities under State Socialism*. Oxford: Oxford University Press, 1985.

Sziráczki, György. "The Development and Functioning of an Enterprise Labour Market in Hungary." *Économies et Sociétés* 3–4 (1983): 517–47.

Szkolny, Michael. "Revolution in Poland." *Monthly Review* 33:2 (June 1981): 1–21.

Thompson, Edward. *The Making of the English Working Class*. New York: Vintage Books, 1963.

Ticktin, Hillel. "The Contradictions of Soviet Society and Professor Bettelheim." *Critique* 6 (1976): 17–44.

Touraine, Alain, François Dubet, Michel Wieviorka, and Jan Strzelecki. *Solidarity: Poland, 1980–81*. Cambridge: Cambridge University Press, 1983.

Turner, Victor. *The Ritual Process: Structure and Anti-Structure*. London: Routledge and Kegan Paul, 1969.

Turovsky, Fyodor. "Society without a Present." In *The Soviet Worker*, edited by Leonard Schapiro and Joseph Godson. London: MacMillan, 1981.

U.S. Department of Commerce, Office of Technology Assessment. *Technology and Steel Industry Competitiveness*. Washington, D.C.: Government Printing Office, 1980.

Walder, Andrew. *Communist Neo-Traditionalism*. Berkeley: University of California Press, 1986.

Wiles, Peter. *Economic Institutions Compared*. Oxford: Basil Blackwell, 1977.

————. "Wages and Incomes Policies." In *The Soviet Worker*, edited by Schapiro and Godson. London: MacMillan, 1981.

Williamson, Oliver. *Markets and Hierarchies*. New York: Free Press, 1975.

———. "The Modern Corporation: Origins, Evolution, Attributes." *Journal of Economic Literature* 19 (1981): 1537–68.

Wright, Erik Olin. *Class, Crisis, and the State*. London: Verso, 1978.

———. *Classes*. London: Verso, 1985.

———. *The Debate on Classes*. London: Verso, 1989.

———. "Women in the Class Structure." *Politics and Society* 17 (1989): 35–66.

Wright, Erik Olin, Carolyn Howe, and Donmoon Cho. "Class Structure and Class Formation: A Comparative Analysis of the United States and Sweden." In *Cross-National Research in Sociology*, edited by Melvin Kohn. New York: Sage Publications, 1989.

Zaslavsky, Victor. *The Neo-Stalinist State*. Armonk, N.Y.: M. E. Sharpe, 1982.

Zinoviev, Alexander. *The Radiant Future*. London: Bodley Head, 1981.

Index

209